BENJAMIN HALL KENNEDY, D.D.

The Revised Latin Primer

Edited and Further Revised by

SIR JAMES MOUNTFORD

D.Litt., D.C.L., LL.D.

 LONGMAN

ADDISON WESLEY LONGMAN LIMITED
*Edinburgh Gate, Harlow, Essex CM20 2JE, England
and Associated Companies throughout the world.*

*New edition 1962
Seventy-fourth impression 1999*

Cover photographs by
J. ALLAN CASH

Printed in Malaysia, LSP

The publisher's policy is to use paper
manufactured from sustainable forests.

ISBN 0 – 582 – 36240 – 7

PREFACE

THE aim of this new edition of *The Revised Latin Primer* is to bring a well-known and popular school book into closer accord with the grammatical conceptions which have established themselves since the last edition. Bearing in mind the convenience of teachers who are accustomed to the older editions, and who will for some time to come find copies of those editions in the hands of their pupils, the publishers have desired to leave not only the enumeration of the paragraphs, but the details of pagination, as far as possible undisturbed. Consequently, no fundamental change has been made in the general plan of the book, and most of the old examples from Latin authors have been retained. The double restriction on the scope of the revision has inevitably precluded some changes which might have been welcomed; but I have not hesitated, when the need was especially urgent, to depart from the enumeration and pagination of former editions. Yet, apart from the four major alterations noted below, the only changes of enumeration which need be indicated are these: 345, n., becomes 441; 363 becomes 438, n. 2; 422 becomes 415b; and 422, nn. 1–3, becomes 422. Attention may also be drawn to the following points:

(1) Some long paragraphs have been subdivided to secure greater lucidity and to make reference easier. The repetitions inherent in the plan of the book have been correlated by cross-references. New indexes have been compiled.

(2) The definitions and rules have frequently been re-written either to avoid positive errors or to correct false implications.

(3) Where space allowed, as in §§ 216 and 217, n. 4, I have preferred to give definite lists of Latin words rather than English equivalents which frequently mislead pupils.

(4) In the old editions the quantities were marked in a somewhat haphazard fashion. The principle now adopted of marking all long vowels and no short vowels is in accordance with the best modern practice, and should leave no room for doubt or misunderstanding. The correct marking of vowels involves the marking of those long vowels which, though they were obvious enough in Roman speech, are now called 'hidden'. It is true that the quantity of a vowel in a closed syllable is sometimes not certainly known or ascertainable; but such cases form a small minority, and there I have chiefly followed the evidence afforded by such authorities as Sommer and Leumann. In §§ 10–17 it seemed advantageous to mark a number

of short vowels; but there is no other divergence from the general principle which has guided me.

(5) Since some knowledge of the methods and results of Comparative Philology is within the grasp of an intelligent pupil, I have not only retained §§ 10–24 and 148–151 in a modified form, but have added cross-references to them in the Accidence.

(6) The Principal Parts of Verbs are now arranged primarily on the basis of the Perfect, and the Supine form is used only to subdivide what would otherwise be rather long lists. Within each group the verbs are arranged in alphabetical order, and the enumeration of the paragraphs will make reference easy.

(7) While retaining the old enumeration of the paragraphs, it has been possible to introduce many changes, especially in the Syntax, and I hope that some at least of the following will be thought improvements: 4b, 8b, 106, 113, 220, 225–6, 316–17, 330–1, 471. In four places I have felt it necessary to discard the old arrangement: 351–363 (the Subjunctive Mood), 433–5 (Cum Temporal), 437–443 (Conditional Sentences), and 458–469 (Oratio Obliqua).

In the preparation of this book I have been fortunate in securing the help of several friends, to whom I desire to express my gratitude. Miss A. Woodward, M.A., of the Royal Holloway College, read much of the manuscript; later she worked over the proofs with great care, as also did Mr. F. H. Dowler, B.A., of the University College of Wales, Aberystwyth. Mr. H. F. Hose, M.A., of Dulwich College, has freely placed his valuable experience of the schoolboy's needs at my disposal in every part of the book. Professor G. E. K. Braunholtz, M.A., of Oxford, not only read and commented on all the paragraphs which deal more closely with Philology, but made many valuable suggestions on a number of syntactical points.

ABERYSTWYTH,   J. F. MOUNTFORD.
January 1930.

Publisher's Note

For this new edition of the *Revised Latin Primer* the typography has been redesigned and it is hoped that users of this standard textbook will appreciate the greater clarity of the modern layout. Care has been taken to retain exactly the same matter on each page so that the new edition can be used side by side with copies of the former one.

At the suggestion of a number of teachers certain small changes have been introduced and these have been carefully reviewed by Sir James Mountford in preparing the present revision.

CONTENTS

In this book the sign ˉ is used to indicate that a *vowel* is pronounced long, as in mēnsa; it is not used to show the length of a *syllable*. See §§ 4b, 8b, 471, and p. 42*.

THE LATIN LANGUAGE

The ancient Romans spoke the language of the district in which they lived, Latium in Italy. Hence their language was called Latin, not Roman.

Latin belongs to the family of languages known as Indo-European, which includes the following main groups:

in Asia:	Indian (as Sanskrit)
	Iranian (as Persian)
in Europe:	Greek (ancient and modern)
	Italic (as Latin, Oscan, Umbrian)
	Celtic (as Welsh, Irish, Gaelic)
	Germanic (as German, English)
	Slavonic (as Russian)

The imperial power of Rome made Latin the general speech of South and Western Europe, and from it are derived the Romance languages (Italian, French, Spanish, Portuguese, and Roumanian).

Note. In Britain, south of the Forth (except Wales and Cornwall), after its conquest by the Angles and Saxons, a branch of the Germanic group, called Anglo-Saxon or Old English, was spoken. But even before the Norman Conquest (A.D. 1066) this language had borrowed many words from Latin, either directly or through French. Similar borrowings have been made ever since; so that to understand the English language thoroughly it is necessary to have a knowledge of Latin.

The earliest specimens of the Latin language we possess are inscriptions, and fragments of songs, hymns, laws, and annals; but literary activity, properly speaking, did not begin at Rome until the third century B.C. In most branches of literature the Romans were deeply indebted to Greek models; for the influence of Greek civilization on Rome began early (with the commerce between the people of Latium and the Greek cities of South Italy), and reached its fullest development after the conquest of Greece by Rome, which was completed in 146 B.C.

1*

The first Latin author known to us is Livius Andronicus, a Greek of Tarentum. Taken prisoner in war, he became a teacher at Rome, and there produced Latin adaptations of Greek plays (240 B.C.). The works of the writers who followed in that and the next century have mostly perished, except the comedies of Plautus and Terence (220–160 B.C.), and a prose work of the elder Cato. The ages regarded as classical are:

I. The Golden Age, comprising (*a*) the Ciceronian (80–43 B.C.) in which the chief poets were Lucretius and Catullus, the chief prose writers Cicero, Caesar, and Sallust; and (*b*) the Augustan (43 B.C.–A.D. 14) in which the chief poets were Virgil, Horace, and Ovid, the chief prose writer Livy.

II. The Silver Age (A.D. 14–120) in which the chief poets were Lucan, Martial, Statius, and Juvenal, the chief prose writers Seneca, Pliny, and Tacitus.

For many centuries after A.D. 120 Latin was used for literary purposes; and until recent times scientific and philosophical works were often written in Latin. The Roman Catholic Church still uses it in its services and for official purposes.

LETTERS

2 The Latin Alphabet contained twenty-three letters:

A B C D E F G H I K L M N O P Q R S T V X Y Z.

Note 1. The small letters did not come into general use until the Middle Ages, and were originally a cursive or running-hand variation of the capitals. The small form of V was u.

Note 2. In early times, C represented a sound like 'g' in *get*. Survivals of this pronunciation are found in the abbreviations C. for Gaius, and Cn. for Gnaeus. Later, C was used for a 'k' sound; the 'g' sound was then represented by C with an added stroke, G; and K went out of use, except in a few words, *e.g.* Kalendae (abbreviated to Kal.).

Note 3. The letters Y and Z were added in Cicero's time; but they were used only in words taken from the Greek, just as French uses W in words taken from English.

SOUNDS

3 The Sounds which made up the Latin language are divided into (*a*) Vowels, which can be sounded alone, and (*b*) Consonants, which can only be sounded in conjunction with a vowel.

VOWELS AND DIPHTHONGS

The vowels were represented by the letters **a, e, i, o, u,** and **y.**

Note. The letters i and u were *also* used to represent consonant sounds. The Romans themselves made no distinction in *writing* between consonant-i (pronounced like *y* in *yet*) and vowel-i, or between consonant-u (pronounced like English *w*) and vowel-u; but in some Latin books consonant-i is represented by j, and consonant-u is still generally represented by v.

b Quantity and Pronunciation of Vowels. A vowel is called 'long' or 'short' according to the time taken in pronunciation. A long vowel takes approximately twice as long to pronounce as a short vowel. In this book all long vowels are indicated by the sign ‾, thus nōlō; occasionally the sign ∪ is used to indicate a short vowel, thus ĕrăt; *all vowels not marked are short.*

The following is *approximately* the pronunciation of the vowels:
- ā (prātum), as *a* in f*a*ther.
- ă (răpit), the same sound shortened, as the first *a* in *a*ha!
- ē (mēta), as *ey* in pr*ey* (without the faint i-sound at the end); still nearer are French *été*, German S*ee*.
- ě (frĕta), as *e* in fr*e*t.
- ī (fīdō), as *i* in mach*i*ne.
- ĭ (plĭcō), as *i* in f*i*t.
- ō (nōtus), as *o* in n*o*te (without the faint u-sound at the end); still nearer are French ch*o*se, German S*o*hn.
- ŏ (nŏta), as *o* in h*o*t.
- ū (tū), as *oo* in English sh*oo*t; or *oû* in French g*oû*t.
- ŭ (cŭtis), as *oo* in English t*oo*k; or *ou* in French g*ou*tte.
- ў (Lȳdia, lȳra = Λυδία, λύρα), as French u.

Note 1. Knowledge of vowel quantities in individual words (except final syllables) can only be gained by experience; but the following principles are of importance:
(*a*) a vowel is long (i) before ng, ns, *e.g.* īnfāns; (ii) when the result of a contraction, *e.g.* nīl (for nĭhĭl).
(*b*) a vowel is short (i) before nt, nd, *e.g.* ămănt (except in compounds like nōndum); (ii) before another vowel or h, *e.g.* mĕus, trăhō (Greek words like Aenēās are exceptions; note also **57, 141**).
For the quantity of final syllables see **473**.
Note 2. Do not confuse the **length of a vowel** with the **length of a syllable.** See **8b**, n. 3.

5a A Diphthong (double sound) is formed by two vowels pronounced continuously. The Latin diphthongs are:

ae (portae) = $\widehat{a+e}$, nearly as *ai* in *ai*sle, French ém*ai*l.

au (aurum) = $\widehat{a+u}$, as *ou* in h*ou*se, German H*au*s.

ei (ei!) = $\widehat{e+i}$, as *ei* in r*ei*n.

eu (seu) = $\widehat{e+u}$, *é-ŏŏ* pronounced in one breath.

oe (poena) = $\widehat{o+e}$, as *oi* in b*oi*l.

ui (huic) = $\widehat{u+i}$, as French *oui*.

Note 1.   The diphthongs ei, eu, ui are rare.   Words like meī, meus, tuī are disyllables, and each vowel is pronounced separately.
Note 2.   There were other diphthongs in early Latin: ai, oi, ou.   See **11** and **12** (3).

5b The diphthongs are long.

Note.   In compound words, prae before a vowel is short, *e.g.* prăeustus (*cf.* **4b**, n. 1, b. ii).

CONSONANTS

6 The production of a consonant involves (1) the vocal chords, (2) some part of the mouth, (3) breath.   Latin consonants are therefore classified in three ways, as:

I. Voiceless (= Hard, = Breathed) without vibration of the vocal chords, or Voiced (= Soft) with vibration of the chords.
II. Velar, formed at the *vēlum* or soft palate; Palatal, formed at the roof of the mouth; Dental, formed at the teeth; Labial, formed with the lips; Labio-dental formed with lips and teeth.   Velars and Palatals are sometimes classed together as Gutturals.
III. Plosives (= Mutes, = Stops), formed by complete interruption of the breath; Fricatives (= Spirants), formed by partial interruption of the breath; Liquids, formed by vibrating the breath with the tongue; Nasals, formed by letting the breath escape through the nose.

TABLE OF CONSONANTS

	Plosives		Fricatives		Liquids	Nasals
	Voiceless	Voiced	Voiceless	Voiced	Voiced	Voiced
Velar	q	g				(ng)
Palatal	c, k	g		cons.-i		(ng)
Dental	t	d	s	(z ?)	l, r	n
Labio-dental			f			
Labial	p	b		cons.-u		m

Note 1. n before c, g, qu, had the sound of *ng* in si*ng*; it was a Velar or Palatal, not a Dental, Nasal.
Note 2. In the combination -gu- after n (*e.g.* anguis) the Plosive is Velar, not Palatal.
Note 3. Consonant-i and consonant-u (v) are sometimes called semi-vowels.
Note 4. x is a compound consonant, = c+s. The pronunciation of z is doubtful; it was either a Voiced Fricative or a compound consonant like *dz* in a*dz*e. h represents a rough breathing.

---

7 Pronunciation of Consonants. Some English letters represent more than one consonant-sound: c in cat is a Palatal Plosive, in cider it is a Dental Fricative. Latin letters generally represent only one consonant-sound. The following are the chief differences between the Latin and English pronunciation:

b before s or t is pronounced as p; so, *urbs.*
c always as in *cat*, never as in *cider.*
g always as in *get*, never as in *gentle.*
consonant-**i** like *y* in *yet*; so, *iūs.*
n before c, g, qu, like *ng* in *sing.*
r is always trilled or rolled.
s always as *ss* in *mass*, never as *s* in *was.*
t always as in *ten*, never as in *motion.*
consonant-**u** (**v**) as *w* in *wall.*
x always as in *axe* (= ks), never as in *exact* (= gs).
z as *z* in *lazy* or as *dz* in a*dze.*

The Aspirates ch, th, ph, found only in borrowed words, were pronounced:

ch like *kh* in *inkhorn*, not like *ch* in *church*, or *ch* in *chorus.*
th like *th* in *hothouse*, not like *th* in *thin*, or *th* in *then.*
ph like *ph* in *taphouse*, not like *ph* in *philosophy.*

Note. For convenience, *ch* is often pronounced as in Scottish *loch*, *th* as in *thin*, and *ph* as English *f.*

Doubled consonants were both pronounced; so -*cc*- in *vacca* like -*kc*- in *bookcase.*

SYLLABLES

8a Syllable Division. A syllable consists of a vowel or diphthong, either alone or with one or more consonants adjoining it: e-ram, prā-vus. Words are divided into syllables thus:

(a) A single consonant between two vowels belongs to the same syllable as the second vowel: so e-ram, e-rā-mus.

(b) In the case of two or more consonants, the division falls before the last consonant, except that combinations containing a Plosive or **f** followed by a Liquid (which are easily pronounced in Latin even at the beginning of a word) go with the second vowel: so mag-nus, but a-grum.

Note 1. The separate parts of compounds are kept distinct: so ab-rumpō.
Note 2. The poets sometimes divide between a Plosive and a Liquid, *e.g.* ag-rum. *Cf.* **471**, n. 1.
Note 3. A syllable ending with a vowel is called an *open syllable*; one ending with a consonant is called a *closed syllable*.
Note 4. The last syllable of a word is called the *ultimate*; the last but one, the *penultimate*; the last but two, the *ante-penultimate*.

8b Quantity of Syllables. A syllable is long if it ends (a) with a long vowel or diphthong, or (b) with two consonants or a compound consonant (x), or (c) with a single consonant, when the following syllable begins with a consonant.

All other syllables are short.

Note 1. The initial consonants of a syllable have no influence on its quantity. For cons.-i between vowels, see p. 42, n.
Note 2. Both long and short vowels are found in long syllables of types (b) and (c), and the quantity of such vowels is said to be 'hidden'. In this book the quantity of long vowels in such syllables is marked, *e.g.* mēnsa. *Cf.* **4b**, n. 1 (a).
Note 3. A short *vowel* in long syllables of types (b) and (c) is sometimes said to be 'long by position'; but the term is misleading, since *the vowel remains short in pronunciation*, as in 'dant'.

---

9 Accent. In classical Latin the accent (stress) fell (a) in words of two syllables on the first, (b) in words of more than two syllables on the penultimate if it were long, otherwise on the antepenultimate.

Note 1. The position of the accent may be indicated by the sign ', thus: mágnus.
Note 2. Words of two or more syllables are rarely accented on the last syllable. Exceptions like illíc (for illíce) are due to the loss of a syllable.
Note 3. The enclitic particles (*e.g.* -que, -ve, -ne) which are always attached to a preceding word, may be regarded as final syllables for purposes of accentuation, *e.g.* mēnsámque.
Note 4. In pre-classical times, Latin words were accented on the first syllable.

SOUND CHANGES

10 A language does not remain constant but is continually being modified to a greater or less extent by the people who speak it. The parent Indo-European language was modified before the various groups, such as the Italic, had a separate existence; and traces of one early kind of change (called Vowel Gradation or Ablaut) are found in all languages of the Indo-European family. Thus in English beside *sing* we have *sang, sung*. So in Latin, in groups of related words, we find variations which are due ultimately to Vowel Gradation:

stāre, stătus	tēgula, tĕgō	sēdēs, sĕdeō
fēcī, făciō	tegō, toga	pendere, pondus
fīdō, fĭdēs	vōx, vŏcō	dōnum, dătus

Before the classical period the Latin language itself had undergone changes, *e.g.* doucō became dūcō. Still later, the Latin sounds were modified as the Romance languages developed, *e.g.* Latin *tēctum* became French *toit*. Such changes however are not haphazard; they are due to speech habits which, as long as they operated, were so constant that they can be expressed as phonetic laws. The most important changes which took place within the history of the Latin language itself are the following:

VOWEL AND DIPHTHONG CHANGE

11 I. **Vowel Weakening.** Some of these changes took place in syllables whether they were accented or unaccented; others took place only in unaccented syllables.

A. CHANGES INDEPENDENT OF ACCENT

ai often became ae: so quaerō for quairō (*cf.* **12, 3**).

ĕl became ŏl except before ĕ, ĭ, or l: so beside velle note volō.

ei became ī: so dīcō for deicō.

i became ĕ before an -r- which had originally been -s- (*cf.* **21b**): so cineris for cinisis, and serō for sisō.

oi often became oe, and then ū: so oinos became oenos, then ūnos (finally ūnus) (*cf.* **12, 3**). This change is not always complete: compare poena with pūniō, and Poenī with Pūnicus.

ou became ū: so dūcō for doucō.

ŏl before any consonant except l became ŭl: so beside colō note cultus. This change combined with the ĕl—ŏl change: so sepultus (not sepeltus or sepoltus) from sepeliō.

ŏ before nc became ŭ: so uncus for oncos.

12 B. CHANGES IN UNACCENTED (*i.e.* not initial; *cf.* **9**, n. 4) SYLLABLES

(1) Short vowels in open syllables (**8a**, n. 3) generally became -ĭ-: so ad*i*gŏ for ad*a*gŏ, obs*i*deŏ for obs*e*deŏ, bon*i*tās for bon*o*tās, gen*i*bus for gen*u*bus; but when -r- followed, a short vowel became -ĕ-: so trād*e*re for trā(ns)d*a*re; and under special conditions (*e.g.* before a Labial) a short vowel became -ŭ-: so auc*u*pis beside auc*e*ps.

(2) In closed syllables, -ă- became -ĕ-: so ref*e*llō for ref*a*llō, and auc*e*ps beside c*a*piō. -ŏ- became -ŭ-, especially in final closed syllables: so on*u*stus for on*o*stos, ann*u*s for ann*o*s; but this change was delayed (at least in writing) until the end of the republic in words where the -ŏ- of a final syllable was immediately preceded by u (v), *e.g.* flāv*o*s, serv*o*s.

(3) Weakening of diphthongs: au became ū, as inclūdō for incl*au*dō; ai and oi became ei, then ī: so inquīrō for inqu*ai*rō, annī for ann*oi* (*cf.* **11**).

13 II. **Vowel Assimilation and Dissimilation.** The vowels of two consecutive syllables tended to become alike (assimilation): so hom*o* for hem*o*. On the other hand, two vowels coming together tended to be different (dissimilation): so sān*o*-tās became sān*i*tās (by weakening of -ŏ- in an open syllable), but soci*o*-tās became soci*e*tās, not soci*i*tās.

14 III. **Vowel Contraction.** When two vowels came together, or were separated only by -h-, they tended to join together into one long vowel or diphthong, and the intervening 'h' (if present) disappeared: so cōgō for coagō, cōpia for co-opia, nēmō for ne-hemō, dēbeō for dēhabeō.

When consonant-u was lost between two like vowels (**21c**) contraction took place: so lātrīna for lavātrīna.

15 IV. **Vowel Loss.** (*a*) Syncope, the loss of an unaccented vowel in the middle of a word: so valdē for validē.

(*b*) Apocope, the dropping of a final vowel: so quīn for quīne, dīc for dīce.

16 V. **Vowel Development.** (*a*) Anaptyxis. A vowel sometimes developed between two consonants, especially between c and l, and between b and l: so saec*u*lum for saeclum, perīc*u*lum for perīclum, stab*u*lum for stablum, m*i*na for mna (μνᾶ).

(*b*) Prothetic Vowels. About the middle of the second century A.D. a vowel (i or e) frequently developed in common speech before initial sc, sp, st. Hence compare French écrire, esprit, étroit, with Latin scrībere, spīritus, strictus.

VI. **Changes of Quantity.** (*a*) Shortening tended to take place:

    (1) Before another vowel: so rĕī for rēī (*cf.* **57**).

    (2) In final syllables ending in any consonant but s: so ōrātŏr beside ōrātōris, spem beside spēs.

    (3) In the last syllable of disyllabic words whose first syllable is short: so bene for benē, quasi for quasī, mihi (generally) for mihī.

  (*b*) Lengthening took place:

    (1) To compensate for an -s- which was lost when followed by a Voiced consonant: so dīgerō for disgerō.

    (2) Before ns, nf: so with ingēns compare ingentis. In such cases the *n* was scarcely sounded and the preceding vowel was probably nasalized; hence the abbreviation cos, for cōnsul.

    (3) Generally in Perfect Passive Participles, when the Voiced Consonants g, d, of a verb-root had become c, t (Voiceless) through assimilation (**20a**, 2, *b*) to the t of the participial suffix. So the past participle of agō was agtos, then āctus. Contrast factus, in which the c does not represent an original g, and the -ă- of the verb-root is not lengthened.

CONSONANT CHANGE

18 Consonants at the beginning of a word. Certain combinations of consonants were difficult to pronounce at the beginning of a word and became simplified: so lātus for tlātus (*cf.* tulī); nātus for gnātus; nix for snix (compare *snow*); mīror for smīror (compare *smile*); rādīx for vrādīx (compare *wort*); lūbricus for slūbricus (compare *slippery*); līs for stlīs.

19 Consonants in the middle of a word. In the case of difficult combinations of consonants in the middle of a word either (1) one or more of them was lost, or (2) one became completely or partly assimilated to the other, or (3) another consonant or vowel (a glide sound) developed between them.

    (1) The loss of one or more consonants often involved a lengthening of a preceding short vowel; see **17** (*b*, 1), and note also nīdus for nisdos (*cf. nest*), vēlum for vegh-slom (*cf.* vehō), scāla for scand-slā. A doubled consonant became single in distō (for dis-stō), pergō (for per-regō), vīsus (for vīssus, earlier vidtos), curūlis (compare currus).

20a (2) **Assimilation of consonants** is complete when the first becomes the same sound as the second, partial when the first changes to one which combines more easily with the second.

    (*a*) Complete: offerō for op-ferō, accidō for at-cadō, differō for dis-ferō, agellus for agerlus, immōtus for in-mōtus.

    (*b*) Partial: *e.g.* a Voiced Plosive becomes Voiceless before another Voiceless consonant, as rēc-tum from regō.

    Sometimes, when the first of two consonants was a Liquid, the second became like the first, as collis for colnis, velle for vel-se (compare es-se).

  (3) A consonant develops between m and l, t, or s: so exemplum for exemlom, ēmptus for ēmtus; sūmpsī for sūmsī. For the development of a vowel see **16**.

20b Dissimilation is seen in lucrum for luclum (contrast piāclum). The termination -ālis became -āris when there was a preceding l: so mīlitāris, familiāris (contrast aequālis).

21a Metathesis. Two sounds sometimes change position, as vespa for vepsa (so English *wasp* for *waps*), tarpessīta for trapezīta.

21b Rhotacism. -s- between vowels changed to -r-. This change is called rnotacism from the Greek name, *rho*, for the letter r: so mōris for mōsis, mēnsārum for mēnsāsōm. This change had ceased to operate before some words received their present form; hence causa (not caura) from caussa, and Mūsa (a borrowed word).

21c Consonant-i and -u. Consonant-i was often dropped between two vowels, as moneō for moneiō. Consonant-u (v) was often dropped between two like vowels and before -o: as, lātrīna for lavātrīna, sīs for sī vīs, parum for parvom; deivos became deos, then deus.

22 Consonants at the end of a word. The last of a group of final consonants was often dropped: so lac for lact, cor for cord, mīles for mīless (earlier mīlets). Final -d after a long vowel is dropped, *e.g.* praedā for praidād, magistrātū for magistrātūd, meritō for meretōd.

23 Dropping of Syllables. When two similar syllables came together, one was apt to be dropped. So sēmodius for sēmimodius, venēficium for venēnificium.

INFLEXION

4 An inflexion is a change in the form of a word (most often at the end) whereby a grammatical relationship between this word and other words is indicated. Words which are inflected consist of a Stem and an Inflexion; and the Stem itself either contains, or is identical with, a primitive element called the Root. Thus amā- is the Stem of amāmus, and amōr- is the Stem of amōrem; the Root of both amā- and amōr- is am-.

Note. In Latin, inflexion is either a Suffix, an addition made after the Stem; or a Prefix, an addition made before the Stem; but some verbs have -n- (called the Nasal Infix, **149**) inserted in the stem in some or all tenses, *e.g.* fingō, finxī, fictum. In ce-cin-ī there is both Suffix (-ī) and Prefix (ce-); the Stem -cin- is a modification of the Root can-. In Latin such modifications of a Root are due either to Vowel Gradation (**10**) or to Vowel Weakening (**11-12**).

PARTS OF SPEECH

25 Words are classified as:

  I. **Nouns** (or **Substantives**), names of persons, places, things, or qualities:

  Caesar, *Caesar*; **Rōma,** *Rome*; **sōl,** *sun*; **fortitūdō,** *bravery*.

  II. **Adjectives,** which define nouns by expressing their qualities:

  Rōma **antiqua,** *ancient Rome*; sōl **clārus,** *the bright sun*.

  III. **Pronouns,** which point out a person, place, thing, or quality without naming it:

  ego, *I*; **ille,** *that, he*.

  IV. **Verbs,** which express an action or state:

  Sōl **dat** lūcem, *the sun gives light*; Rōma **manet,** *Rome remains*.

  V. **Adverbs,** which qualify and limit Verbs, Adjectives, and sometimes other Adverbs:

  Rōma diū flōruit; nunc **minus** potēns est.
  Rome flourished long; now it is less powerful.

  VI. **Prepositions,** which (*a*) indicate the relation of a Noun, Adjective, or Pronoun to other words in the sentence; (*b*) modify the meaning of a verb:

  Per Rōmam errō, *I wander through Rome*; **ad**sum, *I am present*.

  VII. **Conjunctions,** which connect words, phrases, and sentences:

  Caelum suspiciō **ut** lūnam **et** sīdera videam.
  I look up to the sky that I may see the moon and stars.

  VIII. **Interjections,** words of exclamation: **heu, ēheu,** *alas!*

Nouns, Adjectives, and Pronouns are *declined* (**28–75; 91–101**); Verbs are *conjugated* (**103–147**); Adjectives and Adverbs may be modified by *Comparison* (**76–87**); Prepositions, Conjunctions, and Interjections have no inflexions.

There is no Article in Latin. Lūx may mean *a light, the light*, or simply *light*.

Substantives denoting the names of persons or places (as Caesar, Rōma) are called Proper Nouns; all others are Common Nouns.

Common Nouns are either (*a*) Concrete: vir, *a man*, mēnsae, *tables*; or (*b*) Abstract: virtūs, *virtue*; or (*c*) Collective: turba, *a crowd*.

7b Numerals are words which express Number. They are Nouns, as mīlia, *thousands*; or Adjectives, as ūnus, *one*; or Adverbs, as semel, *once*. See **88–90**.

DECLENSION

28 A Declension is a grouping of the forms of Nouns, Adjectives, and Pronouns, according to **Numbers** and **Cases.**

Latin has five declensions.

29 The Numbers are two:

Singular for one: mēnsa, *a table*; gēns, *a nation*.
Plural for more than one: mēnsae, *tables*; gentēs, *nations*.

30 A Case is a form of a Noun, Adjective, or Pronoun standing in a particular relation to other words in the sentence.

Note. This relation is not necessarily indicated by the form alone; for there is not a separate form for every case in both singular and plural. The relation between an ambiguous form and the rest of the sentence is determined by the order of words (as *hominēs canēs amant*) or by the context (as *hominēs piscēs edunt*).

There are six Cases in Latin:

Nominative, the Subject Case.
Vocative, the Case of Address.
Accusative, the Object Case.
Genitive, the *of* Case.
Dative, the *to* or *for* Case.
Ablative, the *from, by, in,* or *with* Case.

All but the Nominative and Vocative are called Oblique Cases.

Examples of the cases:

Nominative	Sōl lūcet,	*the sun shines*
Vocative	Sōl *or* ō sōl,	*O sun!*
Accusative	Sōlem videō,	*I see the sun*
Genitive	Sōlis lūx,	*the light of the sun*
Dative	Sōlī lūx additur,	*light is added to the sun*
Ablative	Sōle lūx ēditur,	*light issues from the sun*

The uses of the cases are described in detail later (**200–295**).

Note. Originally there were two more cases, the Instrumental (or Sociative), and the Locative. The Instrumental has been merged in the Ablative. But the Locative is often found in classical literature: humī, *on the ground*; Rōmae, *at Rome*; Athēnīs, *at Athens*.

RULES OF GENDER

31a Natural gender distinguishes between (1) male, (2) female, and (3) inanimate things. Grammatical gender refers to Nouns, Adjectives, and Pronouns and distinguishes between (1) masculine, (2) feminine, or (3) neuter.

Words denoting a male are masculine: **nauta,** *a sailor.*

Words denoting a female are feminine: **mulier,** *a woman.*

Words denoting inanimate things are either masculine, feminine, or neuter. The grammatical gender of such words may often be determined (A) by the form of the Nominative Singular, or (B) by the meaning.

31b (A) Gender shown by the Form:

(*a*) Masculine are most Substantives in **-us** of the Second and Fourth Declensions, and those in **-er** of the Second Declension.

(*b*) Feminine are nearly all Substantives in **-a** of the First Declension and in **-ēs** of the Fifth Declension.

(*c*) Neuter are Substantives in **-um** of the Second Declension, in **-ū** of the Fourth Declension, and indeclinable nouns, including the infinitive verb-noun (**107**).

51–4.   For nouns of the Third Declension no general rule can be given; but see

(B) Gender shown by Meaning:

(a) Masculine are names of all winds and of most rivers and mountains: Boreās, *north wind*, Tiberis, Olympus.

> Exceptions: Some mountains and a few rivers ending in -a or -ē are feminine: Allia, Lēthē, Aetna, Rhodopē, Alpēs (plur.). Neuter: Pēlion, Sōracte.

(b) Feminine are names of most islands, countries, cities, and trees: Lesbos, Aegyptus, Rōma, pīnus, *pine*.

> Exceptions: Countries ending in -um are neuter: Latium. Pontus is masculine. Cities whose nom. is a plural in -ī are masc.: Coriolī, Delphī; those in -um, -on, -a (plur.) are neuter: Tarentum, Īlion, Arbēla.

Many Second Declension masculine nouns have a corresponding feminine of the First Declension.

fīlius, *son*	deus, *god*	arbiter ⎫ *umpire*
fīlia, *daughter*	dea, *goddess*	arbitra ⎭

> Other pairs are found: rēx, *king*, rēgīna, *queen*; victor, victrīx, *conqueror*; nepōs, *grandson*, neptis, *granddaughter*; socer, socrus, *father-, mother-in-law*.

Nouns which are masculine or feminine according as they refer to male or female, are said to be of common gender:

> Sacerdōs, *priest* or *priestess*, vātēs, *seer*, parēns, *parent*, dux, *leader*, comes, *companion*, cīvis, *citizen*, custōs, *guardian*, iūdex, *judge*, hērēs, *heir*, āles, *bird*, canis, *dog*. *Cf.* **503.**

> Many names of animals, though used of both sexes, have (in grammar) only one gender: aquila, *eagle*, fem.; lepus, *hare*, masc.; passer, *sparrow*, masc. Such words are called Epicene.

> (For Memorial Lines on Gender, see Appendix IV.)

DECLENSION OF SUBSTANTIVES

32 The five Declensions of Nouns are distinguished from each other by the final sound of the stem. They differ clearly also in the termination of the Genitive Singular.

Declension	Final sound of Stem	Genitive Singular
First	-ā	-ae
Second	-o	-ī
Third	{ some consonant / -i }	-is
Fourth	-u	-ūs
Fifth	-ē	-eī or ēī

TABLE OF CASE-ENDINGS

Decl.	I.	II.		III.				IV.		V.
Stem.	-a	-ō		consonant		-i		-u		-ē
				SINGULAR						
	f.	*m.*	*n.*	*m.f.*	*n.*	*f.m.*	*n.*	*m.*	*n.*	*f.*
Nom.	a	us(er)	um	various		is, ēs	e, l, r	us	ū	ēs
Voc.	a	e(er)	um	various		is, ēs	e, l, r	us	ū	ēs
Acc.	am	um	um	em	*var.*	em, im	e, l, r	um	ū	em
Gen.	ae	ī		is		is		us		eī(ēī)
Dat.	ae	ō		ī		ī		ui(u)		eī(ēī)
Abl.	ā	ō		e		ī *or* e		u		ē
				PLURAL						
Nom.	ae	ī	a	ēs	a	ēs	ia	ūs	ua	ēs
Voc.	ae	ī	a	ēs	a	ēs	ia	ūs	ua	ēs
Acc.	ās	ōs	a	ēs	a	ēs, īs	ia	ūs	ua	ēs
Gen.	ārum	ōrum		um		ium		uum		ērum
Dat.	īs	īs		ibus		ibus		ibus		ēbus
Abl.	īs	īs		ibus		ibus		ibus		ēbus

3 The Nominative singular of masculine and feminine nouns ends in **s**, except in Stems in **-ā**, some Stems in **-ro** of the Second Declension, and Stems in **-l, -r, -n,** of the Third.

The Vocative is like the Nominative, except in the singular of Nouns of the Second Declension whose nominative ends in **-us**.

Neuters have the Accusative like the Nominative in both singular and plural.

Neuter plural Nominative, Vocative, and Accusative, always end in **-a**.

In the plural of each Declension the Ablative has the same form as the Dative.

FIRST DECLENSION

34 Stems in -ā. The Nominative Singular is a weakened form of the Stem.

Stem   mēnsā-, *table*, f.

	SING.	PLUR.
Nom.	mēnsa	mēnsae
Voc.	mēnsa	mēnsae
Acc.	mēnsam	mēnsās
Gen.	mēnsae	mēnsārum
Dat.	mēnsae	mēnsīs
Abl.	mēnsā	mēnsīs

Nouns of this declension are mostly feminine. A few are masculine, as scrība, *a notary* (*cf.* **31a**); Hadria, *the Adriatic sea*.

Note 1. An old form of the gen. sing. **-āī** for **-ae** is sometimes used by poets as aulāī. Also an old genitive of familia remains in compounds: pater- (māter-) familiās, *father* (*mother*) *of a family*.

Note 2. The **locative** sing. ends in **-ae**; the plur. in **-īs**: Rōmae, *at Rome*; mīlitiae, *at the war*; Athēnīs, *at Athens*.

Note 3. The gen. plur. is sometimes formed in **-um** instead of **-ārum**, by compounds of -cola, -gena: agricola, *a farmer*; and in some words borrowed from Greek: amphora, drachma. This **-um** is an old form, not a contraction of **-ārum**.

Note 4. Dea and fīlia have dat. and abl. plural **-ābus**, to avoid confusion with the dat. and abl. plur. of deus and fīlius.

SECOND DECLENSION

35a Stems in -o. The Nominative Singular ends in -us or -er Masculine; -um Neuter.

Stem	anno- *year*, m.	puero- *boy*, m.	magistro- *master*, m.	bello- *war*, n.
SINGULAR				
Nom.	annus	puer	magister	bellum
Voc.	anne	puer	magister	bellum
Acc.	annum	puerum	magistrum	bellum
Gen.	annī	puerī	magistrī	bellī
Dat.	annō	puerō	magistrō	bellō
Abl.	annō	puerō	magistrō	bellō
PLURAL				
Nom.	annī	puerī	magistrī	bella
Voc.	annī	puerī	magistrī	bella
Acc.	annōs	puerōs	magistrōs	bella
Gen.	annōrum	puerōrum	magistrōrum	bellōrum
Dat.	annīs	puerīs	magistrīs	bellīs
Abl.	annīs	puerīs	magistrīs	bellīs

Note 1. The nom. sing. termination of nouns in -us, -um was originally -os, -om; and the Acc. Sing. was -om (*cf.* **12,** B (2)).

Note 2. In the nom. sing. of stems in -ro, the o was dropped, an -e- developed before the r, and the -s of the nom. ending was assimilated to the r of the stem: so magistros became magisters, and finally magister. In puer, *boy*, socer, *father-in-law*, gener, *son-in-law*, vesper, *evening*, and compounds of -fer and -ger (*e.g.* sīgnifer, armiger), the -e- is part of the stem.

The following in -us are feminine (besides words feminine by meaning): alvus, *paunch*; colus, *distaff*; humus, *ground*; vannus, *winnowing-fan*; also several from the Greek: arctus, *the Bear constellation*; carbasus, *linen*; plural carbasa, n., *sails*. Neuter in -us (and used in the singular only) are pelagus, *sea*; vīrus, *venom*; vulgus, *crowd* (sometimes masculine).

The following have some exceptional forms:

Stem	fīlio- *son*, m.	viro- *man*, m.	deo- *god*, m.
SINGULAR			
Nom.	fīlius	vir	deus
Voc.	fīlī	vir	deus
Acc.	fīlium	virum	deum
Gen.	fīlī *or* fīliī	virī	deī
D. Abl.	fīliō	virō	deō
PLURAL			
N.V.	fīliī	virī	dī (deī)
Acc.	fīliōs .	virōs	deōs
Gen.	fīliōrum	virōrum *or* virum	deōrum *or* deum
D. Abl.	fīliīs	virīs	dīs (deīs)

Note 1. Like fīlius are declined genius, *guardian spirit*, and many proper names in -ius: Claudius, Vergilius. Neuters in -ium like ingenium, *innate quality*, also have gen. sing. in -ī (not -iī). This contracted gen. sing. in -ī, as fīlī, ingenī, is used by writers of the best age, especially poets. The accent in such words is on the penultimate, even if it is short. Contrast **71**, n.

Note 2. Like vir are declined its compounds: triumvir, decemvir, &c.

Note 3. The locative singular ends in ī; the plural in īs: humī, *on the ground*; bellī, *in time of war*; Mīlētī, *at Miletus*; Philippīs, *at Philippi*.

Note 4. A genitive plural in -um is often found, especially in words denoting coins, sums, weights, and measures: nummus, *coin*; talentum, *talent*. This -um is an old form, not a contraction of -ōrum. Some nouns have genitive plural in -um *or* -ōrum: socius, *ally*; faber, *smith*; līberī, *children*; superī, *the gods*, from adj. superus (**304**).

THIRD DECLENSION

36 Consonant Stems and Stems in -i.   The Third Declension contains—

A. Consonant Stems.

PLOSIVES: (1) **Palatals, c, g**; (2) **Dentals, t, d**; (3) **Labials, p, b.**
FRICATIVE: **s.**
NASALS: **n, m.**
LIQUIDS: **l, r.**

B. Stems in -i.

37 Syllabus of Consonant Stems

Stem-ending	Nominative Sing.	Genitive Sing.	English

Stems in Palatals with -x in Nom. for -cs or -gs.

ac-	fax, f.	facis	torch
āc-	pāx, f.	pācis	peace
ec-	nex, f.	necis	death
ēc-	vervēx, m.	vervēcis	wether
ic-	fornix, m.	fornicis	arch
ic-	iūdex, c.	iūdicis	judge
īc-	rādīx, f.	rādīcis	root
ōc-	vōx, f.	vōcis	voice
uc-	dux, c.	ducis	leader
ūc-	lūx, f.	lūcis	light
eg-	grex, m.	gregis	flock
ēg-	rēx, m.	rēgis	king
eg- (ig-)	rēmex, m.	rēmigis	rower
ig-	strix, f.	strigis	screech-owl
ug-	coniūnx, c.	coniugis	wife or husband
ūg-	wanting	frūgis, f.	fruit

Stems in Dentals drop t, d, before -s in the Nom.

at-	anas, f.	anatis	duck
āt-	aetās, f.	aetātis	age
et-	seges, f.	segetis	corn-crop
et-	pariēs, m.	parietis	room-wall
ēt-	quiēs, f.	quiētis	rest
et- (it-)	mīles, c.	mīlitis	soldier
it-	caput, n.	capitis	head
ōt-	nepōs, m.	nepōtis	grandson
ūt-	virtūs, f.	virtūtis	virtue, courage
ct-	lac, n.	lactis	milk
ad-	vas, m.	vadis	surety
ed-	pēs, m.	pedis	foot
ēd-	mercēs, f.	mercēdis	hire
aed-	praes, m.	praedis	bondsman
ed- (id-)	obses, c.	obsidis	hostage
id-	lapis, m.	lapidis	stone
ōd-	custōs, c.	custōdis	guardian
ud-	pecus, f.	pecudis	beast
ūd-	incūs, f.	incūdis	anvil
aud-	laus, f.	laudis	praise
rd-	cor, n.	cordis	heart

Stems in Labials form Nom. regularly with -s.

ap-	wanting	dapis, f.	banquet
ep- (ip-)	prīnceps, c.	prīncipis	chief
ip-	wanting	stipis, f.	dole (a small coin)
op-	wanting	opis, f.	help
ep- (up-)	auceps, m.	aucupis	fowler

Stems in the Fricative, -s, which, except in vās, becomes -r.

ās-	vās, n.	vāsis	vessel
aes- (aer-)	aes, n.	aèris	copper, bronze
es- (er-)	Cerēs, f.	Cereris	Ceres
is- (er-)	cinis, m.	cineris	cinder
ōs- (ōr-)	honōs, m.	honōris	honour
os- (or-)	tempus, n.	temporis	time
os- (er-)	opus, n.	operis	work
ūs- (ūr-)	crūs, n.	crūris	leg

Stems in Liquids.

al-	sāl, m.	salis	salt
ell-	mel, n.	mellis	honey
il-	mūgil, m.	mūgilis	mullet
ōl-	sōl, m.	sōlis	sun
ul-	cōnsul, m.	cōnsulis	consul
ar-	iubar, n.	iubaris	sunbeam
er-	ānser, m.	ānseris	goose, gander
ēr-	vēr, n.	vēris	spring
ter- (tr-)	māter, f.	mātris	mother
or-	aequor, n.	aequoris	sea
or-	ebur, n.	eboris	ivory
ōr-	soror, f.	sorōris	sister
ur-	vultur, m.	vulturis	vulture
ūr-	fūr, m.	fūris	thief

Stems in Nasals.

en- (in-)	nōmen, n.	nōminis	name
on- (in-)	homō, m.	hominis	man
ōn-	leō, m.	leōnis	lion
iōn-	ratiō, f.	ratiōnis	reason
rn-	carō, f.	carnis	flesh
an-	canis, c.	canis	dog
en-	iuvenis, c.	iuvenis	young person
em-	hiems, f.	hiemis	winter

38 A. Consonant Stems (Genitive Plural in -um).

Many nouns of this group retain in the Nom. Sing. the original vowel of the Stem, which in the oblique cases was modified in accordance with the principles explained in 12.

(1) Stems in **Palatals**: c, g

Stem	iūdic-, *judge*, c.	rādīc-, *root*, f.	rēg-, *king*, m.
SINGULAR			
N. V.	iūdex	rādīx	rēx
Acc.	iūdicem	rādīcem	rēgem
Gen.	iūdicis	rādīcis	rēgis
Dat.	iūdicī	rādīcī	rēgī
Abl.	iūdice	rādīce	rēge
PLURAL			
N. V.	iūdicēs	rādīcēs	rēgēs
Acc.	iūdicēs	rādīcēs	rēgēs
Gen.	iūdicum	rādīcum	rēgum
Dat.	iūdicibus	rādīcibus	rēgibus
Abl.	iūdicibus	rādīcibus	rēgibus

So also: f. vōx, **vōc-**, *voice*; c. dux, **duc-**, *leader*; m. grex, greg-, *flock*.

39   (2) Stems in **Dentals**: t, d

Stem	mīlit-, *soldier*, c.	as ped-, *foot*, m.	capit-, *head*, n.
SINGULAR			
N. V.	mīles	pēs	caput
Acc.	mīlitem	pedem	caput
Gen.	mīlitis	pedis	capitis
Dat.	mīlitī	pedī	capitī
Abl.	mīlite	pede	capite
PLURAL			
N. V.	mīlitēs	pedēs	capita
Acc.	mīlitēs	pedēs	capita
Gen.	mīlitum	pedum	capitum
Dat.	mīlitibus	pedibus	capitibus
Abl.	mīlitibus	pedibus	capitibus

So also: f. virtūs, **virtūt-**, *virtue*; f. seges, **seget-**, *corn*; m. lapis, **lapid-**, *stone*; c. sacerdōs, **sacerdōt-**, *priest, priestess*.

(3) Stems in **Labials: p, b**

Stem $\left.\begin{array}{l}\text{prīncep-}\\\text{prīncip-}\end{array}\right\}$ *chief,* c.

	SINGULAR	PLURAL
N. V.	prīnceps	prīncipēs
Acc.	prīncipem	prīncipēs
Gen.	prīncipis	prīncipum
Dat.	prīncipī	prīncipibus
Abl.	prīncipe	prīncipibus

So also: c. forceps, **forcip-**, *tongs*; m. auceps, **aucup-**, *fowler*; f. trabs, **trab-**, *beam.*

(4) Stems in the **Fricative s**

Stems in -s do not add s in the Nominative Singular, and generally they change -s- into -r- in the other cases (*cf.* **21b**).

Stem	$\left.\begin{array}{l}\text{flōs-}\\\text{flōr-}\end{array}\right\}$ *flower,* m.	$\left.\begin{array}{l}\text{opos-}\\\text{oper-}\end{array}\right\}$ *work,* n.	$\left.\begin{array}{l}\text{crūs-}\\\text{crūr-}\end{array}\right\}$ *leg,* n.
SINGULAR			
N. V.	flōs	opus	crūs
Acc.	flōrem	opus	crūs
Gen.	flōris	operis	crūris
Dat.	flōrī	operī	crūrī
Abl.	flōre	opere	crūre
PLURAL			
N. V.	flōrēs	opera	crūra
Acc.	flōrēs	opera	crūra
Gen.	flōrum	operum	crūrum
Dat.	flōribus	operibus	crūribus
Abl.	flōribus	operibus	crūribus

So also: m. honōs, **honōr-**, *honour*; n. tempus, **tempor-**, *time*; corpus, **corpor-**, *body*; genus, **gener-**, *race*; iūs, **iūr-**, *law.*

Note 1. Vās, **vās-**, n., *a vessel*, keeps s in all the cases, and has second decl. plural: vāsa, vāsōrum, vāsīs, *baggage of an army.* Os, **oss-**, n., *bone*, ās, **ass-**, m., *a coin*, have -ss- in the oblique cases, and gen. plur. ossium, assium.
Note 2. Honōs, *honour*, colōs, *colour*, and similar words changed during classical times to honor, color, &c., in the nom. sing., with gen. -ōris. Arbōs, f., changed to arbor, arboris, *tree.*

42

(5) Stems in **Liquids**: l, r

Stems in -l, -r, do not take s in the Nominative Singular.

Stem	cōnsul-	amōr-	pater-⎫ patr-⎭	aequor-
	consul, m.	*love*, m.	*father*, m.	*sea*, n.
SINGULAR				
N. V.	cōnsul	amor	pater	aequor
Acc.	cōnsulem	amōrem	patrem	aequor
Gen.	cōnsulis	amōris	patris	aequoris
Dat.	cōnsulī	amōrī	patrī	aequorī
Abl.	cōnsule	amōre	patre	aequore
PLURAL				
N. V.	cōnsulēs	amōrēs	patrēs	aequora
Acc.	cōnsulēs	amōrēs	patrēs	aequora
Gen.	cōnsulum	amōrum	patrum	aequorum
Dat.	cōnsulibus	amōribus	patribus	aequoribus
Abl.	cōnsulibus	amōribus	patribus	aequoribus

So also: m. sōl, **sōl-**, *sun*; ōrātor, **ōrātōr-**, *speaker*; carcer, **carcer-**, *prison*; frāter, **frātr-**, *brother*; n. ebur, **ebor-**, *ivory*.

43

(6) Stems in **Nasals**: n, m

Stems ending in -n do not take s in the Nominative Singular; those in -ōn, -on, have -ō in the Nominative.

Stem	leōn-	virgon-⎫ virgin-⎭	nōmen-⎫ nōmin-⎭
	lion, m.	*virgin*, f.	*name*, n.
SINGULAR			
N. V.	leō	virgō	nōmen
Acc.	leōnem	virginem	nōmen
Gen.	leōnis	virginis	nōminis
Dat.	leōnī	virginī	nōminī
Abl.	leōne	virgine	nōmine
PLURAL			
N. V.	leōnēs	virginēs	nōmina
Acc.	leōnēs	virginēs	nōmina
Gen.	leōnum	virginum	nōminum
Dat.	leōnibus	virginibus	nōminibus
Abl.	leōnibus	virginibus	nōminibus

So also: m. latrō, **latrōn-**, *robber*; f. ratiō, **ratiōn-**, *reason*; m. ōrdō, **ōrdin-**, *order*; homō, **homin-**, *man*; n. carmen, **carmin-**, *song*.

There is only one Stem in **m**: hiems, *winter*; Genitive hiemis, f.

B. Stems in -i (Genitive Plural in -ium).

(1) Stems with Nominative Singular in -is, and in -er from stem -ri-:

Stem	cīvi-, *citizen*, c.	imbri-, *shower*, m.
SINGULAR		
N. V.	cīvis	imber
Acc.	cīvem	imbrem
Gen.	cīvis	imbris
Dat.	cīvī	imbrī
Abl.	cīve, -ī	imbre, -ī
PLURAL		
N. V.	cīvēs	imbrēs
Acc.	cīvēs, īs	imbrēs, -īs
Gen.	cīvium	imbrium
Dat.	cīvibus	imbribus
Abl.	cīvibus	imbribus

Declined like cīvis: m. amnis, *river*; ignis, *fire*; f. avis, *bird*.
Declined like imber: f. linter, *boat*; m. ūter, *leathern bottle*.

Note 1. Some words have acc. -im, abl. -ī: tussis, *cough*; sitis, *thirst*; most rivers and towns, Tiberis, *Tiber*; Neāpolis, *Naples*; and sometimes febris, *fever*; puppis, *stern*; turris, *tower*; clāvis, *key*; nāvis, *ship*; restis, *rope*; secūris, *axe*; sēmentis, *sowing*. Ignis usually has abl. ignī. The acc. plur. in -īs is the older form. See 48.
Note 2. Vīs, *force*, is the only stem in -ī. It has acc. sing. vim, abl. sing. vī; plur. vīrēs, vīrium, vīribus. Other forms are rare.
Note 3. Some nouns in -is form their gen. plur. in -um from a consonant-stem, *e.g.* canis, *dog*, iuvenis, *youth*, and (sometimes) mēnsis, *month*. See 48.

45 (2) Stems with Nominative Singular in -ēs:

Stem	nūbi-, *cloud*, f.	
	SINGULAR	PLURAL
N. V.	nūbēs	nūbēs
Acc.	nūbem	nūbēs, -īs
Gen.	nūbis	nūbium
Dat.	nūbī	nūbibus
Abl.	nūbe	nūbibus

So also: f. cautēs, *rock*; mōlēs, *pile*; rūpēs, *crag*.

Note. Some have nom. sing. -ēs. or -is: vallēs or vallis, *valley*; vulpēs or vulpis, *fox*. Famēs, *hunger*, and tābēs, *corruption*, have abl. sing. in -ē (not -ě).

46   (3) Stems which have two consonants before the -i. These generally drop i before the s in the Nominative Singular, and assimilation of consonants takes place (20a):

Stem	monti-, *mountain*, m.	urbi-, *city*, f.
SINGULAR		
N. V.	mōns	urbs
Acc.	montem	urbem
Gen.	montis	urbis
Dat.	montī	urbī
Abl.	monte	urbe
PLURAL		
N. V.	montēs	urbēs
Acc.	montēs, -īs	urbēs, -īs
Gen.	montium	urbium
Dat.	montibus	urbibus
Abl.	montibus	urbibus

So also: f. arx, **arci-**, *citadel*; ars, **arti-**, *art*; stirps, **stirpi-**, *stem*; frōns, **fronti-**, *forehead*; frōns, **frondi-**, *leaf*; m. dēns, **denti-**, *tooth*.

47   (4) Neuter **i**- Stems (with Nominative Singular in -e, -al, -ar):

In the Nominative Singular of these nouns the **i** of the Stem has been changed to **e** or dropped (with shortening of the preceding vowel, **17**).

Stem	cubīli-, *couch*	animāli-, *animal*	calcāri-, *spur*
SINGULAR			
N. V. Acc.	cubīle	anima	calcar
Gen.	cubīlis	animālis	calcāris
Dat. Abl.	cubīlī	animālī	calcārī
PLURAL			
N. V. Acc.	cubīlia	animālia	calcāria
Gen.	cubīlium	animālium	calcārium
Dat. Abl.	cubīlibus	animālibus	calcāribus

So also: conclāve, *room*; sedīle, *seat*; rēte, *net* (abl. sing. -e); tribūnal, *tribunal*; exemplar, *pattern*.

Note. Mare, *sea*, has abl. sing. marī, or (very rarely) mare; the gen. plur. does not occur except for a single instance of the irregular marum in poetry. Baccar, *an aromatic root*, fār (gen. farris), *flour*, iubar, *a sunbeam*, nectar, *nectar*, have abl. sing. -e.

In early times the declension of i-stems differed markedly from that of consonant-stems in having -im (not -em) for the accusative singular of masculine and feminine, -ī (not -e) for the ablative singular, -īs (not -ēs) for the accusative plural of masculine and feminine, and -ium (not -um) for the genitive plural. In Classical Latin these differences are obscured; and for many words the classification remains doubtful, and rests chiefly on analogy with other Latin words, or on comparison with cognate words in other languages. A considerable number of nouns (including many monosyllables in -ns, -rs, -bs, -ps, like *mōns, ars, urbs, stirps*) show the consonant-declension in the singular and the i-declension in the plural; they are sometimes spoken of as Mixed Stems.

49 The following rule with regard to the form of the Genitive Plural may be given for practical convenience:

Nouns with a syllable more in the Genitive Singular than in the Nominative Singular (Imparisyllabic Nouns) have Genitive Plural in -um.

Nouns with the same number of syllables in the Nominative Singular and Genitive Singular (Parisyllabic Nouns) have Genitive Plural in -ium.

The chief exceptions to this rule are the following:

(*a*) Imparisyllabic Nouns which have Genitive Plural in -ium are: glīs, līs, mās, mūs, nox, and Nouns of *one* syllable of which the Nominative Singular ends in -ns, -rs, -bs, -ps, -rx, -lx; and neuters in -al, -ar.*

Often also: fraus, rēn, lār, dōs, Nouns of *two* syllables with Nominative Singular ending in -ns, -rs, and most Nouns in -ās (gen. -ātis). These last and Nouns in -ns are especially variable. Horace writes both parentum and parentium, but the latter is rare.

(*b*) Parisyllabic Nouns which have Genitive Plural in -um are: canis, iuvenis, senex, sēdēs, pater, māter, frāter, accipiter.†

Sometimes also: apis, mēnsis, vātēs, volucris.

* Nouns of one syllable, of which the Stem has two Consonants before i-, are only apparently Imparisyllabic because the Nom. Sing. originally ended in -is (46), and of some both forms are found; *e.g.* orbs and orbis. Similarly, neuters in -al, -ar originally ended -āle, āre (47).

† Pater, māter, frāter, accipiter, are only apparently Parisyllabic because the e of the Nom. Sing. does not appear in the other cases.

50 The following have exceptional forms:

(1) Iuppiter = Iou (once Dieu)+piter (for pater); and bōs, *ox.*

		SINGULAR	PLURAL
N. V.	Iuppiter	bōs	bovēs
Acc.	Iovem	bovem	bovēs
Gen.	Iovis	bovis	boum
Dat.	Iovī	bovī	bōbus or būbus
Abl.	Iove	bove	bōbus or būbus

(2) Two stems in -**u**, declined like consonant nouns: grūs, *crane,* sūs, *pig.*

	SINGULAR	PLURAL	SINGULAR	PLURAL
N. V.	grūs	gruēs	sūs	suēs
Acc.	gruem	gruēs	suem	suēs
Gen.	gruis	gruum	suis	suum
Dat.	gruī	gruibus	suī	suibus (subus)
Abl.	grue	gruibus	sue	suibus (subus)

Iter, n. *journey,* is inflected from the stem itiner-.

Iecur, n. *liver,* is inflected from both iecor- and iecinor-.

Femur, n. *thigh,* is inflected from both femor- and femin-.

Senex, m. *old man,* has Sing. Acc. senem, Gen. senis, Dat. senī, Abl. sene; Plur. N. Acc. senēs, Gen. senum, Dat. Abl. senibus.

Supellex, f. *furniture,* is inflected from supellectil-, with Abl. in ī or e.

Iūsiūrandum, n. *oath,* is declined in both parts: N. V. Acc. iūsiūrandum; Gen. iūrisiūrandī; Dat. iūriiūrandō; Abl. iūreiūrandō. No plural.

Paterfamiliās m., māterfamiliās f., *father, mother of a family,* have pater, māter fully declined in the sing. cases, but familiās remains unaltered (*cf.* 34, n. 1). The plur. patrēsfamiliārum is sometimes found.

Note. The **locative** sing. of the third declension ends in -ī or -e; the plural in -ibus: rūrī, rūre, *in the country;* vesperī, vespere, *in the evening;* Carthāginī, Carthāgine, *at Carthage;* Gādibus, *at Gades (Cadiz).*

GENDER IN THIRD DECLENSION (*apart from meaning*)

51 1. Consonant Stems

Masculine are nouns which end in -ōs, -ō (except -dō, -gō, -iō), -or, -er, and Imparisyllabic nouns in -is, -es, ēs.

Exceptions:

cōs, *whetstone,* dōs, *dowry,* f.; ōs, ōris, *mouth,* n.

ēchō, *echo,* carō, *flesh,* f.

arbor, *tree,* f.; aequor, *sea,* cor, *heart,* marmor, *marble,* n.

linter, *skiff,* f.; cadāver, *corpse,* iter, *journey,* tūber, *tumour,* ūber, *udder,* verber, *lash,* n.; some names of plants, as papāver, *poppy,* n.

merges, *sheaf,* seges, *corn,* teges, *mat,* f.

compēs, *fetter,* mercēs, *hire,* quiēs, *rest,* requiēs, *rest,* f.

Feminine are nouns which end in **-x**, **-ās**, **-ps**, **-dō**, **-gō**, **-iō**, and nouns in **-ūs** of more than one syllable.

Exceptions:
Nouns in **-ex**, **ex** are masculine or common; but forfex, *shears*, lex, *law*, nex, *death*, supellex, *furniture*, f.
calix, *cup*, fornix, *arch*, m.; dux, *leader*, c.
ās, *coin*, m.; fās, *right*, nefās, *wrong*, vās, *vessel*, n.
manceps, *buyer*, m.; mūniceps, *burgess*, c., prīnceps, *chief*, c.
cardō, *hinge*, harpagō, *grappling hook*, ōrdō, *order*, m.
ligō, *hoe*, m.; margō, *brink*, c.
Concrete nouns in **-iō** are masculine: pugiō, *dagger*; pāpiliō, *butterfly*.
Abstract nouns in **-iō** are feminine: ratiō, *reason*; regiō, *region*.

3 Neuter are nouns in **-us**, **-ūs** (if monosyllabic), **-en**, **-ēn**, **-l**, **-ar**, **-ur**.

Exceptions:
lepus, *hare*, m.; pecus (pecudis), *single head of cattle*, f.
mūs, *mouse*, m.; grūs, *crane*, sūs, *pig*, c.
pecten, *comb*, rēn, *kidney*, splēn, *spleen*, tībīcen, *flute-player*, m.
mūgil, *mullet*, sāl, *salt*, sōl, *sun*, m.
lār, *god of the hearth*, m.
furfur, *bran*, lemur, *goblin*, turtur, *turtle dove*, vultur, *vulture*, m.

Note. The following words are not accounted for in **51-53**: vas, *surety*, is masc.; faex, *dregs*, fraus, *deceit*, laus, *praise*, are fem.; aes, *copper*, caput, *head*, lac, *milk*, os (ossis), *bone*, vēr, *spring*, are neuter.

---

54 2. I- Stems

Most Parisyllabic nouns in **-is** and **-ēs** are feminine.

Exceptions: the following are masculine:

acīnacēs, *scimitar*	crīnis, *hair*	mēnsis, *month*	unguis, *nail*	
amnis, *river*	ēnsis, *sword*	orbis, *circle*	vectis, *lever*	
axis, *axle*	fascis, *bundle*	pānis, *bread*	vermis, *worm*	
canālis, *canal*	follis, *bag*	piscis, *fish*	verrēs, *boar*	
caulis, *cabbage*	fūstis, *cudgel*	postis, *post*	cassēs, *nets*	} plur.
collis, *hill*	ignis, *fire*	torris, *firebrand*	mānēs, *shades*	

Generally masculine are callis, *path*; fīnis, *end*; fūnis, *rope*; sentis, *thorn*; torquis, *necklace*; veprēs (plur.), *bramble*. Vīs, *force*, is fem.

Nouns in **-al**, **-ar**, and **-e**, are neuter.
Nouns in **-x**, **-bs**, **-ls**, **-ns**, **-rs** are feminine.

But dēns, *tooth*, bidēns, *fork*, fōns, *fountain*, mōns, *mountain*, occidēns, *west*, oriēns, *east*, pōns, *bridge*, rudēns, *rope*, torrēns, *torrent*, m.; infāns, *infant*, parēns, *parent*, c.

FOURTH DECLENSION

55 Stems in -u. The Nominative of masculine and feminine nouns is formed by adding s; neuters lengthen the vowel of the Stem in Nominative and Accusative Singular.

Stem	gradu-, *step*, m.	genu-, *knee*, n.
SINGULAR		
Nom. Voc.	**gradus**	**genū**
Acc.	**gradum**	**genū**
Gen.	**gradūs**	**genūs**
Dat.	**graduī**	**genū**
Abl.	**gradū**	**genū**
PLURAL		
Nom. Voc.	**gradūs**	**genua**
Acc.	**gradūs**	**genua**
Gen.	**graduum**	**genuum**
Dat. Abl.	**gradibus**	**genibus**

Feminine nouns of this declension are: acus, *needle*; manus, *hand*; porticus, *porch*; tribus, *tribe*; Idūs (plural), *Ides*, and words feminine by meaning. The only neuters in common use are: cornū, *horn*; genū, *knee*; verū, *a spit*.

Note 1. The gen. sing., particularly in early Latin, sometimes ends in -ī, as if from an o-stem of the second declension. So: senātī beside senātūs. *Cf.* **56.**
Note 2. The dat. sing. in -ū (not -uī) is the rule for neuter nouns, and is sometimes found in masc. and fem. nouns.
Note 3. The original form of the dat. and abl. plur., **-u-bus**, is found always in: arcus, *bow*, tribus, *tribe*; generally in: artūs, (pl.) *limbs*, lacus, *lake*, partus, *offspring*; occasionally in other words.

---

56 Some nouns have forms of both **u-** and **o-** Stems, especially names of trees: laurus, *bay*; myrtus, *myrtle*. Colus, f., *distaff*, has Genitive -ī and ūs, Ablative -ō and -ū, Accusative plural -ōs and -ūs.

Domus, f., is thus declined (rarer forms in brackets):

	SINGULAR	PLURAL
N. V.	domus	domūs
Acc.	domum	domōs (*or* domūs)
Gen.	domūs (*or* domī)	domōrum
Dat.	domuī (*or* domŏ)	domibus
Abl.	domō	domibus

The locative domī, *at home*, is often used.

FIFTH DECLENSION

Stems in -ē. The Nominative Singular is formed by adding s to the Stem.

	Stem diē-, *day*		Stem rē-, *thing*	
	SING.	PLUR.	SING.	PLUR.
Nom.	diēs	diēs	rēs	rēs
Voc.	diēs	diēs	rēs	rēs
Acc.	diem	diēs	rem	rēs
Gen.	diēī	diērum	reī	rērum
Dat.	diēī	diēbus	reī	rēbus
Abl.	diē	diēbus	rē	rēbus

The gen. and dat. sing. are generally -eī, not -ēī, in all nouns except those which, like diēs, have stems in -iē. *Cf.* **17**, *a*, 1.

Most nouns of this declension are not declined in the plural. Rēs and diēs are the only nouns which have Genitive, Dative, and Ablative Plural.

All nouns of this declension are feminine except diēs and merīdiēs, *noon*. Diēs also is feminine in the Singular when it means 'an appointed day'.

Note 1. Some nouns have forms both of ā- and ē- Stems. They are declined like māteriēs, *matter*, singular only.

	Stem	māteriā-	and māteriē-
Nom., Voc.		māteria	māteriēs
Acc.		māteriam	māteriem
Gen., Dat.		māteriae	(māteriēī)
Abl.		māteriā	māteriē

Note 2. The contracted gen. and dat. sing. in -ē, as fidē for fideī, is found in Virgil and Horace. An old gen. in -ī occurs in tribūnus plēbī, *tribune of the people*. The locative ends in -ē.

58 *Note 3.* **Rēspūblica,** *the public interest, the republic, the State*:

Nom., Voc.	rēspūblica	rēspūblicae
Acc.	rempūblicam	rēspūblicās
Gen.	reīpūblicae	rērumpūblicārum
Dat.	reīpūblicae	rēbuspūblicīs
Abl.	rēpūblicā	rēbuspūblicīs

DEFECTIVE AND VARIABLE SUBSTANTIVES

59 Many nouns are found only in the Singular, as:

aurum,	*gold*	iūstitia,	*justice*
caelum,	*heaven*	lētum,	*death*
humus,	*ground*	vēr,	*spring*

Note. Occasionally the plural of such words is used with a special meaning: Catōnēs, *men like Cato*, aera, *bronzes, bronze figures*, ignōrantiae, *cases of ignorance*.

60 Many nouns are used only in the Plural:

arma,	*arms*	īnsidiae,	*ambush*
artūs, ·	*limbs*	līberī,	*children*
cūnae,	*cradle*	mānēs,	*departed spirits*
dēliciae,	*pet*	minae,	*threats*
dīvitiae,	*riches*	moenia,	*town walls*
fāstī,	*annals*	nūgae,	*trifles*
fēriae,	*holidays*	nūptiae,	*marriage*
hīberna,	*winter quarters*	penātēs,	*household gods*
indūtiae,	*truce*	tenebrae	*darkness*

And names of towns, days, festivals: Athēnae, Delphī, Kalendae, *Calends*; Bacchanālia, *festival of Bacchus*.

Note. In poetry some words take plural form with singular meaning: mella, *honey*, nivēs, *snow*, silentia, *silence*, rūra, *country*.

61 The Plural of some words has a special meaning (sometimes in addition to the usual meaning):

SINGULAR		PLURAL	
aedēs,	*temple*	aedēs,	*house*
auxilium,	*help*	auxilia,	*allied forces*
castrum,	*fort*	castra,	*camp*
cēra,	*wax*	cērae,	*waxen tablet*
cōpia,	*plenty*	cōpiae,	*forces*
fīnis,	*end*	fīnēs,	*boundaries*
fortūna,	*fortune*	fortūnae,	*possessions*
grātia,	*favour*	grātiae,	*thanks*
impedīmentum,	*hindrance*	impedīmenta,	*baggage*
littera,	*letter of the alphabet*	litterae,	*epistle, literature*
lūdus,	*play, school*	lūdī,	*public games*
opem (acc.),	*help*	opēs,	*wealth*
pars,	*part*	partēs,	*faction, rôle*
sāl,	*salt*	salēs,	*wit*

Some nouns have two or more forms of Declension:

Nom.	Gen.			Nom.	Gen.		
tergum,	-ī,	n.	} back	pecus,	-oris, n.		cattle
tergus,	-oris,	n.		pecus,	-udis, f.		a single beast
ēventum,	-ī,	n.	} event	plēbs,	-is, f.	}	the common
ēventus,	-ūs,	m.		plēbēs,	-eī, f.		people
				Nom.	**Gen. Abl.**		
iūgerum,	-ī,	n.	} acre	vespera, -ae	-ā, f.	}	
(iūger),	-is,	n.		vesper, -ī	-ō, m.	}	evening
				vesper, —	-e, m.		

Quiēs, f., *rest*, -ētis, is a t- Stem only; but its compound requiēs has also two Fifth Decl. forms: requiem, requiē. See also **56, 57,** n. 1.

53 Some o-stems have masculine and neuter forms in singular and plural: baculus, -lum, *a stick*; clipeus, -eum, *a shield*.

Some o-stems have masculine and neuter forms in the plural only: frēnum, *bit*: plural frēnī, frēna; iocus, *jest*: plural iocī, ioca; rāstrum, *harrow*: plural rāstrī, rāstra.

Notice: locus, *place*; loca, *places*, *a district*; locī, (generally) *passages in an author*.

64 In many nouns some of the cases are wanting; thus:

	feast, f.	*fruit*, f.	*help*, f.	*prayer*, f.	*change*, f.
N. V.	—	—	—	—	—
Acc.	dapem	frūgem	opem	precem	vicem
Gen.	dapis	frūgis	opis	—	vicis
Dat.	dapī	frūgī	—	precī	—
Abl.	dape	frūge	ope	prece	vice

These have full plural with Genitive -um (except vicium).

65 Some nouns are used in the Ablative Singular only.

coāctū,	*by force*	nātū,	*by birth*
concessū,	*by permission*	noctū,	*by night*
iussū,	*by command*	rogātū,	*by request*
iniussū,	*without command*	sponte,	*by choice*

66 Some neuters have Nominative and Accusative Singular only: fās, *right*, nefās, *wrong*, īnstar, *likeness*, *size*, nihil, *nothing*.

Māne is used as Accusative and Ablative Singular.

Nēmō, *nobody*, has only Accusative nēminem, Dative nēminī. For Genitive and Ablative, nūllīus and nūllō are used.

2*

DECLENSION OF GREEK NOUNS

FIRST DECLENSION

67 At an early date many Greek nouns were borrowed by Latin and received a Latin form. Nouns of the first Greek declension, whatever the ending of their nominative singular had been in Greek, took the ending **-a** in Latin and were declined throughout like mēnsa. Such borrowed words are: nauta, *sailor*, māchina, *contrivance*.

Note. These early borrowings were made from the Doric dialect of Greek (ναύτας, μαχανά) not from the Attic (ναύτης, μηχανῇ).

At a later date the Greek forms, especially of proper names, were brought in by the poets; and thus in many instances both Greek and Latin forms of the same word are found, while of some words, used chiefly in poetry, the Greek forms alone occur.

MASCULINE NOUNS IN **-ās, -ēs,** AND FEMININE NOUNS IN **-ē**

		SINGULAR	
N.	Aenēās	Atrīdēs (-a)	Cybelē (-a)
V.	Aenēā	Atrīdē (-ā, -a)	Cybelē (-a)
A.	Aenēān	Atrīdēn	Cybelēn (-am)
G.	Aenēae	Atrīdae	Cybelēs (-ae)
D.	Aenēae	Atrīdae	Cybelae
Abl.	Aenēā	Atrīdē (-ā)	Cybelē (ā)

Plural in all cases like that of mēnsa.

Note 1. Patronymics (*family names*) are usually in the Greek form, as Atrīdēs (*son of Atreus*), Pēlīdēs (*son of Peleus*); and though they sometimes have -a for -ēs in the nom. they always retain the Greek acc. in -ēn. Those in -adēs, -idēs have gen. pl. in -um: Aeneadum, Dardanidum.
Note 2. Names denoting nationality and ending in -ātēs, -ītēs, or -ōtēs, as Eleātēs (inhabitant of Elea), generally have -em or -am in the acc.

SECOND DECLENSION

Greek nouns of the Second Declension, especially names of persons and places, often keep their Greek forms in the nominative and accusative, but the other cases generally take the Latin forms.

SINGULAR

Nom.	Dēlos, f.	Pēlion, n.
Acc.	Dēlon, -um	Pēlion
Gen.	Dēlī	Pēliī
D. Abl.	Dēlō	Pēliō

Note 1. The fem. words of this Declension are chiefly names of towns, islands, plants, and precious stones.

Note 2. Nouns ending in -ros sometimes take the Latin ending -er in the nom., as Euander (or -dros).

Note 3. The Greek plural forms are rare, but plural nom. in -oe, as Canēphoroe, and plur. gen. in -ōn, as Būcolicōn, are sometimes found.

THIRD DECLENSION

69 These nouns are very numerous, and have many different endings in the Nominative Singular.   Examples of declension:

SINGULAR

N. V.	hērōs, m., *hero*	lynx, c., *lynx*	crātēr m., *mixing bowl*
Acc.	hērō-a, -em	lync-em, -a	crātēra, -rem
Gen.	hērōis	lyncis	crātēros, -ris
Dat.	hērōī	lyncī	crātērī
Abl.	hērōe	lynce	crātēre

PLURAL

N. V.	hērōes	lynces	crātēres
Acc.	hērōas	lync-as, -ēs	crātēras
Gen.	hērōum	lyncum	crātērum
Dat.	hērōibus	lyncibus	crātēribus
Abl.	hērōibus	lyncibus	crātēribus

The masculine and feminine accusative singular endings in **-em** and **-a** are both frequent. Genitive singular usually is **-is,** but the Greek ending **-os** is often found in poetry. The dative singular is generally in **-ī** but sometimes in **-i,** as in Greek. The ablative singular is generally in **-e.** The masculine and feminine nominative plural is always in **-es,** and in the accusative plural the Greek **-as** is usual.

Poēma, poēmatis, n., *poem,* is regularly declined, but Cicero has dative and ablative plural poēmatīs. Poēsis, f., *poetry,* has accusative poēs-in *or*-im, ablative poēsī.

Tigris, *tiger,* is declined throughout like cīvis; but also as a consonant-stem in **-d,** forming plural: tigrides, tigridas, tigridum (without dative and ablative).

PROPER NAMES

Proper names in **-ēs,** as Sōcratēs, have vocative **-es** or **-ē**; accusative **-em** or **-ēn**; genitive **-is** or **-ī**; dative **-ī**; ablative **-e.** A few like Thalēs also have accusative **-ēta**; genitive **-ētis**; dative **-ētī**; ablative **-ēte.**

Proper names in **-is,** as Paris, have some forms from a consonant stem and some from an i-stem. So, vocative **-is** or **-i**; accusative **-im, -in, -ida,** or **-idem**; genitive **-idis** or **-idos**; dative **-idi** or **-idī**; ablative **-ide.**

Proper names in **-eus,** as Orpheus, have vocative **-eu**; accusative **-eum** or **-ea**; genitive **-eī** or **-eos**; dative **-eī** or **-eō**; ablative **-eō.** These endings are frequently scanned by the poets as one syllable.

Proper names in **-ōn** often drop the **-n** in the nominative: as Platō, genitive Platōnis.

Feminine proper names in **-ō,** like Dīdō, generally are declined **-ōnem, -ōnis**; but they also have accusative in **-ō,** and genitive in **-ūs.**

ADJECTIVES AND ADVERBS

DECLENSION OF ADJECTIVES

70 Adjectives are declined by Gender, Number, and Case. They fall into two main classes: (A) Adjectives declined like nouns of the first and second declensions; (B) Adjectives declined like nouns of the third declension.

71 A. Like nouns of the first and second declensions are declined Adjectives of three endings in **-us, -a, -um** or **-er, -a, -um**.

Stem	bono-	bonā-	bono-

good

SINGULAR	M.	F.	N.
Nom.	bonus	bona	bonum
Voc.	bone	bona	bonum
Acc.	bonum	bonam	bonum
Gen.	bonī	bonae	bonī
Dat.	bonō	bonae	bonō
Abl.	bonō	bonā	bonō
PLURAL			
Nom.	bonī	bonac	bona
Voc.	bonī	bonae	bona
Acc.	bonōs	bonās	bona
Gen.	bonōrum	bonārum	bonōrum
Dat.	bonīs	bonīs	bonīs
Abl.	bonīs	bonīs	bonīs

Note. Adjectives in **-ius, -ia, -ium,** as eximius, *excellent*, have masc. voc. sing. in **-ie**; masc. and neut. gen. sing. in **-iī**. In these two cases they differ from nouns like fīlius and ingenium (**35b**, n. 1).

Stem	tenero-	tenera-	tenero-
		tender	

SINGULAR	M.	F.	N.
Nom.	tener	tenera	tenerum
Voc.	tener	tenera	tenerum
Acc.	tenerum	teneram	tenerum
Gen.	tenerī	tenerae	tenerī
Dat.	tenerō	tenerae	tenerō
Abl.	tenerō	tenerā	tenerō

PLURAL			
N. V.	tenerī	tenerae	tenera
Acc.	tenerōs	tenerās	tenera
Gen.	tenerōrum	tenerārum	tenerōrum
D. Abl.	tenerīs	tenerīs	tenerīs

So also: asper, *rough*; lacer, *torn*; līber, *free*; miser, *wretched*; prōsper, *prosperous*; frūgifer, *fruit-bearing*, plūmiger, *feathered*, and other compounds of -fer and -ger. Satur, *full*, has fem. satura, neut. saturum.

Stem	nigro-	nigrā-	nigro-
		black	

SINGULAR	M.	F.	N.
Nom.	niger	nigra	nigrum
Voc.	niger	nigra	nigrum
Acc.	nigrum	nigram	nigrum
Gen.	nigrī	nigrae	nigrī
Dat.	nigrō	nigrae	nigrō
Abl.	nigrō	nigrā	nigrō

PLURAL			
N. V.	nigrī	nigrae	nigra
Acc.	nigrōs	nigrās	nigra
Gen.	nigrōrum	nigrārum	nigrōrum
D. Abl.	nigrīs	nigrīs	nigrīs

Note. All adjectives in -er, -a, -um are declined like niger, except those mentioned under tener. Dexter, *on the right hand*, may be declined like tener, or like niger.

B. Like nouns of the third declension are declined (1) Adjectives which have two (rarely three) endings in the Nominative Singular; (2) Adjectives which have one ending for all genders in Nominative Singular.

(1) Adjectives with Nominative Singular in -is, Masculine and Feminine; in -e, Neuter: Stems in -i.

Stem   trīsti-, *sad*

| | SINGULAR | | PLURAL | |
	M. F.	N.	M. F.	N.
N. V.	tristis	triste	tristēs	tristia
Acc.	tristem	triste	tristēs, -īs	tristia
Gen.	tristis	tristis	tristium	tristium
D. Abl.	tristī	tristī	tristibus	tristibus

Some stems in -ri form the Masculine Nominative Singular in -er:

Stem   ācri-, *keen*

SINGULAR	M.	F.	N.
N. V.	ācer	ācris	ācre
Acc.	ācrem	ācrem	ācre
Gen.	ācris	ācris	ācris
Dat. Abl.	ācrī	ācrī	ācrī

PLURAL			
N. V.	ācrēs	ācrēs	ācria
Acc.	ācrēs, -īs	ācrēs, -īs	ācria
Gen.	ācrium	ācrium	ācrium
D. Abl.	ācribus	ācribus	ācribus

The other adjectives like **ācer** are: celeber, *famous*; salūber, *healthy*; alacer, *brisk*; campester, *level*; equester, *equestrian*; pedester, *pedestrian*; palūster, *marshy*; puter, *crumbling*; silvester, *woody*; terrester, *earthly*; volucer, *winged*.

Note 1. In celer, celeris, celere, *swift*, the Stem itself ends in -eri and the e is therefore kept throughout. The noun celerēs, *patricians*, has gen. pl. celerum.

Note 2. Names of months are adjectives (agreeing with mēnsis, m., Kalendae, f., Nōnae, f., Īdūs, f.): Aprīlis is declined like trīstis; September, Octōber, November, December like ācer; the rest like bonus. *Cf.* **498.**

74   (2) Adjectives with Nominative Singular the same for all genders:

(a) Stems in -i.

Stem   fēlīci-, *happy*

	M. F. SING.	N.	M. F. PLUR.	N.
N. V.	fēlix	fēlix	fēlīcēs	fēlīcia
Acc.	fēlīcem	fēlix	fēlīcēs, -īs	fēlīcia
Gen.	fēlīcis	fēlīcis	fēlīcium	fēlīcium
Dat. Abl.	fēlīcī	fēlīcī	fēlīcibus	fēlīcibus

Stem   ingenti-, *huge*

	M. F. SING.	N.	M. F. PLUR.	N.
N. V.	ingēns	ingēns	ingentēs	ingentia
Acc.	ingentem	ingēns	ingentēs, -īs	ingentia
Gen.	ingentis		ingentium	
Dat. Abl.	ingentī		ingentibus	

Like ingēns are declined all Present Participles.

Note 1. In all adjectives from i-stems the abl. sing. generally ends in i when the adj. is used with a substantive, and in e when the adj. stands in place of a substantive. This rule applies especially to Present Participles: ā sapientī virō, *by a wise man*, ā sapiente, *by a philosopher*. But in the ablative absolute construction (237) the ablative always ends in e: viridantī quercū cīnctus, *wreathed with green oak*; viridante quercū, *when the oak is green*.

Note 2. Some adjectives with stems in -ti have genitive plural in -um as well as -ium: cōnsors, cōnsortum or cōnsortium. In Participles, however, the gen. plur. is almost always in -ium.

---

75 (b) Consonant Stems

Stem   veter-, *old*

	M. F. SING.	N.	M. F. PLUR.	N.
N. V.	vetus	vetus	veterēs	vetera
Acc.	veterem	vetus	veterēs	vetera
Gen.	veteris	veteris	veterum	veterum
Dat.	veterī	veterī	veteribus	veteribus
Abl.	vetere	vetere	veteribus	veteribus

The most important adjectives with consonant-stems are: caelebs, -ibis, *unmarried*; compos, -otis, *possessing*; dīves, -itis, *rich*; inops, -opis, *poor*; memor, -oris, *mindful*; particeps, -cipis, *sharing*; pauper, -eris, *poor*; sōspes, -itis, *safe*; superstes, -stitis, *surviving*.

Note 1. Dīves has contracted forms also: nom. dīs; acc. dītem; gen. dītis; dat. and abl. dītī; the plural forms commonly used are: nom. and acc. dītēs (m., f.), dītia (n.); gen. dīvitum and dītium; dat. and abl. dītibus.

Note 2. Inops and memor have abl. sing. in -ī.

Frūgī, *thrifty*, and nēquam, *wicked*, are used as indeclinable adjectives.

COMPARISON OF ADJECTIVES

76 Adjectives are compared in three degrees:

   (1) Positive: **dūrus,** *hard.*
   (2) Comparative: **dūrior,** *harder (rather hard, too hard)* **(309).**
   (3) Superlative: **dūrissimus,** *hardest (very hard)* **(310).**

The Comparative is formed from the Positive by adding the suffix **-ior (-ius)** to the last consonant of the Stem; the Superlative generally by adding **-issimus (-a, -um)** to the last consonant of the Stem.

Stem	Positive	Comparative	Superlative
dūr-o-	dūrus, *hard*	dūr-ior	dūr-issimus
trīst-i-	trīstis, *sad*	trīst-ior	trīst-issimus
audāc-i-	audāx, *bold*	audāc-ior	audāc-issimus

77 The Comparative is declined as a consonant-stem, with Nominative Singular endings **-ior** *m.f.,* **-ius** *n.*

	M. F. SING.	N.	M. F. PLUR.	N.
N. V.	trīstior	trīstius	trīstiōrēs	trīstiōra
Acc.	trīstiōrem	trīstius	trīstiōrēs	trīstiōra
Gen.	trīstiōris		trīstiōrum	
Dat.	trīstiōrī		trīstiōribus	
Abl.	trīstiōre		trīstiōribus	

78 The Superlative is declined from **o-** and **ā-** Stems, like bonus.
Adjectives with Stems in **-ro, -ri,** form the Superlative by doubling
the last consonant of the Stem and adding **-imus.** Words like niger
(71) have **e** before **r** in the Superlative.

Stem	Positive	Comparative	Superlative
tenero-	tener	tenerior	tenerrimus
nigro-	niger	nigrior	nigerrimus
celeri-	celer	celerior	celerrimus

Six adjectives with Stems in **-ili** also form the Superlative by
doubling the last consonant of the Stem and adding **-imus**:

facilis,	*easy*	similis,	*like*	gracilis,	*slender*
difficilis,	*difficult*	dissimilis,	*unlike*	humilis,	*lowly*
facili-		facilis	facilior	facillimus	

79 Many Participles are compared like adjectives:

amāns,	*loving*	amantior	amantissimus
parātus,	*ready*	parātior	parātissimus

Irregular Comparison

80a   (1) Some Comparatives and Superlatives are formed from Stems
distinct from that of the Positive:

Positive	Comparative	Superlative
bonus, *good*	melior, *better*	optimus, *best*
malus, *bad*	peior,* *worse*	pessimus, *worst*
parvus, *small*	minor, *less*	minimus, *least*
multus, *much*	plūs, *more*	plūrimus, *most*
magnus, *great*	maior*	maximus
nēquam (indecl.), *wicked*	nēquior	nēquissimus
frūgī (indecl.), *honest*	frūgālior	frūgālissimus
senex, *old*	∫ senior	nātū maximus
	⎰ nātū maior	
iuvenis, *young*	∫ iūnior	nātū minimus
	⎰ nātū minor	

Note 1.   Senior, iūnior are not used as true comparatives of senex, iuvenis, but
with the meaning *old rather than young,* and *young rather than old.*

Note 2.   Dīves has comp. dīvitior and dītior; superl. dīvitissimus and dītissimus.
Vetus has comp. veterior (rare) and vetustior (from vetustus); superl. veterrimus.

Note 3.   The consonant-i between vowels in words like peior, maior, eius, huius,
was pronounced as a doubled consonant; consequently the first *syllable* of such
words is long even though the *vowel* preceding the i is short.

Plūs is used in the Singular only as a neuter noun; in the Plural as an adjective.

	SINGULAR	M. F. PLURAL	N.
N. V., Acc.	plūs	plūrēs	plūra
Gen.	plūris	plūrium	
Dat.	—	plūribus	
Abl.	plūre	plūribus	

(2) Adjectives ending in **-dicus, -ficus, -volus** (cf. dīcō, faciō, volō), form the Comparative and Superlative as if from forms in -dīcēns, -ficēns, -volēns.

Positive	Comparative	Superlative
maledicus, *evil-speaking*	maledīcentior	maledīcentissimus
beneficus, *beneficent*	beneficentior	beneficentissimus
benevolus, *well-wishing*	benevolentior	benevolentissimus
Also: egēnus, *needy* (cf. egeō)	egentior	egentissimus
prōvidus, *provident* (cf. videō)	prōvidentior	prōvidentissimus

82 (3) Adjectives in **-eus, -ius, -uus** are generally compared by means of the adverbs magis, maximē; as dubius, *doubtful*, magis dubius, *more doubtful*, maximē dubius, *most doubtful*.

Note. Adjectives in **-quus** are compared regularly, the first u being consonantal: aequus, *level*, aequior, aequissimus; so, antīquus, *ancient*. Ēgregius, *excellent*, has comparative ēgregior; strēnuus, *vigorous*, sometimes has strēnuior.

---

83 (4) Some adjectives have no Comparative forms; some no Superlative; of some the Comparative and Superlative are found without the Positive: ōcior, *swifter*, ōcissimus, *swiftest*.

84 Some Comparatives denoting relations of place have no Positive, but correspond to Adverbs or Prepositions from the same Stem.

Adverb		Comparative Adj.	Superlative Adj.
*extrā,	outside	exterior	extrēmus, extimus
intrā,	within	interior	intimus
*suprā,	above	superior	suprēmus, summus
*īnfrā,	below	īnferior	īnfimus, īmus
citrā,	on this side	citerior	citimus
ultrā,	beyond	ulterior	ultimus
prae,	before	prior	prīmus, *first*
*post,	after	posterior	postrēmus, *last*
prope,	near	propior	proximus
(dē, *down*)		dēterior, *worse*	dēterrimus, *worst*

---

* *Note.* The adjectives exterus, superus, īnferus, posterus, are, however, sometimes found.

Formation and Comparison of Adverbs

85a Most Adverbs differ from cognate adjectives in having: (1) -ē or -ō for the -ī of the genitive singular masculine of adjectives of the first and second declension: dignē, *worthily*, from dignus, pulchrē, *beautifully*, from pulcher, tūtō, *safely*, from tūtus.

(2) -iter, -ter, or -er for the -is of the genitive singular of adjectives of the third declension: fortiter, *bravely*, from fortis, audācter, *boldly*, from audāx, cōnstanter, *firmly*, from cōnstāns.

A few Adverbs are simply the accusative singular neuter of adjectives: facile, *easily*, from facilis.

Note. The acc. or abl. of some nouns and pronouns are used as adverbs: partim, *partly*, aliās, *at other times*; prīncipiō, *in the beginning*, aliquā, *somehow*. From participial stems note, *e.g.* statim, *at once* (*cf.* stō), cursim, *in haste* (*cf.* currō). Such words have no comparative or superlative.

85b The Comparative of an Adverb regularly consists of the accusative singular neuter of the comparative of the adjective; and the Superlative of an Adverb generally ends in -issimē.

Adjective		*Adverb*		*Comparative*	*Superlative*
dignus,	*worthy*	dignē,	*worthily*	dignius	dignissimē
tūtus,	*safe*	tūtō,	*safely*	tūtius	tūtissimē
fortis,	*brave*	fortiter,	*bravely*	fortius	fortissimē
audāx,	*bold*	audācter,	*boldly*	audācius	audācissimē
cōnstāns,	*firm*	cōnstanter,	*firmly*	cōnstantius	cōnstantissimē
facilis,	*easy*	facile,	*easily*	facilius	facillimē

86 When an adjective is irregular in comparison (**80a**), the corresponding Adverb is irregular also:

Adverb		*Comparative*	*Superlative*
bene,	*well*	melius	optimē
male,	*ill*	peius (*cf.* p. 42*)	pessimē
paulum,	*little*	minus	minimē
multum,	*much*	plūs	plūrimum
magnopere,	*greatly*	magis	maximē
—		ōcius, *more quickly*	ōcissimē
nēquiter,	*wickedly*	nēquius	nēquissimē

Note. Magis, *more* (in degree); plūs, *more* (in quantity).

87 Notice also:

diū,	*long*	diūtius	diūtissimē
intus,	*within*	interius	intimē
(prae,	*before*)	prius	prīmum, prīmō
post,	*after*	posterius	postrēmō
prope,	*near*	propius	proximē
saepe,	*often*	saepius	saepissimē
nūper,	*lately*	—	nūperrimē
—		potius, *rather*	potissimum, *especially*

Numerals

Numeral Adjectives are of three kinds:

1. Cardinals; answering the question, *How many?*
2. Ordinals; answering the question, *Which in order of number?*
3. Distributives; answering the question, *How many each?*

Numeral Adverbs answer the question, *How many times?*

Ūnus, *one*, from o- and ā- Stems, is declined as follows:

| | SINGULAR | | | PLURAL | | | |
	M.	F.	N.	M.	F.	N.	
Nom.	ūnus	ūna	ūnum	ūnī		ūnae	ūna
Acc.	ūnum	ūnam	ūnum	ūnōs		ūnās	ūna
Gen.	ūnīus	ūnīus	ūnīus	ūnōrum		ūnārum	ūnōrum
Dat.	ūnī	ūnī	ūnī	ūnīs		ūnīs	ūnīs
Abl.	ūnō	ūnā	ūnō	ūnīs		ūnīs	ūnīs

The i of the gen. sing. is sometimes short.   For words declined like ūnus see **101a.**

Duo, *two* is an o- Stem, and trēs, *three*, an i- Stem.

	M.	F.	N.	M. and F.	N.
Nom.	duo	duae	duo	trēs	tria
Acc.	duōs, duo	duās	duo	trēs(-i)	tria
Gen.	duōrum	duārum	duōrum	trium	trium
D. Abl.	duōbus	duābus	duōbus	tribus	tribus

Duum is sometimes used for duōrum, duārum.   **Ambō,** *both,* is declined like duo, except that it has ō in the nom. and acc. of m. and n.

Note 1.   The **Cardinals** from quattuor to centum are indeclinable.   Hundreds from *two* to *nine hundred* are o- and ā- Stems: ducentī, ducentae, ducenta.   Mīlle (*a thousand*) is an indeclinable adjective; but mīlia (*thousands*) is a neuter substantive declined like animālia.   *Cf.* **311.**

Note 2.   In **Compound Numbers** between twenty and ninety-nine, the order is the same as in English.   Either the smaller number with **et** comes first, or the larger without **et**: septem et trīgintā, *seven and thirty*; or trīgintā septem, *thirty-seven*.   Ūnus usually stands first: ūnus et vīgintī, *twenty-one*.   In numbers above a hundred the larger comes first, with or without **et.**

Thousands are expressed by putting (1) the numeral adverbs bis, ter, &c., before mīlle: bis mīlle; or (2) cardinal numbers before mīlia: duo mīlia.   Mīlia is followed by a genitive: duo mīlia hominum, *two thousand men.*

Note 3.   The **Ordinals** and **Distributives** are o- and ā- Stems: singulī, singulae, singula.   Besides indicating *how many each*, the distributives are also used in place of the Cardinals with nouns that are plural in form but singular in meaning: bīna castra, *two camps.*   *Cf.* **312–3.**

ARABIC NUMERALS	ROMAN NUMERALS	CARDINALS	ORDINALS	DISTRIBUTIVES	NUMERAL ADVERBS
		answering the question Quot? *how many?*	answering the question Quotus? *which in order of number?* m. -*us*, f. -*a*, n. -*um*.	answering the question Quotēnī? *how many each?* m. -ī, f. -*ae*, n. *a*	answering the question Quotiēns? *how many times?*
1	I	ūnus	prīmus (prior), *first*	singulī, *one each*	semel, *once*
2	II	duo	secundus (alter), *second*	bīnī, *two each*	bis, *twice*
3	III	trēs	tertius	ternī *or* trīnī	ter
4	IIII or IV	quattuor	quārtus	quaternī	quater
5	V	quīnque	quīntus	quīnī	quīnquiēns
6	VI	sex	sextus	sēnī	sexiēns
7	VII	septem	septimus	septēnī	septiēns
8	VIII	octō	octāvus	octōnī	octiēns
9	IX	novem	nōnus	novēnī	noviēns
10	X	decem	decimus	dēnī	deciēns
11	XI	ūndecim	ūndecimus	ūndēnī	ūndeciēns
12	XII	duodecim	duodecimus	duodēnī	duodeciēns
13	XIII	tredecim	tertius decimus	ternī dēnī	terdeciēns
14	XIV	quattuordecim	quārtus decimus	quaternī dēnī	quattuordeciēns
15	XV	quīndecim	quīntus decimus	quīnī dēnī	quīndeciēns
16	XVI	sēdecim	sextus decimus	sēnī dēnī	sēdeciēns
17	XVII	septendecim	septimus decimus	septēnī dēnī	septiēns deciēns
18	XVIII	duodēvīgintī	duodēvīcēnsimus	duodēvīcēnī	duodēviciēns
19	XIX	ūndēvīgintī	ūndēvīcēnsimus	ūndēvīcēnī	ūndēviciēns
20	XX	vīgintī	vīcēnsimus	vīcēnī	vīciēns
21	XXI	ūnus et vīgintī	ūnus et vīcēnsimus	vīcēnī singulī	semel et vīciēns
22	XXII	duo et vīgintī	alter et vīcēnsimus	vīcēnī bīnī	bis et vīciēns
28	XXVIII	duodētrīgintā	duodētrīcēnsimus	duodētrīcēnī	duodētrīciēns
29	XXIX	ūndētrīgintā	ūndētrīcēnsimus	ūndētrīcēnī	ūndētrīciēns
30	XXX	trīgintā	trīcēnsimus	trīcēnī	trīciēns
40	XL	quadrāgintā	quadrāgēnsimus	quadrāgēnī	quadrāgiēns

[46]

50	L	**quīnquāgintā**	quīnquāgēnsimus	quīnquāgēni	quīnquāgiēns
60	LX	**sexāgintā**	sexāgēnsimus	sexāgēni	sexāgiēns
70	LXX	**septuāgintā**	septuāgēnsimus	septuāgēni	septuāgiēns
80	LXXX	**octōgintā**	octōgēnsimus	octōgēni	octōgiēns
90	XC	**nōnāgintā**	nōnāgēnsimus	nōnāgēni	nōnāgiēns
98	IIC	**octō et nōnāgintā**	duodēcentēnsimus	duodēcentēni	duodēcentiēns
99	XCIX	**ūndēcentum**	ūndēcentēnsimus	ūndēcentēni	ūndēcentiēns
100	C	**centum**	centēnsimus	centēni	centiēns
101	CI	**centum et ūnus**	centēnsimus prīmus	centēni singuli	centiēns semel
126	CXXVI	**centum vīgintī sex**	centēnsimus vīcēnsimus sextus	centēni vīcēni sēni	centiēns vīciēns sexiēns
200	CC	**ducentī, ae, a**	ducentēnsimus	ducēni	ducentiēns
300	CCC	**trecentī**	trecentēnsimus	trecēni	trecentiēns
400	CCCC	**quadringentī**	quadringentēnsimus	quadringēni	quadringentiēns
500	IƆ or D	**quīngentī**	quīngentēnsimus	quīngēni	quīngentiēns
600	IƆC	**sescentī**	sescentēnsimus	sescēni	sescentiēns
700	IƆCC	**septingentī**	septingentēnsimus	septingēni	septingentiēns
800	IƆCCC	**octingentī**	octingentēnsimus	octingēni	octingentiēns
900	IƆCCCC	**nōngentī**	nōngentēnsimus	nōngēni	nōngentiēns
1,000	CIƆ or M	**mille**	mīllēnsimus	singula mīlia	mīliēns
2,000	CIƆCIƆ	**duo mīlia**	bis mīllēnsimus	bīna mīlia	bis mīliēns
5,000	IƆƆ	**quīnque mīlia**	quīnquiēns mīllēnsimus	quīna mīlia	quīnquiēns mīliēns
10,000	CCIƆƆ	**decem mīlia**	deciēns mīllēnsimus	dēna mīlia	deciēns mīliēns
50,000	IƆƆƆ	**quīnquāgintā mīlia**	quīnquāgiēns mīllēnsimus	quīnquāgēna mīlia	quīnquāgiēns mīliēns
100,000	CCCIƆƆƆ	**centum mīlia**	centiēns mīllēnsimus	centēna mīlia	centiēns mīliēns
500,000	IƆƆƆƆ	**quīngenta mīlia**	quīngentiēns mīllēnsimus	quīngēna mīlia	quīngentiēns mīliēns
1,000,000	CCCCIƆƆƆƆ	**deciēns centēna mīlia**	deciēns centiēns mīllēnsimus	deciēns centēna mīlia	deciēns centiēns mīliēns

Note 1. Some of the Cardinals formed with duodē-, ūndē- are rare. Such forms for 68, 69 and 98 never occur.

Note 2. The endings -ēnsimus and -iēns are often written -ēsimus, -iēs (*cf.* **17**, *b*, 2).

Note 3. MULTIPLICATIVES, answering the question, *how many fold?* are: simplex, duplex, triplex, **&c.**, centuplex, *a hundredfold* (gen. -**plicis**, from Stem **plic-**, *fold*).

[47]

PRONOUNS AND PRONOMINAL ADJECTIVES

91 There are the following kinds of Pronoun: (1) Personal, (2) Reflexive, (3) Possessive, (4) Demonstrative, (5) Definitive, (6) Intensive, (7) Relative, (8) Interrogative, (9) Indefinite.

Personal and Reflexive Pronouns are used only as Substantives; Possessive Pronouns only as Adjectives; the others as Substantives or Adjectives.

PERSONAL PRONOUNS

92a There are three Persons:

First: The person speaking: *I* or *we.*
Second: The person spoken to: *thou* or *you* (s. and pl.).
Third: The person or thing spoken of: *he, she, it, they*

	1st Person		SINGULAR		2nd Person
Nom.	**ego,**	*I*		**tū,**	*thou, you* (Voc. also)
Acc.	**mē,**	*me*		**tē,**	*thee, you*
Gen.	**mei,**	*of me*		**tui,**	*of thee, of you*
Dat.	**mihi,**	*to me*		**tibi,**	*to thee, to you*
Abl.	**mē,**	*(from) me*		**tē,**	*(from) thee, (from) you*

			PLURAL		
Nom.	**nōs,**	*we*		**vōs,**	*you* (Voc. also)
Acc.	**nōs,**	*us*		**vōs,**	*you*
Gen.	{ **nostrī** / **nostrum** }, *of us*			{ **vestrī** / **vestrum** }, *of you*	
Dat.	**nōbīs,**	*to us*		**vōbīs,**	*to you*
Abl.	**nōbīs,**	*(from) us*		**vōbīs,**	*(from) you*

Note 1. The second -i of mihi and tibi sometimes retains its original length (*cf.* 17, *a,* 3). A dative mī also occurs.

Note 2. Nostrī, vestrī, are called Objective Genitives: memor nostrī, *mindful of us* (263). Nostrum, vestrum, are called Partitive Genitives, because they are used after words which express a part: ūnus nostrum, *one of us* (259).

For the Personal Pronoun of the 3rd Person, *he, she, it,* the Demonstrative **is, ea, id,** is used (*cf.* 94),

92b

REFLEXIVE PRONOUN (3rd Person, *cf.* 316)

Acc.	**sē** or **sēsē,**	*himself, herself, itself,* or *themselves.*
Gen.	**sui,**	*of himself,* &c.
Dat.	**sibi,**	*to himself,* &c.
Abl.	**sē** or **sēsē,**	*(from) himself,* &c.

Note. The second -i of sibi is sometimes long (*cf.* 17, *a,* 3).

These forms serve for both numbers of all three genders. The oblique cases of ego and tū serve as reflexives of the First and Second Persons.

POSSESSIVE PRONOUNS (Adjectival only, 91)

SINGULAR	1st Person:	**meus,**	**mea,**	**meum,**	*my*
	2nd Person:	**tuus,**	**tua,**	**tuum,**	*thy, your*
PLURAL	1st Person:	**noster,**	**nostra,**	**nostrum,**	*our*
	2nd Person:	**vester,**	**vestra,**	**vestrum,**	*your*

Suus, sua, suum, *his, her, its, their,* is the Possessive of the Reflexive Pronoun (*cf.* 317).

Note. Meus, tuus, suus are declined like bonus: noster, vester, like niger. Meus has voc. sing. masc. mī. The other possessives, except noster, have no vocative.

DEMONSTRATIVE PRONOUNS

Is, *that*, or *he, she, it*

	SINGULAR			PLURAL		
	M.	F.	N.	M.	F.	N.
Nom.	**is**	**ea**	**id**	**iī (eī, ī)**	**eae**	**ea**
Acc.	**eum**	**eam**	**id**	**eōs**	**eās**	**ea**
Gen.	**eius***	**eius***	**eius***	**eōrum**	**eārum**	**eōrum**
Dat.	**eī**	**eī**	**eī**	**eīs, iīs**	**eīs, iīs**	**eīs, iīs**
Abl.	**eō**	**eā**	**eō**	**eīs, iīs**	**eīs, iīs**	**eīs, iīs**

Hic, *this* (*near me*), or *he, she, it*

	SINGULAR			PLURAL		
	M.	F.	N.	M.	F.	N.
Nom.	**hic†**	**haec**	**hoc†**	**hī**	**hae**	**haec**
Acc.	**hunc**	**hanc**	**hoc†**	**hōs**	**hās**	**haec**
Gen.	**huius***	**huius***	**huius***	**hōrum**	**hārum**	**hōrum**
Dat.	**huic**	**huic**	**huic**	**hīs**	**hīs**	**hīs**
Abl.	**hōc**	**hāc**	**hōc**	**hīs**	**hīs**	**hīs**

Ille, *that* (*yonder*), or *he, she, it*

	SINGULAR			PLURAL		
	M.	F.	N.	M.	F.	N.
Nom.	**ille**	**illa**	**illud**	**illī**	**illae**	**illa**
Acc.	**illum**	**illam**	**illud**	**illōs**	**illās**	**illa**
Gen.	**illīus**	**illīus**	**illīus**	**illōrum**	**illārum**	**illōrum**
Dat.	**illī**	**illī**	**illī**	**illīs**	**illīs**	**illīs**
Abl.	**illō**	**illā**	**illō**	**illīs**	**illīs**	**illīs**

Note. The second -i of the gen. sing. is sometimes short.

Iste, *that* (*near you*), is declined like ille.

* See p. 42, note 3.

† Generally pronounced hicc, hocc (from hodce, 96, note 3). These *syllables* are therefore generally long.

95

DEFINITIVE PRONOUN

Īdem, *same*

SINGULAR

	M.	F.	N.
Nom.	īdem	eadem	idem
Acc.	eundem	eandem	idem
Gen.	eiusdem*	eiusdem*	eiusdem*
Dat.	eīdem	eīdem	eīdem
Abl.	eōdem	eādem	eōdem

PLURAL

	M.	F.	N.
Nom.	īdem *or* eīdem	eaedem	eadem
Acc.	eōsdem	eāsdem	eadem
Gen.	eōrundem	eārundem	eōrundem
Dat.	īsdem *or* eīsdem		
Abl.	īsdem *or* eīsdem		

96

INTENSIVE PRONOUN

Ipse, *self*

	SINGULAR			PLURAL		
	M.	F.	N.	M.	F.	N.
Nom.	ipse	ipsa	ipsum	ipsī	ipsae	ipsa
Acc.	ipsum	ipsam	ipsum	ipsōs	ipsās	ipsa
Gen.	ipsīus	ipsīus	ipsīus	ipsōrum	ipsārum	ipsōrum
Dat.	ipsī	ipsī	ipsī	ipsīs	ipsīs	ipsīs
Abl.	ipsō	ipsā	ipsō	ipsīs	ipsīs	ipsīs

Ipsĭus also occurs in genitive singular.

Note 1. Īdem (for is-dem), and ipse (for is-pse), are emphatic forms of **is**. The logically accurate forms eapse, eampse (for ipsa, ipsam), &c., sometimes occur. For ipsissimus, see 320, n.

Note 2. The suffixes -met, -te, -pte *or* -pse are added to some cases of pronouns for emphasis:

(*a*) -met may be joined (1) to ego and its cases, except gen. plur.: egomet, *I myself*; (2) to the cases of tū, except nom. sing. and gen. plur.; vōsmet, *you yourselves*; (3) to sē and its cases, except suī: sibimet; (4) to the cases of suus: suamet facta.

(*b*) -te is joined to tū: tūte; tūtemet, *thou thyself, you yourself.*

(*c*) -pte is joined especially to the abl. sing. of the possessive pronouns: meōpte cōnsiliō, *by my advice.*

Note 3. The -c at the end of some forms of the Pronoun hic, is a demonstrative particle whose full form is -ce. It is sometimes found with other demonstrative forms as: huiusce, hōsce; istīc, istaec, istuc (for istud-ce); illīc, illaec, illuc.

---

* See p. 42, note 3.

RELATIVE PRONOUN
Quī, *who, which*

	M.	F.	N.	M.	F.	N.
	SINGULAR			PLURAL		
Nom.	quī	quae	quod	quī	quae	quae
Acc.	quem	quam	quod	quōs	quās	quae
Gen.	cuius*	cuius*	cuius*	quōrum	quārum	quōrum
Dat.	cui	cui	cui	quibus *or* quīs		
Abl.	quō	quā	quō	quibus *or* quīs		

INTERROGATIVE PRONOUN
Quis, *who? what?*

	M.	F.	N.		M.	F.	N.
Nom. {	quis / quī	(quis) / quae	quid / quod	*Acc.* {	quem / quem	quam / quam	quid / quod

In all other Cases singular and plural the Interrogative is like the Relative.

INDEFINITE PRONOUN
Quis, *anyone* or *anything*

	M.	F.	N.		M.	F.	N.
Nom. {	quis / quī	qua / quae	quid / quod	*Acc.* {	quem / quem	quam / quam	quid / quod

In the other Cases singular and plural the Indefinite is like the Relative, except that qua or quae may be used in neuter nominative and accusative plural.

Quis, both Interrogative and Indefinite, and its compounds (*cf.* 102), are used **chiefly** as Substantives; **quī** and its compounds **chiefly** as Adjectives.

Quid and its compounds are used **only** as Substantives; **quod** and its compounds **only** as Adjectives.

EXAMPLES:

Is quī venit,	*The man who comes*	(quī, relative)
Quis venit?	*Who comes?*	(quis, interrogative)
Quī homō venit?	*What man comes?*	(quī, interrogative)
Aliquid amārī,	*Some bitterness*	
Aliquod verbum,	*Some word*	

* See p. 42, Note 3.

100   COMPOUND PRONOUNS

MASCULINE	FEMININE	NEUTER	
quicumque, **quisquis,**	**quaecumque,** **quisquis,**	**quodcumque,** **quidquid** or **quicquid,**	} *whosoever*, or *whatsoever*
quidam,	**quaedam,**	**quiddam (quoddam),**	{ *a certain person* or *thing*
aliquis, **aliquī,**	**aliqua,** **aliqua,**	**aliquid,** **aliquod,**	} *someone* or *something*
quispiam,	**quaepiam,**	**quippiam (quodpiam),**	*someone*
quivīs, **quīlibet,**	**quaevīs,** **quaelibet**	**quidvīs (quodvīs),** **quidlibet (quodlibet),**	} *anyone you like*
quisquam,	——	**quidquam** or **quicquam,**	*anyone at all*
quisque,	**quaeque,**	**quidque (quodque),**	{ *each one* *severally*
ūnusquisque,	**ūnaquaeque,**	**ūnumquidque** (**ūnumquodque**),	} *each single one*
ecquis,	**ecqua,**	**ecquid (ecquod),**	{ *Is there any* *who?*
quisnam,	**quaenam,**	**quidnam (quodnam),**	*Who, pray?*

Note 1. Quisquis is found only in nom., acc., and abl.

Note 2. Quisquam is used as a substantive, sing. only, chiefly in negative sentences: haud quisquam, *not anyone*; the adjective which corresponds to it is ūllus.

Note 3. In Compound Pronouns, quī, quis, follow their own declension in the oblique cases; the prefix or suffix is unaltered (alicuius, cuiusque, cuivīs, quamlibet) except that in ūnusquisque both ūnus and quisque are declined.

The following Pronominal Adjectives form the Genitive Singular in
-īus or -ius, and the Dative Singular in -ī: **ūllus**, *any*; **nūllus**, *none*;
sōlus, *sole*; **tōtus**, *whole*; **alius**, *other, another*; **alter**, *one of two, the
other*; **uter**, *which of two?*, *whichever of two*; **neuter**, *neither*.
   Ūllus, nūllus, sōlus, tōtus are declined like ūnus (89).

Note. Nūllīus, gen. sing., and nūllō, abl. sing. of nūllus, are used as gen. and
abl. sing. of nēmō, *nobody* (66).

Alius is declined:

	SINGULAR			PLURAL		
	M.	F.	N.	M.	F.	N.
Nom.	alius	alia	aliud	aliī	aliae	alia
Acc.	alium	aliam	aliud	aliōs	aliās	alia
Gen.	alīus	alīus	alīus	aliōrum	aliārum	aliōrum
Dat.	aliī	aliī	aliī	aliīs	aliīs	aliīs
Abl.	aliō	aliā	aliō	aliīs	aliīs	aliīs

   In place of the gen. sing. of alius, the gen. sing. of alter or the adjective aliēnus
is used, to avoid confusion with the nom. sing.

c Alter is declined:

SINGULAR	M.	F.	N.
Nom.	alter	altera	alterum
Acc.	alterum	alteram	alterum
Gen.	alterīus	alterīus	alterīus
Dat.	alterī	alterī	alterī
Abl.	alterō	alterā	alterō
PLURAL	M.	F.	N.
Nom.	alterī	alterae	altera
Acc.	alterōs	alterās	altera
Gen.	alterōrum	alterārum	alterōrum
Dat. Abl.	alterīs	alterīs	alterīs

The gen. sing. is often alterīus.

   Like alter, but without **e** before **r** in all cases except the Nominative
Singular Masculine, are declined **uter** and **neuter**. These are seldom
used in the plural.

Note 1. Uter forms compounds by taking nearly all the same suffixes as quis
and quī: utercumque, *whichever of two*; utervīs, uterlibet. In alteruter, *one or
the other,* usually, the second part only is declined, but sometimes both parts are
declined.

54 PRONOUNS

102 TABLE OF CORRELATIVE PRONOUNS, ADJECTIVES AND ADVERBS

Interrogative	Demonstrative	Relative	Indefinite (1)
quis, quĭ, *who? which?*	is, *that*	quī, *who, which*	(sĭ) quis, (*if*) *any one*
uter, *which of two?*	alter, *one of two, other of two*		
quālis, *of what kind?*	tālis, *of such a kind*	quālis, *as*	
quantus, *how great?*	tantus, *so great*	quantus, *as (great)*	
quot, *how many?*	tot, *so many*	quot, *as (many)*	
ubi, *where?*	ibi, *there*	ubi, *where*	sīcubi, *if anywhere*
unde, *whence?*	inde, *thence*	unde, *whence*	sīcunde, *if from any quarter*
quŏ, *whither?*	eŏ, *thither*	quŏ, *whither*	(sī) quŏ, (*if*) *anywhither*
quā, *by what way?*	eā, *by that way*	quā, *by what way*	(sī) quā, (*if*) *by any way*
quam, *how?*	tam, *so*	quam, *as*	
quandŏ, *when?*	tum, *then*	{ quandŏ, *when* ubi, *when* cum, *when* }	(sī) quandŏ, (*if*) *ever*
quotiēns, *how often?*	totiēns, *so often*	quotiēns, *as (often)*	

Indefinite (2)	*Distributive*	*Universal Relative*
aliquis, *some one*	quisque, *each*	quīcumque, *whoever, whatever*
alteruter, *one or other of two*	uterque, *each of two*	utercumque, *whichever of two*
		quāliscumque, *of what kind soever*
aliquantus, *some (in quantity)*		quantuscumque, *however great*
aliquot, *some (in number)*		quotcumque, *however many*
alicubi, *somewhere*	ubique, *everywhere*	ubicumque, *wheresoever*
alicunde, *from some quarter*	undique, *from every side*	undecumque, *whencesoever*
aliquō, *somewhither*		quōcumque, *whithersoever*
aliquā, *by some way*		quācumque, *by whatsoever way*
aliquandō, *at some time*		quandōcumque, *whensoever*
aliquotiēns, *at some (various) times*		quotiēnscumque, *however often*

VERBS

103 The **Verb** has:

The **Three Persons**—First, Second, Third. ⎤
The **Two Numbers**—Singular and Plural. |
Six **Tenses**—(1) Present, (2) Future Simple, | The Verb
    (3) Past Imperfect, (4) Perfect, (5) Future ⎬ Finite
    Perfect, (6) Pluperfect. |
Three Moods—(1) Indicative, (2) Imperative, |
    (3) Subjunctive. ⎦

The **Infinitives** (Verbal Substantives). ⎤
Three Participles (Verbal Adjectives). |
The **Gerund** and **Gerundive** (Verbal Substan- ⎬ The Verb
    tive and Adjective). | Infinite
Two Supines (Verbal Substantives). |
Two Voices—(1) Active, (2) Passive. ⎦

The Verb Finite is so called because it is limited by Mood and Persons; while the Verb Infinite is not so limited.

104
PERSON AND NUMBER

The inflexion of a verb according to Person and Number is effected by adding personal suffixes:

su-**m**,	*I am*, am-**ō**, *I love*	su-**mus**,	*we are*
es (for es-s), *thou art, you are*		es-**tis**,	*you are*
es-**t**,	*he (she, it) is*	su-**nt**,	*they are*

CHIEF PERSONAL ENDINGS IN THE INDICATIVE AND SUBJUNCTIVE MOODS

		ACTIVE VOICE	PASSIVE VOICE
Singular	1	**-m** *or* **-ō**	**-r**
	2	**-s**	**-ris** *or* **-re**
	3	**-t**	**-tur**
Plural	1	**-mus**	**-mur**
	2	**-tis**	**-minī**
	3	**-nt**	**-ntur**

In the Perfect Indicative the endings are: **-ī, -is-tī, -it; -imus, -is-tis, -ērunt** (or **-ēre**).

The Imperative Mood has only the Second and Third Persons Singular and Plural, not the First.

TENSES (*cf.* **336–343**)

The six tenses of the **Indicative** represent an action or state as being: (1) Present, Future, or Past; (2) Incomplete or Complete; (3) Momentary or Continuous.

In English, by means of auxiliary Verbs, such differences can be more accurately expressed than in Latin; some tenses in Latin correspond to two tenses in English, of which one is momentary, the other continuous. Thus, rogō, *I ask*, has the following tenses in the Indicative:

Present {	Present	*incomplete*	rogō	{ *I ask* / *I am asking*
	Perfect	*complete*	rogāvī	*I have asked*
Future {	Fut. Simple	*incomplete*	rogābō	{ *I shall ask* / *I shall be asking*
	Fut. Perf.	*complete*	rogāverō	*I shall have asked*
Past {	Perfect } Imperf. }	*incomplete*	{ rogāvī / rogābam	{ *I asked* / *I was asking*
	Pluperf.	*complete*	rogāveram	*I had asked*

Note 1. Latin has no tenses corresponding to English *I have been asking, I shall have been asking, I had been asking.* To express such ideas, Latin resorts to idiomatic uses of the Present and Imperf. with **iam diū, iam dūdum, iam pridem**: iam diū rogō, *I have long been asking*; iam diū rogābam, *I had long been asking.*

Note 2. Latin has no separate tenses corresponding to the Greek Aorist and Perfect; the Latin Perfect fills the place of two Tenses: the Aorist, *I asked*, and the Perfect, *I have asked.*

The Present, the Future Simple, and the Future Perfect are called **Primary** Tenses.

The Imperfect and the Pluperfect are called **Historic** Tenses.

The Perfect in the sense of *I have asked* is **Primary**; in the sense of *I asked* it is **Historic**.

3

105b The **Subjunctive** has four Tenses, of which the Present and Perfect are Primary, the Imperfect and Pluperfect are Historic. The use and meanings of these tenses are given **351–363, 411.**

MOOD (*cf.* **344–363**)

106 Moods are groups of verb-forms which (either by themselves or in relation to a particular context) represent the verbal activity (or state) as being real, willed, desired, hypothetical, &c.

Note 1. There is not a separate mood for every conceivable aspect of verbal activity; and some aspects can be expressed by more than one mood.

The **Indicative** mood makes a statement or enquiry about a fact, or about something which will be a fact in the future:

amō, *I love*; amat? *does he love?* si vēnerit, vidēbit. *if he comes, he will see*; nōn ēmit, *he did not buy.*

The **Imperative** mood expresses the will of a speaker as a command, request, or entreaty:

amā, *love (thou)!* mihi ignōsce, *pardon me!* valē, *farewell!*

The **Subjunctive** mood represents a verbal activity as willed, desired, conditional, or prospective:

istam nē relīquerīs, *do not leave her!* dī prohibeant, *may the gods forbid!* sī veniās, videās, *if you were to come, you would see.*

Note 2. In the Paradigms the tenses of the Subjunctive are given without any English translation, because their meanings vary so much according to the context that any one rendering is misleading. See also **363.**

THE VERB INFINITE (*cf.* **364–394**)

107 The **Infinitive** is a Verb Noun expressing a verbal activity in general, without limit of person or number: amāre, *to love*; amāvisse, *to have loved*; amārī, *to be loved.*

The **Gerund** is a Verbal Noun, active in meaning. It has no plural: amandum, *the loving.*

The **Gerundive** is a Participle or Verbal Adjective, passive in meaning: amandus (-a, -um), *fit to be loved.*

The **Supines** are Cases of a Verbal Substantive: amātum, *in order to love*; amātū, *for* or *in loving.*

The **Participles** have partly the properties of Verbs and partly those of Adjectives; there are three besides the Gerundive:

(*a*) Act. Pres.	amāns,	*loving* (declined like ingēns).	
(*b*) Act. Fut.	amātūrus,	*about to love*	(declined like
(*c*) Pass. Perf.	amātus,	*loved*	bonus).

Note. The three Participles wanting are: (*a*) Active Perfect, (*b*) Passive Present, (*c*) Passive Future.

VOICE

8 The **Active Voice** expresses what the Subject of a Verb is or does: sum, *I am*; valeō, *I am well*; amō, *I love*; regō, *I rule.*

The **Passive Voice** expresses (*a*) what is done to the Subject of the Verb: amor, *I am loved*; regor, *I am ruled*; (*b*) the verbal activity regarded impersonally: ītur, *one goes.*

09 Deponent Verbs are Verbs which have (*a*) indicative, subjunctive and imperative moods passive in form but active in meaning; (*b*) present and future participle, future infinitive, supine, and gerund active in form and meaning; (*c*) gerundive passive in form and meaning; (*d*) past participles passive in form but generally active in meaning.

110 Verbs in the Active Voice and Deponent Verbs are:

(*a*) Transitive, having a direct object: eum amō, *I love him*; vōs hortor, *I exhort you.*

(*b*) Intransitive, not having a direct object; stō, *I stand*; loquor, *I speak.*

Only Transitive Verbs have the full Passive Voice.

THE CONJUGATIONS

111 A **Conjugation** is a grouping of verb-forms. The four regular conjugations are distinguished by the final sound of the Present Stem, which is most clearly seen before the suffix **-re** (or **-ere**) of the Present Infinitive Active:

CONJUGATION	STEM ENDING	PRES. INFIN. ACT.
First	-ā	-āre
Second	-ē	-ēre
Third	consonant (or -u)	-ere
Fourth	-ī	-īre

Deponent Verbs are also divided into four Conjugations with the same Stem endings.

112 The following forms (called Principal Parts) must be known in order to give the full Conjugation (*cf.* **147**).

	A- Stems	E- Stems	Consonant and U- Stems	I- Stems

Active Voice

	A- Stems	E- Stems	Consonant and U- Stems	I- Stems
1 Pers. Pres. Indic.	amō	moneō	regō	audiō
Infin. Pres.	amāre	monēre	regere	audīre
Perfect	amāvī	monuī	rēxī	audīvī
Supine in -um	amātum	monitum	rēctum	audītum

Passive Voice (and Deponent Verbs)

	A- Stems	E- Stems	Consonant and U- Stems	I- Stems
1 Pers. Pres. Indic.	amor	moneor	regor	auior
Infin. Pres.	amārī	monērī	regī	audīrī
Partic. Perf.	amātus	monitus	rēctus	audītus
Gerundive	amandus	monendus	regendus	audiendus

Alongside of Perfects in -ĭvī and derived forms, we sometimes find shorter forms:

audiī *beside* audīvī	audiērunt *beside* audīvērunt
audīstī *beside* audīvistī	audīsse *beside* audīvisse

Alongside of Perfects in -āvī, -ēvi, -ōvī and derived forms, we sometimes find shorter forms, in which -vi-, -ve-, or -vē- do not appear:

amāstī *beside* amāvistī	amārim *beside* amāverim
dēlēstī *beside* dēlēvistī	dēlērunt *beside* dēlēvērunt
nōstī *beside* nōvistī	nōram *beside* nōveram

For -ērunt (3rd person plural Perfect Active) -ēre was often used: amāvēre, implēvēre, audīvēre. The ending -ērunt itself is really a compromise between -ēre and an ending -ĕrunt (which survived in popular speech).

The 2nd person singular in the Passive ends in -ris or -re: amābāris, amābāre. In the Present Indicative, Cicero prefers the ending in -ris, and so avoids confusion with the Present Infinitive Active and Present Imperfect Passive.

An old form of the Present Infinitive Passive in -ier is sometimes found in poetry: amārier for amārī.

In the 4th Conjugation, forms like audībō for the Future, and audībam for the Imperfect, are sometimes found instead of audiam and audiēbam; but they are not part of the ordinary classical usage.

In the 3rd and 4th Conjugations, the Gerund and Gerundive sometimes end in -undum, -undus (-a, -um).

The endings of the 2nd person singular and the 1st and 2nd person plural in the Future Perfect Indicative are: -is, -imus, -itis; in the Perfect Subjective they are: -īs-, -īmus, -ītis. The poets, however, treat the -i- in both these tenses as either long or short.

PERIPHRASTIC CONJUGATION

114 The Active Future Participle with the auxiliary verb **sum** forms an Active Periphrastic Conjugation:

amātūrus (-a) sum (eram, &c.), *I am (was) about to love.*

amātūrī (-ae) sumus (erāmus), *We are (were) about to love.*

The Gerundive with the auxiliary verb **sum** forms a Passive Periphrastic Conjugation:

amandus (-a) sum (eram), *I am (was) fit to be loved.*

amandī (-ae) sumus (erāmus), *We are (were) fit to be loved.*

115 * The Verb **Sum**, *I am* (sum, fuī, esse, futūrus).

This verb is formed from two roots: **es-**, *to be*, and **fu-**, *to be* or *to become*. **es-** sometimes appears as **s-** (*e.g.* sum); and between vowels **-s-** becomes **-r-**, as: eram (*cf.* 21b).

TENSE	INDICATIVE	
Present	sum,	*I am*
	es,	*you* (s.) *are*
	est,	*he is*
	sumus,	*we are*
	estis,	*you* (pl.) *are*
	sunt,	*they are*
Future Simple	erō,	*I shall be*
	eris,	*you* (s.) *will be*
	erit,	*he will be*
	erimus,	*we shall be*
	eritis,	*you* (pl.) *will be*
	erunt,	*they will be*
Imperfect	eram,	*I was*
	erās,	*you* (s.) *were*
	erat,	*he was*
	erāmus,	*we were*
	erātis,	*you* (pl.) *were*
	erant,	*they were*
Perfect	fuī,	*I have been* or *I was*
	fuistī,	*you* (s.) *have been* or *you* (s.) *were*
	fuit,	*he has been* or *he was*
	fuimus,	*we have been* or *we were*
	fuistis,	*you* (pl.) *have been* or *you* (pl.) *were*
	fuērunt,	*they have been* or *they were*
Future Perfect	fuerō,	*I shall have been*
	fueris,	*you* (s.) *will have been*
	fuerit,	*he will have been*
	fuerimus,	*we shall have been*
	fueritis,	*you* (pl.) *will have been*
	fuerint,	*they will have been*
Pluperfect	fueram,	*I had been*
	fuerās,	*you* (s.) *had been*
	fuerat,	*he had been*
	fuerāmus,	*we had been*
	fuerātis,	*you* (pl.) *had been*
	fuerant,	*they had been*

* It is necessary first to conjugate the irregular Verb of Being, sum, *I am*, esse, *to be*, because it is used as an auxiliary in the conjugation of other Verbs.

SUBJUNCTIVE	IMPERATIVE
sim sīs sit sīmus sītis sint	es, estō, *be* (s.) estō, *let him be* este, estōte, *be* (pl.) suntō, *let them be*

THE VERB INFINITE

Infinitives

Present   esse, *to be*
Perfect   fuisse, *to have been*

essem essēs esset essēmus essētis essent

Future $\left\{ \begin{array}{l} \text{futūrus esse} \\ \text{fore} \end{array} \right\}$ *to be about to be*

Participles

Present   (*none*)
Future   futūrus, *about to be*
Gerunds and Supines (*none*)

fuerim fuerīs fuerit fuerīmus fuerītis fuerint

Note 1. In the Pres. Subj. the forms siem, siēs, siet, sient, and fuam, fuās, fuat, fuant sometimes occur. In the Imperf. Subj. the forms forem, forēs, foret, forent are frequent.

Note 2. Some compounds of Sum have a Pres. Participle: absēns, praesēns.

Note 3. Like Sum are conjugated its compounds: absum, *am absent*; adsum, *am present*; dēsum, *am wanting*; īnsum, *am in* or *among*; intersum, *am among*; obsum, *hinder*; praesum, *am set over*; prōsum, *am of use*; subsum, *am under*; supersum, *survive*. In prōsum **d** appears between ō and e: prōdest.

fuissem fuissēs fuisset fuissēmus fuissētis fuissent

116 FIRST CONJUGATION A- STEMS

Active Voice

TENSE	INDICATIVE	
Present	amō,	*I love* or *I am loving*
	amās,	*you* (s.) *love* or *you* (s.) *are loving*
	amat,	*he loves* or *he is loving*
	amāmus,	*we love* or *we are loving*
	amātis,	*you* (pl.) *love* or *you* (pl.) *are loving*
	amant,	*they love* or *they are loving*
Future Simple	amābō,	*I shall love*
	amābis,	*you* (s.) *will love*
	amābit,	*he will love*
	amābimus,	*we shall love*
	amābitis,	*you* (pl.) *will love*
	amābunt,	*they will love*
Imperfect	amābam,	*I was loving*
	amābās,	*you* (s.) *were loving*
	amābat,	*he was loving*
	amābāmus,	*we were loving*
	amābātis,	*you* (pl.) *were loving*
	amābant,	*they were loving*
Perfect	amāvī,	*I have loved* or *I loved*
	amāvistī,	*you* (s.) *have loved* or *you* (s.) *loved*
	amāvit,	*he has loved* or *he loved*
	amāvimus,	*we have loved* or *we loved*
	amāvistis,	*you* (pl.) *have loved* or *you* (pl.) *loved*
	amāvērunt,	*they have loved* or *they loved*
Future Perfect	amāverō,	*I shall have loved*
	amāveris,	*you* (s.) *will have loved*
	amāverit,	*he will have loved*
	amāverimus,	*we shall have loved*
	amāveritis,	*you* (pl.) *will have loved*
	amāverint,	*they will have loved*
Pluperfect	amāveram,	*I had loved*
	amāverās,	*you* (s.) *had loved*
	amāverat,	*he had loved*
	amāverāmus,	*we had loved*
	amāverātis,	*you* (pl.) *had loved*
	amāverant,	*they had loved*

SUBJUNCTIVE	IMPERATIVE
amem amēs amet amēmus amētis ament	amā, amātō, *love* (s.) amātō, *let him love* amāte, amātōte, *love* (pl.) amantō, *let them love*

THE VERB INFINITE

Infinitives

amārem amārēs amāret amārēmus amārētis amārent	Present Perfect Future	amāre, *to love* amāvisse, *to have loved* amātūrus esse, *to be about to love*

amāverim
amāverīs
amāverit
amāverīmus
amāverītis
amāverint

Gerund

amandum, *the loving*

Supines

amātum, *in order to love*
amātū, *in* or *for loving*

amāvissem
amāvissēs
amāvisset
amāvissēmus
amāvissētis
amāvissent

Participles

Present	amāns, *loving*
Future	amātūrus, *about to love*

3*

117 SECOND CONJUGATION Ē- STEMS

Active Voice

TENSE	INDICATIVE	
Present	moneō,	*I advise* or *I am advising*
	monēs,	*you* (s.) *advise* or *you* (s.) *are advising*
	monet,	*he advises* or *he is advising*
	monēmus,	*we advise* or *we are advising*
	monētis,	*you* (pl.) *advise* or *you* (pl.) *are advising*
	monent,	*they advise* or *they are advising*
Future Simple	monēbō,	*I shall advise*
	monēbis,	*you* (s.) *will advise*
	monēbit,	*he will advise*
	monēbimus,	*we shall advise*
	monēbitis,	*you* (pl.) *will advise*
	monēbunt,	*they will advise*
Imperfect	monēbam,	*I was advising*
	monēbās,	*you* (s.) *were advising*
	monēbat,	*he was advising*
	monēbāmus,	*we were advising*
	monēbātis,	*you* (pl.) *were advising*
	monēbant,	*they were advising*
Perfect	monuī,	*I have advised* or *I advised*
	monuistī,	*you* (s.) *have advised* or *you* (s.) *advised*
	monuit,	*he has advised* or *he advised*
	monuimus,	*we have advised* or *we advised*
	monuistis,	*you* (pl.) *have advised* or *you* (pl.) *advised*
	monuērunt,	*they have advised* or *they advised*
Future Perfect	monuerō,	*I shall have advised*
	monueris,	*you* (s.) *will have advised*
	monuerit,	*he will have advised*
	monuerimus,	*we shall have advised*
	monueritis,	*you* (pl.) *will have advised*
	monuerint,	*they will have advised*
Pluperfect	monueram,	*I had advised*
	monuerās,	*you* (s.) *had advised*
	monuerat,	*he had advised*
	monuerāmus,	*we had advised*
	monuerātis,	*you* (pl.) *had advised*
	monuerant,	*they had advised*

SUBJUNCTIVE	IMPERATIVE
moneam moneās moneat moneāmus moneātis moneant	monē, monētō, *advise* (s.) monētō, *let him advise* monēte, monētōte, *advise* (pl.) monentō, *let them advise*

THE VERB INFINITE

monērem monērēs monēret monērēmus monērētis monērent	*Infinitives* Present monēre, *to advise* Perfect monuisse, *to have advised* Future monitūrus esse, *to be about to advise*
monuerim monuerīs monuerit monuerīmus monuerītis monuerint	*Gerund* monendum, *the advising*

Supines

monitum,   *in order to advise*

monitū,   *in or for advising*

monuissem monuissēs monuisset monuissēmus monuissētis monuissent	*Participles* Present monēns, *advising* Future monitūrus, *about to advise*

118 THIRD CONJUGATION CONSONANT (AND **U**) STEMS

Active Voice

TENSE	INDICATIVE	
Present	regō,	*I rule* or *I am ruling*
	regis,	*you* (s.) *rule* or *you* (s.) *are ruling*
	regit,	*he rules* or *he is ruling*
	regimus,	*we rule* or *we are ruling*
	regitis,	*you* (pl.) *rule* or *you* (pl.) *are ruling*
	regunt,	*they rule* or *they are ruling*
Future Simple	regam,	*I shall rule*
	regēs,	*you* (s.) *will rule*
	reget,	*he will rule*
	regēmus,	*we shall rule*
	regētis,	*you* (pl.) *will rule*
	regent,	*they will rule*
Imperfect	regēbam,	*I was ruling*
	regēbās,	*you* (s.) *were ruling*
	regēbat,	*he was ruling*
	regēbāmus,	*we were ruling*
	regēbātis,	*you* (pl.) *were ruling*
	regēbant,	*they were ruling*
Perfect	rēxī,	*I have ruled* or *I ruled*
	rēxistī,	*you* (s.) *have ruled* or *you* (s.) *ruled*
	rēxit,	*he has ruled* or *he ruled*
	rēximus,	*we have ruled* or *we ruled*
	rēxistis,	*you* (pl.) *have ruled* or *you* (pl.) *ruled*
	rēxērunt,	*they have ruled* or *they ruled*
Future Perfect	rēxerō,	*I shall have ruled*
	rēxeris,	*you* (s.) *will have ruled*
	rēxerit,	*he will have ruled*
	rēxerimus,	*we shall have ruled*
	rēxeritis,	*you* (pl.) *will have ruled*
	rēxerint,	*they will have ruled*
Pluperfect	rēxeram,	*I had ruled*
	rēxerās,	*you* (s.) *had ruled*
	rēxerat,	*he had ruled*
	rēxerāmus,	*we had ruled*
	rēxerātis,	*you* (pl.) *had ruled*
	rēxerant,	*they had ruled*

Note:—Faciō, dīcō, dūcō, and the compounds of dūcō, in the 2nd person of the Pres. Imperative have fac, dīc, dūc, &c.

SUBJUNCTIVE	IMPERATIVE
regam regās regat regāmus regātis regant	rege, regitō, *rule* (s.) regitō, *let him rule* regite, regitōte, *rule* (pl.) reguntō, *let them rule*

THE VERB INFINITE

Infinitives

	SUBJUNCTIVE		
regerem regerēs regeret regerēmus regerētis regerent	Present	regere, *to rule*
	Perfect	rēxisse, *to have ruled*
	Future	rēctūrus esse, *to be about to rule*

rēxerim
rēxerīs
rēxerit
rēxerīmus
rēxerītis
rēxerint

Gerund

regendum, *the ruling*

Supines

rēctum, *in order to rule*

rēctū, *in or for ruling*

rēxissem
rēxissēs
rēxisset
rēxissēmus
rēxissētis
rēxissent

Participles

Present regēns, *ruling*

Future rēctūrus, *about to rule*

119 FOURTH CONJUGATION I- STEMS

Active Voice

TENSE	INDICATIVE	
Present	audiō,	I hear or I am hearing
	audīs,	you (s.) hear or you (s.) are hearing
	audit,	he hears or he is hearing
	audīmus,	we hear or we are hearing
	audītis,	you (pl.) hear or you (pl.) are hearing
	audiunt,	they hear or they are hearing
Future Simple	audiam,	I shall hear
	audiēs,	you (s.) will hear
	audiet,	he will hear
	audiēmus,	we shall hear
	audiētis,	you (pl.) will hear
	audient,	they will hear
Imperfect	audiēbam,	I was hearing
	audiēbās,	you (s.) were hearing
	audiēbat,	he was hearing
	audiēbāmus,	we were hearing
	audiēbātis,	you (pl.) were hearing
	audiēbant,	they were hearing
Perfect	audīvī,	I have heard or I heard
	audīvistī,	you (s.) have heard or you (s.) heard
	audīvit,	he has heard or he heard
	audīvimus,	we have heard or we heard
	audīvistis,	you (pl.) have heard or you (pl.) heard
	audīvērunt,	they have heard or they heard
Future Perfect	audīverō,	I shall have heard
	audīveris,	you (s.) will have heard
	audīverit,	he will have heard
	audīverimus,	we shall have heard
	audīveritis,	you (pl.) will have heard
	audīverint,	they will have heard
Pluperfect	audīveram,	I had heard
	audīverās,	you (s.) had heard
	audīverat,	he had heard
	audīverāmus,	we had heard
	audīverātis,	you (pl.) had heard
	audīverant,	they had heard

Subjunctive	Imperative
audiam audiās audiat audiāmus audiātis audiant	audī, audītō, *hear* (s.) audītō, *let him hear* audīte, audītōte, *hear* (pl.) audiuntō, *let them hear*

The Verb Infinite

Infinitives

audīrem audīrēs audīret audīrēmus audīrētis audīrent	Present Perfect Future	audīre, *to hear* audīvisse, *to have heard* audītūrus esse, *to be about to hear*

Gerund

audiendum, *the hearing*

audīverim
audīverīs
audīverit
audīverīmus
audīverītis
audīverint

Supines

audītum, *in order to hear*

audītū, *in* or *for hearing*

Participles

| audīvissem
audīvissēs
audīvisset
audīvissēmus
audīvissētis
audīvissent | Present
Future | audiēns, *hearing*
audītūrus, *about to hear* |

120 FIRST CONJUGATION A- STEMS

Passive Voice

TENSE	INDICATIVE	
Present	amor,	*I am* or *I am being loved*
	amāris,	*you* (s.) *are* or *you* (s.) *are being loved*
	amātur,	*he is* or *he is being loved*
	amāmur,	*we are* or *we are being loved*
	amāminī,	*you* (pl.) *are* or *you* (pl.) *are being loved*
	amantur,	*they are* or *they are being loved*
Future Simple	amābor,	*I shall be loved*
	amāberis (-re),	*you* (s.) *will be loved*
	amābitur,	*he will be loved*
	amābimur,	*we shall be loved*
	amābiminī,	*you* (pl.) *will be loved*
	amābuntur,	*they will be loved*
Imperfect	amābar,	*I was being loved*
	amābāris (-re),	*you* (s.) *were being loved*
	amābātur,	*he was being loved*
	amābāmur,	*we were being loved*
	amābāminī,	*you* (pl.) *were being loved*
	amābantur,	*they were being loved*
Perfect	amātus sum,	*I have been* or *I was loved*
	amātus es,	*you* (s.) *have been* or *you* (s.) *were loved*
	amātus est,	*he has been* or *he was loved*
	amātī sumus,	*we have been* or *we were loved*
	amātī estis,	*you* (pl.) *have been* or *you* (pl.) *were loved*
	amātī sunt,	*they have been* or *they were loved*
Future Perfect	amātus erō,	*I shall have been loved*
	amātus eris,	*you* (s.) *will have been loved*
	amātus erit,	*he will have been loved*
	amātī erimus,	*we shall have been loved*
	amātī eritis,	*you* (pl.) *will have been loved*
	amātī erunt,	*they will have been loved*
Pluperfect	amātus eram,	*I had been loved*
	amātus erās,	*you* (s.) *had been loved*
	amātus erat,	*he had been loved*
	amātī erāmus,	*we had been loved*
	amātī erātis,	*you* (pl.) *had been loved*
	amātī erant,	*they had been loved*

SUBJUNCTIVE	IMPERATIVE
amer amēris (-re) amētur amēmur amēminī amentur	amāre, amātor, *be loved* (s.) amātor, *let him be loved* amāminī, *be loved* (pl.) amantor, *let them be loved*
amārer amārēris (-re) amārētur amārēmur amārēminī amārentur	**THE VERB INFINITE** *Infinitives*
amātus sim amātus sīs amātus sit amātī sīmus amātī sītis amātī sint	Present amārī, *to be loved* Perfect amātus esse, *to have been loved* Future amātum īrī (387)
	Participle Perfect amātus, *loved*, or *having been loved*
amātus essem amātus essēs amātus esset amātī essēmus amātī essētis amātī essent	*Gerundive* amandus, *fit to be loved*

121 SECOND CONJUGATION E- STEMS

Passive Voice

TENSE	INDICATIVE	
Present	moneor,	I am or I am being advised
	monēris,	you (s.) are or you (s.) are being advised
	monētur,	he is or he is being advised
	monēmur,	we are or we are being advised
	monēminī,	you (pl.) are or you (pl.) are being advised
	monentur,	they are or they are being advised
Future Simple	monēbor,	I shall be advised
	monēberis (-re),	you (s.) will be advised
	monēbitur,	he will be advised
	monēbimur,	we shall be advised
	monēbiminī,	you (pl.) shall be advised
	monēbuntur,	they will be advised
Imperfect	monēbar,	I was being advised
	monēbāris (-re,)	you (s.) were being advised
	monēbātur,	he was being advised
	monēbāmur,	we were being advised
	monēbāminī,	you (pl.) were being advised
	monēbantur,	they were being advised
Perfect	monitus sum,	I have been or I was advised
	monitus es,	you (s.) have been or you (s.) were advised
	monitus est,	he has been or he was advised
	monitī sumus,	we have been or we were advised
	monitī estis,	you (pl.) have been or you (pl.) were advised
	monitī sunt,	they have been or they were advised
Future Perfect	monitus erō,	I shall have been advised
	monitus eris,	you (s.) will have been advised
	monitus erit,	he will have been advised
	monitī erimus,	we shall have been advised
	monitī eritis,	you (pl.) will have been advised
	monitī erunt,	they will have been advised
Pluperfect	monitus eram,	I had been advised
	monitus erās,	you (s.) had been advised
	monitus erat,	he had been advised
	monitī erāmus,	we had been advised
	monitī erātis,	you (pl.) had been advised
	monitī erant,	they had been advised

SUBJUNCTIVE	IMPERATIVE
monear moneāris (-re) moneātur moneāmur moneāminī moneantur	monēre, monētor, *be advised* (s.) monētor, *let him be advised* monēminī, *be advised* (pl.) monentor, *let them be advised*
monērer monērēris (-re) monērētur monērēmur monērēminī monērentur	**THE VERB INFINITE**
monitus sim monitus sīs monitus sit monitī sīmus monitī sītis monitī sint	*Infinitives* Present monērī, *to be advised* Perfect monitus esse, *to have been advised* Future monitum īrī (**387**)
	Participle Perfect monitus, *advised,* or *having been advised* *Gerundive* monendus, *fit to be advised*
monitus essem monitus essēs monitus esset monitī essēmus monitī essētis monitī essent	

122 THIRD CONJUGATION CONSONANT (AND U) STEMS

Passive Voice

TENSE	INDICATIVE	
Present	regor,	I am, or I am being ruled
	regeris,	you (s.) are or you (s.) are being ruled
	regitur,	he is or he is being ruled
	regimur,	we are or we are being ruled
	regiminī,	you (pl.) are or you (pl.) are being ruled
	reguntur,	they are or they are being ruled
Future Simple	regar,	I shall be ruled
	rēgēris (-re),	you (s.) will be ruled
	regētur,	he will be ruled
	regēmur,	we shall be ruled
	regēminī,	you (pl.) will be ruled
	regentur,	they will be ruled
Imperfect	regēbar,	I was being ruled
	regēbāris (-re),	you (s.) were being ruled
	regēbātur,	he was being ruled
	regēbāmur,	we were being ruled
	regēbāminī,	you (pl.) were being ruled
	regēbantur,	they were being ruled
Perfect	rēctus sum,	I have been or I was ruled
	rēctus es,	you (s.) have been or you (s.) were ruled
	rēctus est,	he has been or he was ruled
	rēctī sumus,	we have been or we were ruled
	rēctī estis,	you (pl.) have been or you (pl.) were ruled
	rēctī sunt,	they have been or they were ruled
Future Perfect	rēctus erō,	I shall have been ruled
	rēctus eris,	you (s.) will have been ruled
	rēctus erit,	he will have been ruled
	rēctī erimus,	we shall have been ruled
	rēctī eritis,	you (pl.) will have been ruled
	rēctī erunt,	they will have been ruled
Pluperfect	rēctus eram,	I had been ruled
	rēctus erās,	you (s.) had been ruled
	rēctus erat,	he had been ruled
	rēctī erāmus,	we had been ruled
	rēctī erātis,	you (pl.) had been ruled
	rēctī erant,	they had been ruled

SUBJUNCTIVE	IMPERATIVE
regar regāris (-re) regātur regāmur regāminī regantur	regere, regitor, *be ruled* (s.) regitor, *let him be ruled* regiminī, *be ruled* reguntor, *let them be ruled*
regerer regerēris (-re) regerētur regerēmur regerēminī regerentur	

THE VERB INFINITE

Infinitives

Present	regī, *to be ruled*	
Perfect	rēctus esse, *to have been ruled*	
Future	rēctum īrī (**387**)	

with subjunctive forms:

rēctus sim
rēctus sīs
rēctus sit
rēctī sīmus
rēctī sītis
rēctī sint

Participle

Perfect   rēctus, *ruled*, or *having been ruled*

Gerundive

regendus, *fit to be ruled*

with subjunctive forms:

rēctus essem
rēctus essēs
rēctus esset
rēctī essēmus
rēctī essētis
rēctī essent

123 FOURTH CONJUGATION I- STEMS

Passive Voice

TENSE	INDICATIVE	
Present	audior,	I am or I am being heard
	audīris,	you (s.) are or you (s.) are being heard
	audītur,	he is or he is being heard
	audīmur,	we are or we are being heard
	audīminī,	you (pl.) are or you (pl.) are being heard
	audiuntur,	they are or they are being heard
Future Simple	audiar,	I shall be heard
	audiēris (-re),	you (s.) will be heard
	audiētur,	he will be heard
	audiēmur,	we shall be heard
	audiēminī,	you (pl.) will be heard
	audientur,	they will be heard
Imperfect	audiēbar,	I was being heard
	audiēbāris (-re),	you (s.) were being heard
	audiēbātur,	he was being heard
	audiēbāmur,	we were being heard
	audiēbāminī,	you (pl.) were being heard
	audiēbantur,	they were being heard
Perfect	audītus sum,	I have been or I was heard.
	audītus es,	you (s.) have been or you (s.) were heard
	audītus est,	he has been or he was heard
	audītī sumus,	we have been or we were heard
	audītī estis,	you (pl.) have been or you (pl.) were heard
	audītī sunt,	they have been or they were heard
Future Perfect	audītus erō,	I shall have been heard
	audītus eris,	you (s.) will have been heard
	audītus erit,	he will have been heard
	audītī erimus,	we shall have been heard
	audītī eritis,	you (pl.) will have been heard
	audītī erunt,	they will have been heard
Pluperfect	audītus eram,	I had been heard
	audītus erās,	you (s.) had been heard
	audītus erat,	he had been heard
	audītī erāmus,	we had been heard
	audītī erātis,	you (pl.) had been heard
	audītī erant,	they had been heard

Subjunctive	Imperative
audiar audiāris (-re) audiātur audiāmur audiāminī audiantur	audīre, audītor, *be heard* (s.) audītor, *let him be heard* audīminī, *be heard* (pl.) audiuntor, *let them be heard*

| audīrer
audīrēris (-re)
audīrētur
audīrēmur
audīrēminī
audīrentur | |

The Verb Infinite

Infinitives

Present	audīrī, *to be heard*	
Perfect	audītus esse, *to have been heard*	
Future	audītum īrī **(387)**	

audītus sim
audītus sīs
audītus sit
audītī sīmus
audītī sītis
audītī sint

Participle

Perfect   audītus, *heard*, or *having been heard*

Gerundive

audiendus, *fit to be heard*

audītus essem
audītus essēs
audītus esset
audītī essēmus
audītī essētis
audītī essent

124 Deponent Verb (cf. 109)

Ūtor, ūtī, ūsus, use (THIRD CONJUGATION)

TENSE	INDICATIVE	
Present	ūtor,	I use or I am using
	ūteris,	you (s.) use or you (s.) are using
	ūtitur,	he uses or he is using
	ūtimur,	we use or we are using
	ūtiminī,	you (pl.) use or you (pl.) are using
	ūtuntur,	they use or they are using
Future Simple	ūtar,	I shall use
	ūtēris (-re),	you (s.) will use
	ūtētur,	he will use
	ūtēmur,	we shall use
	ūtēminī,	you (pl.) will use
	ūtentur,	they will use
Imperfect	ūtēbar,	I was using
	ūtēbāris (-re),	you (s.) were using
	ūtēbātur,	he was using
	ūtēbāmur,	we were using
	ūtēbāminī,	you (pl.) were using
	ūtēbantur,	they were using
Perfect	ūsus sum,	I have used or I used
	ūsus es,	you (s.) have used or you (s.) used
	ūsus est,	he has used or he used
	ūsī sumus,	we have used or we used
	ūsī estis,	you (pl.) have used or you (pl.) used
	ūsī sunt,	they have used or they used
Future Perfect	ūsus erō,	I shall have used
	ūsus eris,	you (s.) will have used
	ūsus erit,	he will have used
	ūsī erimus,	we shall have used
	ūsī eritis,	you (pl.) will have used
	ūsī erunt,	they will have used
Pluperfect	ūsus eram,	I had used
	ūsus erās,	you (s.) had used
	ūsus erat,	he had used
	ūsī erāmus,	we had used
	ūsī erātis,	you (pl.) had used
	ūsī erant,	they had used

SUBJUNCTIVE	IMPERATIVE
ūtar ūtāris (-re) ūtātur ūtāmur ūtāminī ūtantur	ūtere, ūtitor, *use* (s.) ūtitor, *let him use* ūtiminī, *use* (pl.) ūtuntor, *let them use*

THE VERB INFINITE
Infinitives

ūterer ūterēris (-re) ūterētur ūterēmur ūterēminī ūterentur	Present	ūtī, *to use*
	Perfect	ūsus esse, *to have used*
	Future	ūsūrus esse, *to be about to use*

Gerund

ūsus sim ūsus sīs ūsus sit ūsī sīmus ūsī sītis ūsī sint	ūtendum, *using*

Supines

ūsum, *to use*

ūsū   *in* or *for using*

Participles

Present	ūtēns, *using*
Future	ūsūrus, *about to use*
Perfect	ūsus, *having used*

ūsus essem ūsus essēs ūsus esset ūsī essēmus ūsī essētis ūsī essent	

Gerundive

ūtendus, *fit to be used*

125   DEPONENT VERBS of the four Conjugations

Vēnor	vēnātus sum	vēnārī, *hunt*	Ūtor	ūsus sum	ūtī, *use*
Vereor	veritus sum	verērī, *fear*	**Partior**	partītus sum	partīrī, *divide*

INDICATIVE

TENSE	1ST CONJ.	2nd CONJ.	3rd CONJ.	4th CONJ.
Pres.	vēnor	vereor	ūtor	partior
Fut. S.	vēnābor	verēbor	ūtar	partiar
Imperf.	vēnābar	verēbar	ūtēbar	partiēbar
Perf.	vēnātus sum	veritus sum	ūsus sum	partītus sum
Fut. Perf.	vēnātus erō	veritus erō	ūsus erō	partītus erō
Pluperf.	vēnātus eram	veritus eram	ūsus eram	partītus eram

SUBJUNCTIVE

Pres.	vēner	verear	ūtar	partiar
Imperf.	vēnārer	verērer	ūterer	partīrer
Perf.	vēnātus sim	veritus sim	ūsus sim	partītus sim
Pluperf.	vēnātus essem	veritus essem	ūsus essem	partītus essem

IMPERATIVE

	vēnāre	verēre	ūtere	partīre
	vēnātor	verētor	ūtitor	partītor

THE VERB INFINITE

Infinitives

Pres.	vēnārī	verērī	ūtī	partīrī
Perf.	vēnātus esse	veritus esse	ūsus esse	partītus esse
Fut.	vēnātūrus esse	veritūrus esse	ūsūrus esse	partītūrus esse

Participles

Pres.	vēnāns	verēns	ūtēns	partiēns
Fut.	vēnātūrus	veritūrus	ūsūrus	partītūrus
Perf.	vēnātus	veritus	ūsus	partītus

Gerund

	vēnandum	verendum	ūtendum	partiendum

Gerundive

	vēnandus	verendus	ūtendus	partiendus

Supines

in -um	vēnātum	veritum	ūsum	partītum
in -ū	vēnātū	veritū	ūsū	partītū

Note. Some Deponents have an Active form also: pūnior and pūniō, *punish.*

; Many Perfect Participles of Deponent Verbs are used passively as well as actively; as cōnfessus from cōnfiteor, *confess*; imitātus from imitor, *imitate*; meritus from mereor, *deserve*; pollicitus from polliceor, *promise*.

7 Some Verbs have a Present of Active form but a Perfect of Passive form: they are called **Semi-deponents**:

audeō,	*dare*	ausus sum	gaudeō,	*rejoice*	gāvīsus sum
fīdō,	*trust*	fīsus sum	soleō,	*am wont*	solitus sum

:8 Some Verbs have an Active form with Passive meaning; they are called **Quasi-Passive** (*cf.* 303):

exsulō,	*am banished*	liceō,	*am put up for sale*
vāpulō,	*am beaten*	vēneō,	*am on sale*
fīō **(141)**,	*am made*		

129 Some Verbs have Perfect Participles with Active meaning, like the Deponent Verbs:

adolēscō,	*grow up*	adolēvi,	*I grew up*	adultus,	*having grown up*
cēnō,	*sup*	cēnāvī,	*I supped*	cēnātus,	*having supped*
iūrō,	*swear*	iūrāvī,	*I swore*	iūrātus,	*having sworn*
pōtō,	*drink*	pōtāvī,	*I drank*	pōtus,	*having drunk*
prandeō,	*dine*	prandī,	*I dined*	prānsus	*having dined*

130 **Inceptive** Verbs, with Present Indicative in **-scō** (Third Conjugation), express beginning of action, and are derived from Verb-Stems or from Nouns:

pallēscō,	*turn pale,*	from palleō
nigrēscō,	*turn black,*	from niger

The vowel preceding the termination in such verbs is always long.

131 **Frequentative** Verbs (First Conjugation) express repeated or intenser action. They end in **-tō** or **-sō**.

rogitō, *ask repeatedly* (rogō); cursō, *run about* (currō).

132 **Desiderative** Verbs (Fourth Conjugation) express desire of action. They are formed from Supine Stems and end in **-uriō**.

ēsuriō, *I desire to eat, am hungry* (edō, **140**).

MIXED CONJUGATION

133 Verbs in **-iō**, with Present Infinitive in **-ere**. In forms derived from the Present stem, these verbs take the endings of the 4th Conjugation, wherever the latter have two successive vowels. Such forms are given below in heavy type.

Forms from Present Stem, cap-i-, *take*

		ACTIVE VOICE			PASSIVE VOICE	
		INDIC.	SUBJUNC.		INDIC.	SUBJUNC.
Present		**capiō** capis capit **capimus** capitis **capiunt**	**capiam** **capiās** **capiat** **capiāmus** **capiātis** **capiant**	Present	**capior** caperis capitur **capimur** **capiminī** **capiuntur**	**capiar** **capiāris (-re)** **capiātur** **capiāmur** **capiāminī** **capiantur**
Future Simple		**capiam** **capiēs** **capiet** **capiēmus** **capiētis** **capient**		Future Simple	**capiar** **capiēris (-re)** **capiētur** **capiēmur** **capiēminī** **capientur**	
Imperfect		**capiēbam** **capiēbās** **capiēbat** **capiēbāmus** **capiēbātis** **capiēbant**	caperem caperēs caperet caperēmus caperētis caperent	Imperfect	**capiēbar** **capiēbāris (-re)** **capiēbātur** **capiēbāmur** **capiēbāminī** **capiēbantur**	caperer caperēris (-re) caperētur caperēmur caperēminī caperentur
Imperative	Sing.	2. cape, capitō 3. capitō			2. capere, capitor 3. capitor	
Imperative	Plur.	2. capite, capitōte 3. **capiuntō**			2. **capiminī** 3. **capiuntor**	

Infin. Pres. capere
Gerund. **capiendum**
Pres. Partic. **capiēns**

Infin. Pres. capī
Gerundive **capiendus**

The Verbs whose Present stem is conjugated like capiō are:

capiō, cupiō *and* faciō,
fodiō, fugiō *and* iaciō, } and their
pariō, rapiō, sapiō, quatiō } compounds,
Compounds of speciō *and* laciō { obsolete Verbs,
Deponent: gradior, patior, morior,
And in some tenses, potior, orior (see **161**)

take, desire, make,
dig, flee, throw,
bring forth, seize, know, shake
look at, entice

step, suffer, die
get possession of, arise

IRREGULAR VERBS

Those verbs are called irregular which are formed from more than one root (as **sum, ferō**) or whose tense-forms differ from those of the regular conjugations (*cf.* **148**).

Dō, *I give,* **dare, dedī, datum.**

This verb differs from amō in that its Present and Supine Stems, **da-,** have a short vowel which is retained in all derived forms except: **dō, dās; dā** (imperative); **dāns**; and the Present Subjunctive.

Note. The pres. subj. is: dem, dēs, det, dēmus, dētis, dent; but the forms: duim, duīs, duit, duint, and: duam, duās, duat, duant occasionally occur.

The compounds of **dō** belong to the third conjugation, except **circumdō,** *surround,* and **vēnumdō,** *sell,* which are conjugated like **dō.**

Possum, *I can,* **posse, potuī.**

	INDIC.	SUBJUNC.		INDIC.	SUBJUNC.
Present	possum	possim	**Perfect**	potuī	potuerim
	potes	possīs		potuistī	potueris
	potest	possit		potuit	potuerit
	possumus	possīmus		potuimus	potuerīmus
	potestis	possītis		potuistis	potuerītis
	possunt	possint		potuērunt	potuerint
Future Simple	poterō		**Future Perfect**	potuerō	
	poteris			potueris	
	poterit			potuerit	
	poterimus			potuerimus	
	poteritis			potueritis	
	poterunt			potuerint	
Imperfect	poteram	possem	**Pluperfect**	potueram	potuissem
	poterās	possēs		potuerās	potuissēs
	poterat	posset		potuerat	potuisset
	poterāmus	possēmus		potuerāmus	potuissēmus
	poterātis	possētis		potuerātis	potuissētis
	poterant	possent		potuerant	potuissent

Infinitives: Present, posse; Perfect, potuisse.

Potēns is used as an Adjective, *powerful, able,* never as a Participle.

136 Ferō, *bear,* **ferre, tulī, lātum.**

	ACTIVE VOICE			PASSIVE VOICE	
	INDIC.	SUBJUNC.		INDIC.	SUBJUNC.
Present	ferō fers fert ferimus fertis ferunt	feram ferās ferat ferāmus ferātis ferant	Present	feror ferris fertur ferimur feriminī feruntur	ferar ferāris (-re) ferātur ferāmur ferāminī ferantur
Future Simple	feram ferēs feret ferēmus ferētis ferent		Future Simple	ferar ferēris (-re) ferētur ferēmur ferēminī ferentur	
Imperfect	ferēbam ferēbās ferēbat ferēbāmus ferēbātis ferēbant	ferrem ferrēs ferret ferrēmus ferrētis ferrent	Imperfect	ferēbar ferēbāris (-re) ferēbātur ferēbāmur ferēbāminī ferēbantur	ferrer ferrēris (-re) ferrētur ferrēmur ferrēminī ferrentur
Imperative	Sing.	2. fer, fertō 3. fertō		2. ferre, fertor 3. fertor	
	Plur.	2. ferte, fertōte 3. feruntō		2. feriminī 3. feruntor	
Infin. Pres. ferre Gerund ferendum Pres. Partic. ferēns			Infin. Pres. ferrī Gerundive ferendus		

Forms derived from the Perfect and Supine stems are regular.

Eō (for eiō), *go*, īre, iī, itum

	INDIC.	SUBJUNC.	IMPERATIVE
Present	eō	eam	ī, ītō
	īs	eās	ītō
	it	eat	
	īmus	eāmus	īte, ītōte
	ītis	eātis	euntō
	eunt	eant	
Future Simple	ībō		
	ībis		THE VERB INFINITE
	ībit		*Infinitives*
	ībimus		
	ībitis		Present īre
	ībunt		Perfect īsse, īvisse
			Future itūrus esse
Imperfect	ībam	īrem	
	ībās	īrēs	*Gerund*
	ībat	īret	eundum
	ībāmus	īrēmus	
	ībātis	īrētis	
	ībant	īrent	*Supines*
Perfect	iī	ierim	itum
	īstī	ierīs	itū
	iit	ierit	
	iimus	ierīmus	*Participles*
	īstis	ierītis	Present iēns (Acc. euntem)
	iērunt	ierint	Future itūrus

In tenses derived from the Perfect stem, forms in īv- (*e.g.* īvī, īverō, īveram) exist but are rare. In compounds, -iistī, -iistis are sometimes used for -īstī, -īstis.

The Impersonal ītur, itum est, *there is (was) a going*, is often used. For eundum est see **382**.

Transitive compounds of eō, admit the full Passive inflexion: adeor, *I am approached*.

138 Queō, *can*, nequeō, *cannot*, are conjugated like eō in the forms which occur; the Perfect, however, usually ends in -īvī.

Ambiō, *go round, canvass*, is conjugated like audiō.

139

Volō, *am willing, wish.*
Nōlō, *am unwilling, do not wish*
Mālō, *prefer, wish rather.*

Nōlō is compounded of ne and volō; mālō of magis and volō.

		INDICATIVE		IMPERATIVE
Present	volō	nōlō	mālō	nōlī, nōlītō
	vīs	nōn vīs	māvīs	nōlītō
	vult	nōn vult	māvult	
	volumus	nōlumus	mālumus	
	vultis	nōn vultis	māvultis	nōlīte, nōlītōte
	volunt	nōlunt	mālunt	nōluntō
Future Simple	volam	(nōlam)	(mālam)	Volō and mālō have no
	volēs	nōlēs	(māles)	Imperative
	volet	nōlet	mālet	
	volēmus	(nōlēmus)	(mālēmus)	
	volētis	(nōlētis)	(mālētis)	THE VERB INFINITE
	volent	(nōlent)	mālent	
Imperf.	volēbam	nōlēbam	mālēbam	*Infinitive*
	volēbās	nōlēbās	mālēbās	
	&c.	&c.	&c.	Present { velle / nōlle / mālle
		SUBJUNCTIVE		*Gerunds*
Present	velim	nōlim	mālim	(volendum)
	velīs	nōlīs	mālīs	(nōlendum)
	velit	nōlit	mālit	—
	velīmus	nōlīmus	mālīmus	
	velītis	nōlītis	mālītis	
	velint	nōlint	mālint	*Supines*
				None
Imperfect	vellem	nōllem	māllem	
	vellēs	nōllēs	māllēs	
	vellet	nōllet	māllet	*Participles*
	vellēmus	nōllēmus	māllēmus	
	vellētis	nōllētis	māllētis	Present { volēns / (nōlēns)
	vellent	nōllent	māllent	—

The Perfect-Stem forms are regular:

Volu-ī	-erō	-eram	-erim	-issem	Infin. {	voluisse
Nōlu-ī	-erō	-eram	-erim	-issem		nōluisse
Mālu-ī	-erō	-eram	-erim	-issem		māluisse

Edō, *I eat,* **esse, ēdī, ēsum**

Pres. Indic. Act.:	edō, ēs, ēst; edimus, ēstis, edunt.
Imperf. Subj. Act.:	ēssem, ēssēs, ēsset, &c.
Imperat. Act.:	ēs, ēstō; ēstō; ēste, ēstōte; eduntō.
Infin. Pres.:	ēsse.
Pres. Indic. Pass.:	ēstur.
Imperf. Subj. Pass.:	ēssētur.

Most of these forms are distinguished from forms of **esse,** *to be,* by the long vowel of **ēs-.**

The other forms of this verb are regular; except that **edim, edīs, edit, edint,** are often found in the Present Subjective.

Compounds of **edō** are similarly conjugated; except that **comedō** has Past Participle **comēstus** or **comēsus.**

Fīō, (1) *I become,* (2) *I am made,* **fierī.** .

The forms of **fīō** take the place of passive forms of the Present stem of **faciō,** *I make.*

The **ī** of the stem becomes short in **fit** and before **-er.**

		INDIC.	SUBJUNC.	IMPERATIVE
Present		fīō	fīam	
		fīs	fīās	(fī)
		fit	fīat	(fīte)
		(fīmus)	fīāmus	
		(fītis)	fīātis	
		fīunt	fīant	Pres. Infin.: fierī
Future Simple		fīam		
		fīēs		
		fīet		
		fīēmus		*Note.* When **fīō** means *I become,*
		fīētis		a Fut. Infin. and Fut. Part. are
		fīent		supplied by **fore** and **futūrus.** When
Imperfect		fīēbam	fierem	**fīō** means *I am made,* a Fut. Infin.
		fīēbās	fierēs	and Gerundive are supplied by
		fīēbat	fieret	**factum īrī** and **faciendus.**
		fīēbāmus	fierēmus	
		fīēbātis	fierētis	
		fīēbant	fierent	

Fīō has no other forms. The meaning *I have become* is represented by **sum,** *I am;* the meaning *I have been made* is represented by **factus sum.**

4

DEFECTIVE VERBS

142a Defective verbs are those which lack a considerable number of forms.

Coepī, *I have begun, I began,* **Meminī,** *I remember,* **Ōdī,** *I hate,* are limited mainly to Perfect-stem forms. Meminī and ōdī, though Perfect in form, are Present in meaning.

Indicative

Perfect	coepī	meminī	ōdī
Fut. Perfect	coeperō	meminerō	ōderō
Pluperfect	coeperam	memineram	ōderam

Subjunctive

Perfect	coeperim	meminerim	ōderim
Pluperfect	coepissem	meminissem	ōdissem

Infinitive, Imperative, Participles

Perf. Infin.	coepisse	meminisse	ōdisse
Fut. Infin.	coeptūrus esse	*none*	ōsūrus esse
Imperative	*none*	mementō ⎱ mementōte ⎰	*none*
Perf. Part.	coeptus	*none*	ōsus, *hating*
Fut. Part.	coeptūrus	*none*	ōsūrus

Note 1. Coepī also has perf. passive forms: **coeptus sum,** &c., which are used mainly when coepī governs a passive infinitive, as: urbs aedificārī coepta est, *the city began to be built.*

Note 2. Incipiō, *I begin,* supplies the present-stem forms which coepī lacks.

Note 3. The fut. perf. and pluperf. of meminī and ōdī have the meanings of a fut. simple and imperfect respectively.

Note 4. The participle ōsus is active and present in meaning. Ōsus sum occasionally occurs in the sense of ōdī.

Nōvī (Perfect of nōscō, *I get to know*) means *I have got to know, I know*; nōverō, *I shall know*; nōveram (nōram **113**), *I knew*; nōvisse (nōsse)**,** *to know,* &c.

Aiō, *I say* or *affirm*:

Ind. Pres.	**aiō, ais, ait, — — aiunt.**
Impf.	**aiēbam, aiēbās, aiēbat, aiēbāmus, aiēbātis, aiēbant.**
Subj. Pres.	**aiat** and **aiant.**
Participle	**aiēns.**

Note 1. Except in ais, ait, the -i- is consonantal and the first *syllable* is long (*cf.* p. 42 footnote).

Inquam, *I say*:

Ind. Pres.	**inquam,**	**inquis,**	**inquit,**	**inquimus, inquitis,**	**inquiunt**
Impf.	—	—	**inquiēbat**	— —	**inquiēbant**
Fut. S.	—	**inquiēs,**	**inquiet**		
Perf.	—	**inquīstī,**	**inquit**		
Imper.		**inque**	—	**inquitō**	

Fārī, *to speak*:

Indic. Pres.	**fātur.**		Indic. Fut.	**fābor** and **fābitur.**
Imper.	**fāre,** *speak thou.*			
Participles:	Pres. Acc. **fantem**;		Perf.	**fātus.**
Gerund:	**fandī, fandō**;		Gerundive:	**fandus.**

Quaesō, *entreat* (an old form of quaerō), has first person plural **quaesumus.**

The following Imperatives are found:

apage, *be gone.*
avē (havē), avēte, *hail.* Infin. **avēre,** *to have a desire.*
cedo, cette, *give.*
salvē, salvēte, *hail.* Infin. **salvēre,** *to be well.*

Note 2. Age, agite, *come*, and valē, valēte, *farewell*, are used with special meaning; but the verbs agō, *I do*, valeō, *I am well*, are fully conjugated.

IMPERSONAL VERBS

143 **Impersonal Verbs (288–295)** have only the Third Person Singular of each tense, an Infinitive, and a Gerund. They do not have a personal Subject in the Nominative.

144 The principal are the following:

Present		Perfect	Infinitive
miseret,	*it moves to pity*	miseruit	miserēre
piget,	*it vexes*	piguit	pigēre
paenitet,	*it repents*	paenituit	paenitēre
pudet,	*it shames*	puduit	pudēre
taedet,	*it wearies*	taeduit	taedēre
decet,	*it is becoming*	decuit	decēre
dēdecet,	*it is unbecoming*	dēdecuit	dēdecēre
libet,	*it pleases*	libuit	libēre
licet,	*it is lawful*	licuit	licēre
oportet,	*it behoves*	oportuit	oportēre
rēfert,	*it concerns*	rētulit	rēferre

Note 1.   Decet, dēdecet have also 3rd pers. plur.: decent, dēdecent.
Note 2.   Some passive forms are found: miseritum est, pigitum est, puditum est, pertaesum est.   Other forms are occasionally found: paenitendus, pudendus.

145 Some Impersonals express change of weather and time:

fulgurat,	*it lightens*	**tonat,**	*it thunders*
ningit,	*it snows*	**lūcēscit,**	*it dawns*
pluit,	*it rains*	**vesperāscit,**	*it grows late*

146 Of some Verbs which have all the personal forms, the Third Person Singular is used impersonally with special meaning:

accēdit,	*it is added*	ēvenit,	*it turns out*
accidit,	*it happens*	expedit,	*it is expedient*
appāret,	*it is evident*	fallit, fugit,	*it escapes one*
attinet,	*it belongs*	interest,	*it concerns*
cōnstat,	*it is agreed*	iuvat,	*it delights*
contingit,	*it befalls*	pertinet,	*it pertains*
convenit,	*it suits*	placet,	*it seems good*
dēlectat,	*it charms*	restat,	*it remains*

Intransitive Verbs also are used impersonally in the **Passive (299):** ītur, *one goes, a journey is made.*

DERIVATION FROM THE THREE TENSE STEMS

I. From the **Present-Stem**

Pres. Indic. Act.	am-ō	mone-ō	reg-ō	audi-ō
,, ,, Pass.	-or	e-or	-or	i-or
,, Subj. Act.	-em	e-am	-am	i-am
,, ,, Pass.	-er	e-ar	-ar	i-ar
Imperf. Indic. Act.	ā-bam	ē-bam	-ēbam	i-ēbam
,, ,, Pass.	ā-bar	ē-bar	-ēbar	i-ēbar
,, Subj. Act.	ā-rem	ē-rem	-ērem	ī-rem
,, ,, Pass.	ā-rer	ē-rer	-erer	ī-rer
Fut. Indic. Act.	ā-bō	ē-bō	-am	i-am
,, ,, Pass.	ā-bor	ē-bor	-ar	i-ar
Imperative Act.	ā	ē	-e	ī
,, Pass.	ā-re	ē-re	-ere	ī-re
Infin. Pres. Act.	ā-re	ē-re	-ere	ī-re
,, ,, Pass.	ā-rī	ē-rī	-ī	ī-rī
Partic. Pres. Act.	ā-ns	ē-ns	-ēns	i-ēns
Gerund	a-ndum	e-ndum	-endum	i-endum
Gerundive	a-ndus	e-ndus	-endus	i-endus

II. From the **Perfect-Stem**

Perfect Indic. Act.	amāv-ī	monu-ī	rēx-ī	audīv-ī
,, Subj. ,,	-erim	-erim	-erim	-erim
Fut. Perf. Indic. Act.	-erō	-erō	-erō	-erō
Plup. ,, ,,	-eram	-eram	-eram	-eram
,, Subj. ,,	-issem	-issem	-issem	-issem
Infin. Perf. ,,	-isse	-isse	-isse	-isse

III. From the **Supine-Stem***

Supine I.	amāt-um	monit-um	rēct-um	audīt-um
Infin. Fut. Pass. }	-um īrī	-um īrī	-um īrī	-um īrī
Supine II.	-ū	-ū	-ū	-ū
Partic. Fut. Act. }	-ūrus	-ūrus	-ūrus	-ūrus
Partic. Perf. Pass. }	-us	-us	-us	-us
Perf. Indic. Pass. }	-us sum	-us sum	-us sum	-us sum
Perf. Subj. Pass. }	-us sim	-us sim	-us sim	-us sim
Fut. Perf. Pass. }	-us erō	-us erō	-us erō	-us erō
Plup. Ind. Pass. }	-us eram	-us eram	-us eram	-us eram
Plup. Subj. Pass. }	-us essem	-us essem	-us essem	-us essem
Infin. Pass.	-us esse	-us esse	-us esse	-us esse

* See 151.

FORMATION OF THE STEMS IN VERBS

148 The forms of the Latin Verb vary in many respects from those of the parent and related languages. The verbs in the older language belonged to two principal classes:

    I. Verbs in which the Personal endings were joined immediately to the verb-root (or a modification of it).

    II. Verbs in which the Personal endings were separated from the verb-root (or a modification of it) by a so-called Thematic vowel (-e-, or -o-, which often appears in Latin verbs as -i-).

Of the first class there are very few remains in Latin; for most of the verbs which belonged to it have gone over into the second class. The following 'irregular' verbs, however, retain some athematic forms:

sum, *I am*; **dō,** *I give*; **eō,** *I go*; **volō,** *I wish*; **edō,** *I eat*; **fīō,** *I become* (and compounds of all these except dō).

With reg-i-s	compare, *e.g.*	es (for es-s); ēs (for ēs-s).
,, reg-i-t	,,	es-t; ēs-t; vol-t (vult).
,, reg-i-mus	,,	ī-mus; da-mus; fī-mus.
,, reg-i-tis	,,	es-tis; ēs-tis; ī-tis; vol-tis.
,, reg-e-rem	,,	es-sem; ī-rem; vel-lem.

Sum alone retains the athematic ending -m (for -mi) of the first person singular Present Indicative; but the -u- in sum (and sunt) is derived from a thematic vowel.

All other Latin verbs belong to the second class. Owing to phonetic changes, the presence of the thematic vowel is often obscured.

PERSONAL ENDINGS IN ATHEMATIC AND THEMATIC VERBS

		ACTIVE VOICE		PASSIVE VOICE
		Athematic	Thematic	
Singular	1	-m	-ō	-r
	2	-s	-s	-ris *or* -re
	3	-t	-t	-tur
Plural	1	-mus	-mus	-mur
	2	-tis	-tis	-minī
	3	-nt	-nt	-ntur

PRESENT-STEM FORMATION

The Thematic Verbs can be divided into groups according to the manner in which their Present-stems are formed from the Verb-root.

I. The Present-stem is formed from the Verb-root merely by the addition of the Thematic vowel (originally -e- or -o-):

leg-i-t; pet-i-t; veh-i-t; cēd-i-t; dīc-i-t; dūc-i-t.

II. Reduplicated Presents. Of this class there are very few remains in Latin. To the Verb-root is prefixed a syllable consisting of the first consonant of the Verb-root with the vowel -i:

gignō: for gi-gnō; *cf.* the participle gen-itus and genus, *race.*
sistō: for si-stō; *cf.* the participle sta-tus.
serō: for si-sō (*cf.* 11); *cf.* the participle sa-tus.

III. With -t- between the Verb-root and the Thematic vowel:

plec-t-ō; flec-t-ō (*cf.* flexī, for flec-sī); nec-t-ō (*cf.* nexuī).

IV. Nasalized Stems:

(*a*) with -n- between the Verb-root and the Thematic vowel:

cernō (from cri-n-ō; *cf.* crē-vī); ster-n-ō (*cf.* strā-vī); pōnō (from po-si-n-ō; *cf.* po-si-tus); sper-n-ō *cf.* sprē-vī). Some verbs in -llō (for -lnō) belong to this class: pellō, tollō.

(*b*) the -n- is inserted within the Verb-root and is called a Nasal Infix (24, n.). In some verbs the infix appears only in the Present stem: frangō (*cf.* frēgī, frāctus). In other verbs the infix is found in all the stems: iungō, iūnxī, iūnctus (*cf.* iugum). A few verbs have such an infix in Present and Perfect stems only:

pingō, pīnxī (*cf.* pictus). The -n- becomes -m- before Labials: rumpō (*cf.* rūpī, ruptus).

V. The suffix -scō is added:

(*a*) directly to the Verb-root: nō-scō (*cf.* nō-tus); crē-scō (*cf.* crē-tus).

(*b*) is separated from the Verb-root by ā-, ē-, or ī-. Inceptive Verbs (130) which are derived from other Verbs or from nouns are often formed in this way:

congel-ā-scō (*cf.* gelō);   cal-ē-scō (*cf.* caleō);
gem-ī-scō (*cf.* gemō);   dūr-ē-scō (*cf.* dūrus).

VI. With -i- (originally consonantal) between the Verb-root and the Thematic vowel. To this class belongs not only verbs of the 4th conjugation and verbs like capiō (133), but also verbs of the first and second conjugations:

amō (for amāiō);   fleō (for flēiō);   moneō (for moneiō).

PRESENT-STEM FORMATION

150 The Perfect-stem of Latin verbs is formed, not from the Present-stem, but from the Verb-root, in the following ways:

I. By Reduplication. This is the oldest way of forming the Perfect, and arose from a doubling of the root-syllable. The Reduplicating syllable consists of the initial consonant(s) of the Verb-root followed by a vowel (originally -e-), as pe-pend-ī, from pendō. But in Latin, the -e- of the Reduplicating syllable is often assimilated (13) to the vowel of the Verb-root:

mo-mord-ī (*cf.* mordeō); pu-pug-ī (*cf.* pu-n-gō).

In compounds the -e- is often dropped:

reppulī (*cf.* repellō; pellō, pepulī).

In many verbs which form their Perfect by Reduplication, the vowel of the Verb-root is weakened (*cf.* **12**):

ce-cin-ī (*cf.* canō); fe-fell-ī (*cf.* fallō).

When the Verb-root begins with s followed by another consonant (sc, sp, st), the Reduplicating syllable begins with the two consonants, but the Verb-root drops the s-:

spo-pond-ī (*cf.* spondeō); ste-t-ī (*cf.* stō).

Note. Many Reduplicating Perfects in Latin have lost the Reduplicating syllable entirely, as: tulī, for tetulī (but not the compound rettulī).

II. By change in the vowel of the Verb-root.

(*a*) By Lengthening:

sēdī (*cf.* sedeō); ēmī (*cf.* emō); vīdī (*cf.* videō); vīcī (*cf.* vi-n-cō); fūgī (*cf.* fugiō); fōdī (*cf.* fodiō).

(*b*) By a change of vowel accompanied by lengthening:

ēgī (*cf.* agō); fēcī (*cf.* faciō); frēgī (*cf.* fra-n-gō).

The reasons for these vowel changes are various and complicated.

III. Without change in the Verb-root:

verrī (*cf.* verrō); vertī (*cf.* vertō); scandī (*cf.* scandō); prandī (*cf.* prandeō); strīdī (*cf.* strīdeō); and compounds of -cendō, -fendō, -hendō.

Note 2. Many verbs which seem to belong to this class originally formed their Perfect by Reduplication, as: incidī (for incecidī from incidō; *cf.* cadō, cecidī).

IV. With the suffix **-s-**, which corresponds to some Aorist forma-
tions in Greek. So:

> carp-sī (*cf.* carpō). This addition involved other consonant changes:
> -cs-, -gs-, and -hs- became -x-: dīxī (*cf.* dīcō); pīnxī (*cf.* pingō); vēxī
> (*cf.* vehō). d and t combined with -s- to form -ss- (assimilation)
> which was simplified to -s-: clausī (*cf.* claudō); sēnsī (*cf.* sentiō).
> g was lost when preceded by l or r: fulsī (*cf.* fulgeō); mersī (*cf.* mergō).
> p was inserted between m and s: sūm-p-sī (*cf.* sūmō).

V. With the suffix **-v-** (or **-u-**), a Perfect formation peculiar to
Latin. So:

> amā-vī; flē-vī; mon-uī; sprē-vī; audī-vī.

THE PAST PARTICIPLE, SUPINES, AND FUTURE PARTICIPLE

51 The stem of the Past Participle ends in **-to**. This suffix was originally
added directly to the Verb-root, as cap-tus. When it is preceded by
a consonant, the laws of consonant-change (**19–20a**) and the principle
of vowel-lengthening (**17**) apply: āctus (*cf.* agō). In verbs which
have a Perfect in -āvī, -ēvī, or -īvī, the participial ending -tus is
preceded by a long vowel, as amātus (*cf.* amāvī); dēlētus (*cf.* dēlēvī);
audītus (*cf.* audīvī); in verbs which have a Perfect in -uī, the participle
is in -tus or -itus, as: doctus (*cf.* docuī); monitus (*cf.* monuī).

The Supines in -um and -ū are not directly related to the Past
Participial-stem in -to; they are cases of a Verbal Substantive (4th
declension) whose stem ends in **-tu**. Whatever differences there may
have been between the formation of the Participial-stem and the
Supine-stem, they are obscured in classical Latin; and the Supines
now differ from the Nominative masculine singular of the Past Participle only by the substitution of -um and -ū for -us.

The Supine in -um is traditionally given in dictionaries and
grammars as the Fourth Principal Part of Active Verbs; but many
Supines so given were never used by Latin authors, and their forms
are only inferred from the Past or Future Participles.

The origin of the Future Participle is uncertain; in form it differs
from the Past Participle in having -ūrus instead of -us.

TABLE OF PRINCIPAL PARTS OF VERBS*

Present	Infinitive	Perfect	Supine

152   First Conjugation: Ā-Stems

Usual Form

amō	amāre	amāvī	amātum

Exceptions

PERFECT in **-uī**:

crepō	-āre	crepuī	crepitum	*creak*
cubō	-āre	cubuī	cubitum	*lie down*
domō	-āre	domuī	domitum	*tame*
ēnecō	-āre	ēnecuī	ēnectum	*kill*
fricō	-āre	fricuī	frictum ⎱ fricātum ⎰	*rub*
micō	-āre	micuī ⎱ -micāvī ⎰	-micātum	*glitter*
plicō	-āre	plicāvī ⎱ plicuī ⎰	plicātum ⎱ plicitum ⎰	*fold*
secō	-āre	secuī	sectum	*cut*
sonō	-āre	sonuī	sonitum	*sound*
tonō	-āre	tonuī	—	*thunder*
vetō	-āre	vetuī	vetitum	*forbid*

PERFECT with **Reduplication**:

stō	-āre	stetī ⎱ -stitī ⎰	statum	*stand*

PERFECT with **Lengthened Vowel**:

iuvō	-āre	iūvī	iūtum	*help*
lavō	-āre	lāvī	lautum ⎱ lōtum ⎰	*wash*

Note 1. sonō, stō, iuvō, lavō have Fut. Part. -ātūrus.

Note 2. For dō, see **135a**; for most of its compounds, see **154d**.

Note 3. Compounds of stō have Perfect -stetī only if the preposition is disyllabic: circumstetī (contrast īnstitī).

---

* Forms printed with a hyphen, as -plicāvī, -plicātum, are used only in compounds.

Second Conjugation: Ē-Stems

Usual Form

moneō   monēre   monuī   monitum

Exceptions

PERFECT in **-uī**; but SUPINE in **-tum** or **-sum**:

cēnseō	-ēre	cēnsuī	cēnsum	*deem, vote*
doceō	-ēre	docuī	doctum	*teach*
misceō	-ēre	miscuī	mixtum	*mix*
teneō	-ēre	tenuī	-tentum	*hold*
torreō	-ēre	torruī	tostum	*scorch*

PERFECT in **-vī**:

aboleō	-ēre	abolēvī	abolitum	*destroy*
cieō	-ēre	cīvī	citum	*stir up*
dēleō	-ēre	dēlēvī	dēlētum	*blot out*
fleō	-ēre	flēvī	flētum	*weep*
neō	-ēre	nēvī	notum	*spin*
-pleō	-ēre	-plēvī	-plētum	*fill*

PERFECT in **-sī**:

algeō	-ēre	alsī	—	*be cold*
ārdeō	-ēre	ārsī	arsum	*burn* (intr.
augeō	-ēre	auxī	auctum	*increase* (tr.)
fulgeō	-ēre	fulsī	—	*shine*
haereō	-ēre	haesī	haesum	*stick*
indulgeō	-ēre	indulsī	indultum	*indulge*
iubeō	-ēre	iussī	iussum	*command*
lūceō	-ēre	lūxī	—	*shine*
lūgeō	-ēre	lūxī	luctum	*mourn*
maneō	-ēre	mānsī	mānsum	*remain*
mulceō	-ēre	mulsī	mulsum	*soothe*
mulgeō	-ēre	mulsī	multum	*milk*
rīdeō	-ēre	rīsī	rīsum	*laugh*
suādeō	-ēre	suāsī	suāsum	*advise*
tergeō	-ēre	tersī	-tersum	*wipe*
torqueō	-ēre	torsī	tortum	*twist*
turgeō	-ēre	tursī	—	*swell*
urgeō	-ēre	ursī	—	*press*

Note 1. Many verbs of this conjugation have only Pres. and Perf. stems (*e.g.* arceō, *ward off*).

Note 2. The compounds of cieō belong to the 4th conjugation, as: acciō, accīre, accīvī, accītus.

Note 3. Ārdeō, haereō, have Fut. Part. ārsūrus, haesūrus.

PERFECT with **Reduplication**:

mordeō	-ēre	momordī	morsum	*bite*
pendeō	-ēre	pependī	—	*hang* (intr.)
spondeō	-ēre	spopondī	spōnsum	*pledge*
tondeō	-ēre	totondī	tōnsum	*shear*

PERFECT with **Lengthened Vowel**:

caveō	-ēre	cāvī	cautum	*beware*
faveō	-ēre	fāvī	fautum	*favour*
foveō	-ēre	fōvī	fōtum	*cherish*
moveō	-ēre	mōvī	mōtum	*move* (tr.)
paveō	-ēre	pāvī	—	*fear*
sedeō	-ēre	sēdī	sessum	*sit*
videō	-ēre	vīdī	vīsum	*see*
voveō	-ēre	vōvī	vōtum	*vow*

PERFECT without Change:

ferveō	-ēre	fervī (ferbuī)	—	*be hot*
langueō	-ēre	languī	—	*be weary*
prandeō	-ēre	prandī	prānsum	*lunch, dine*
strīdeō	-ēre	strīdī	—	*creak*

154a

Third Conjugation: Consonant and U- Stems

Consonant Stems

PERFECT in **-sī,** and SUPINE in **-tum**:

carpō	-ere	carpsī	carptum	*pluck*
cingō	-ere	cīnxī	cīnctum	*surround*
cōmō*	-ere	cōmpsī	cōmptum	*adorn*
coquō	-ere	coxī	coctum	*cook*
dēmō*	-ere	dēmpsi	dēmptum	*take away*
dīcō	-ere	dīxī	dictum	*say*
dīligō†	-ere	dīlēxī	dīlēctum	*love*
dūcō	-ere	dūxī	ductum	*lead*
fingō	-ere	fīnxī	fīctum	*feign*
adflīgō	-ere	-flīxī	-flīctum	*smite down*
gerō	-ere	gessī	gestum	*carry on*
intellegō†	-ere	intellēxī	intellēctum	*understand*
iungō	-ere	iūnxī	iūnctum	*join, attach*
neglegō†	-ere	neglēxī	neglēctum	*neglect*

* Compound of emō, which has Perf. ēmī.
† Compound of legō, which has Perf. lēgī.

ningit	-ere	nīnxit	—	*it snows*
nūbō	-ere	nūpsī	nūptum	*marry*
pergō‡	-ere	perrēxī	perrēctum	*proceed*
pingō	-ere	pīnxī	pictum	*paint*
plangō	-ere	plānxī	plānctum	*smite*
prōmō*	-ere	prōmpsī	prōmptum	*bring out*
regō	-ere	rēxī	rēctum	*rule*
rēpō	-ere	rēpsī	—	*creep*
scalpō	-ere	scalpsī	scalptum	*scratch*
scrībō	-ere	scrīpsī	scriptum	*write*
sculpō	-ere	sculpsī	sculptum	*carve*
serpō	-ere	serpsī	—	*crawl*
stringō	-ere	strīnxī	strictum	*bind*
sūmō*	-ere	sūmpsī	sūmptum	*take*
surgō‡	-ere	surrēxī	surrēctum	*arise*
tegō	-ere	tēxī	tēctum	*cover*
temnō	-ere	-tempsī	-temptum	*despise*
tingō	-ere	tīnxī	tīnctum	*dye*
trahō	-ere	trāxī	tractum	*draw*
ungō (unguō)	-ere	ūnxī	ūnctum	*anoint*
ūrō	-ere	ussī	ustum	*burn* (tr.)
vehō	-ere	vēxī	vectum	*carry*
vīvō	-ere	vīxī	vīctum	*live*

4b PERFECT in **-sī**, and SUPINE in **-sum**:

cēdō	-ere	cessī	cessum	*yield*
claudō	-ere	clausī	clausum	*shut*
dīvidō	-ere	dīvīsī	dīvīsum	*divide*
fīgō	-ere	fīxī	fīxum	*fix*
flectō	-ere	flexī	flexum	*bend* (tr.)
laedō	-ere	laesī	laesum	*hurt*
lūdō	-ere	lūsī	lūsum	*play*
mergō	-ere	mersī	mersum	*drown*
mittō	-ere	mīsī	missum	*send*
pectō	-ere	pexī	pexum	*comb*
plaudō	-ere	plausī	plausum	*applaud*
premō	-ere	pressī	pressum	*press* (tr.)
rādō	-ere	rāsī	rāsum	*scrape*
rōdō	-ere	rōsī	rōsum	*gnaw*
spargō	-ere	sparsī	sparsum	*sprinkle*
trūdō	-ere	trūsī	trūsum	*thrust*
vādō	-ere	(in)vāsī	(in)vāsum	*go* (*attack*)

* Compound of emō, which has Perf. ēmī.
‡ Compound of regō, which has Perf. rēxī.

154c   PERFECT in **-vi**:

cernō	-ere	crēvī	crētum	*sift, discern*
linō	-ere	lēvī	litum	*smear*
serō	-ere	sēvī	satum	*sow*
sinō	-ere	sīvī	situm	*allow*
spernō	-ere	sprēvī	sprētum	*despise*
sternō	-ere	strāvī	strātum	*strew*
abolēscō	-ere	abolēvī	—	*decay*
adolēscō	-ere	adolēvī	adultum	*grow up*
cognōscō	-ere	cognōvī	cognitum	*get to know*
crēscō	-ere	crēvī	crētum	*grow*
nōscō	-ere	nōvī	nōtum	*get to know*
obsolēscō	-ere	obsolēvī	obsolētum	*grow out of use*
pāscō	-ere	pāvī	pāstum	*feed* (tr.)
quiēscō	-ere	quiēvī	quiētum	*rest*
suēscō	-ere	suēvī	suētum	*grow accustomed*

Note. The Perf. of Inceptive verbs (130) is the same as that of the verbs from which they are derived: flōrēscō, *begin to bloom*; Perf. flōruī (*cf.* flōreō).

     PERFECT in **-īvī**:

arcessō	-ere	arcessīvī	arcessītum	*send for*
capessō	-ere	capessīvī	capessītum	*take in hand*
incessō	-ere	incessīvī	—	*attack*
lacessō	-ere	lacessīvī	lacessītum	*provoke*
petō	-ere	petīvī	petītum	*seek*
quaerō	-ere	quaesīvī	quaesītum	*seek*
terō	-ere	trīvī	trītum	*rub*

     PERFECT in **-uī**:

alō	-ere	aluī	altum	*nourish*
colō	-ere	coluī	cultum	*till, worship*
cōnsulō	-ere	cōnsuluī	cōnsultum	*consult*
cumbō	-ere	-cubuī	cubitum	*lie*
excellō	-ere	excelluī	—	*excel*
fremō	-ere	fremuī	fremitum	*bellow*
gemō	-ere	gemuī	gemitum	*groan*
gignō	-ere	genuī	genitum	*produce*
metō	-ere	messuī	messum	*reap*
molō	-ere	moluī	molitum	*grind*
nectō	-ere	nexuī	nexum	*bind*
occulō	-ere	occuluī	occultum	*hide*
-pescō	-ere	-pescuī	—	*restrain*
pōnō	-ere	posuī	positum	*place*
serō	-ere	seruī	sertum	*join, interweave*
strepō	-ere	strepuī	strepitum	*roar*
texō	-ere	texuī	textum	*weave*
tremō	-ere	tremuī	—	*tremble*
vomō	-ere	vomuī	vomitum	*vomit*

PERFECT with **Reduplication**:

addō	-ere	addidī	additum	*add*
cadō	-ere	cecidī	cāsum	*fall*
caedō	-ere	cecīdī	caesum	*beat, kill*
canō	-ere	cecinī	cantum	*sing*
currō	-ere	cucurrī	cursum	*run*
discō	-ere	didicī	—	*learn*
fallō	-ere	fefellī	falsum	*deceive*
pangō	-ere	pegigī, pēgī	pāctum	*fix, make*
parcō	-ere	pepercī	parsum	*spare*
pellō	-ere	pepulī	pulsum	*drive*
pendō	-ere	pependī	pēnsum	*hang* (tr. & intr.)
poscō	-ere	poposcī	—	*demand*
pungō	-ere	pupugī	pūnctum	*prick*
sistō	-ere	stitī	—	*make to stand*
tangō	-ere	tetigī	tāctum	*touch*
tendō	-ere	tetendī	tentum (tēnsum)	*stretch*
tundō	-ere	tutudī	tūsum (tūnsum)	*bruise*

Note 1. Like addō, are most other compounds of dō: *e.g.* crēdō, trādō (*cf.* **135a**).

Note 2. Sistō and its compounds (*e.g.* dēsistō, *leave off*), are Reduplicated Presents (**149**) from stō.

PERFECT with **Lengthened Vowel**:

agō	-ere	ēgī	āctum	*do*
emō	-ere	ēmī	ēmptum	*buy*
frangō	-ere	frēgī	frāctum	*break* (tr.)
fundō	-ere	fūdī	fūsum	*pour* (tr.)
legō	-ere	lēgī	lēctum	*choose, read*
linquō	-ere	līquī	-lictum	*leave*
rumpō	-ere	rūpī	ruptum	*break* (tr.)
vincō	-ere	vīcī	victum	*conquer*

Note 3. The following compounds of emō have Perf. -psī: cōmō, *comb, adorn*, dēmō, *remove*, prōmō, *bring out*, sūmō, *take up*.

Note 4. The following compounds of legō have Perf. -lēxī: dīligō, *love*, intellegō, *understand*, neglegō, *neglect*.

154e PERFECT in -**ī** (without **Reduplication** or **Lengthening**):

bibō	-ere	bibī	—	*drink*
-cendō	-ere	-cendī	-cēnsum	*kindle*
-cūdō	-ere	-cūdī	-cūsum	*stamp*
-fendō	-ere	-fendī	-fēnsum	*strike*
findō*	-ere	fidī	fissum	*cleave*

* Originally reduplicating.

mandŏ	-ere	mandī	mānsum	*chew*
pandŏ	-ere	pandī	passum	*open, spread* (tr.)
percellŏ*	-ere	perculī	perculsum	*thrill*
prehendŏ	-ere	prehendī	prehēnsum	*grasp*
psallŏ	-ere	psallī	—	*play on strings*
scandŏ	-ere	-scendī	-scēnsum	*climb*
scindŏ*	-ere	-scidī	scissum	*tear*
sīdŏ	-ere	sēdī	sessum	*settle* (intr.)
solvŏ	-ere	solvī	solūtum	*loose*
tollŏ*	-ere	sus-tulī	sub-lātum	*remove*
vellŏ	-ere	vellī, vulsī	vulsum	*rend*
verrŏ	-ere	verrī	versum	*sweep*
vertŏ	-ere	vertī	versum	*turn* (tr.)
vīsŏ	-ere	vīsī	vīsum	*visit*
volvŏ	-ere	volvī	volūtum	*roll* (tr.)

154f VERBS in **-uō**:

acuŏ	-ere	acuī	acūtum	*sharpen*
adnuŏ	-ere	adnuī	—	*nod*
arguŏ	-ere	arguī	—	*prove*
congruŏ	-ere	congruī	—	*come together*
exuŏ	-ere	exuī	exūtum	*put off*
fluŏ	-ere	flūxī	—	*flow*
imbuŏ	-ere	imbuī	imbūtum	*tinge*
induŏ	-ere	induī	indūtum	*put on*
luŏ	-ere	luī	-lūtum	*wash, atone*
metuŏ	-ere	metuī	—	*fear*
minuŏ	-ere	minuī	minūtum	*lessen*
pluit	-ere	pluit	—	*rain*
ruŏ	-ere	ruī	rutum†	*rush, fall*
spuŏ	-ere	spuī	spūtum	*spit*
statuŏ	-ere	statuī	statūtum	*set up*
sternuŏ	-ere	sternuī	—	*sneeze*
-stinguŏ	-ere	-stīnxī	-stīnctum	*quench*
struŏ	-ere	strūxī	strūctum	*build*
suŏ	-ere	suī	sūtum	*sew*
tribuŏ	-ere	tribuī	tribūtum	*assign, render*

154g **Mixed Conjugation**

capiŏ	-ere	cēpī	captum	*take*
cupiŏ	-ere	cupīvī	cupītum	*desire*
-cutiŏ	-ere	-cussī	-cussum	*shake*
faciŏ	-ere	fēcī	factum	*do*
fodiŏ	-ere	fōdī	fossum	*dig*
fugiŏ	-ere	fūgī	—	*flee*
iaciŏ	-ere	iēcī	iactum	*hurl*
-liciŏ	-ere	lexī	-lectum	*entice*

* Originally reduplicating.   † Fut. participle: ruitūrus.

pariō	-ere	peperī	partum	*bring forth*
rapiō	-ere	rapuī	raptum	*snatch*
sapiō	-ere	sapīvī	—	*taste*
-spiciō	-ere	-spexī	-spectum	*gaze*
quatiō	-ere	—	quassum	*shake* (tr.)

Note 1. Fugiō has Fut. Part. fugitūrus; pariō has paritūra.
Note 2. Like -liciō are alliciō, illiciō, polliciō; but ēliciō has Perf. ēlicuī, Supine ēlicitum.

Fourth Conjugation: Ī- Stems

Usual Form

audiō   audīre   audīvī   audītum

Exceptions

PERFECT in -**īvī**; but SUPINE in -**tum**:

sepeliō	-īre	sepelīvī	sepultum	*bury*

PERFECT in -**uī**:

aperiō	-īre	aperuī	apertum	*open* (tr.)
operiō	-īre	operuī	opertum	*cover*
saliō	-īre	saluī	—	*dance*

PERFECT in -**sī**:

amiciō	-īre	—	amictum	*clothe*
fulciō	-īre	fulsī	fultum	*prop*
hauriō	-īre	hausī	haustum	*drain*
referciō	-īre	refersī	refertum	*fill*
saepiō	-īre	saepsī	saeptum	*hedge in*
sanciō	-īre	sānxī	sānctum	*hallow*
sarciō	-īre	sarsī	sartum	*patch*
sentiō	-īre	sēnsī	sēnsum	*feel*
vinciō	-īre	vīnxī	vīnctum	*bind*

PERFECT in -**ī**:

comperiō*	-īre	comperī	compertum	*find*
reperiō*	-īre	repperī	repertum	*discover*
veniō	-īre	vēnī	ventum	*come*

DEPONENT AND SEMI-DEPONENT VERBS

156   ## First Conjugation: Ā- Stems (Perfect -ātus sum)

About 160, all regular.

157   ## Second Conjugation: Ē- Stems (Perfect -itus sum)

Exceptions

fateor	-ērī	fassus sum	*confess*
reor	-ērī	ratus sum	*think*

* Originally reduplicating; compounds of pariō (**154g**).

158   SEMI-DEPONENT:

audeō	-ēre	ausus sum	—	*dare*
gaudeō	-ēre	gāvīsus sum	—	*rejoice*
soleō	-ēre	solitus sum	—	*be wont*

159   **Third and Mixed Conjugations** (Perfect -tus *or* -sus sum)

adipīscor	-ī	adeptus sum	*acquire*
amplector	-ī	amplexus sum	*embrace*
expergīscor	-ī	experrēctus sum	*waken*
fruor	-ī	frūctus sum	*enjoy*
fungor	-ī	fūnctus sum	*perform*
gradior	-ī	gressus sum	*step*
īrāscor	-ī	īrātus sum	*be angry*
lābor	-ī	lāpsus sum	*glide*
līquor	-ī	—	*melt*
loquor	-ī	locūtus sum	*speak*
-minīscor	-ī	-mentus sum	*have in mind*
morior	-ī	mortuus sum	*die*
nancīscor	-ī	nactus, nānctus sum	*obtain*
nāscor	-ī	nātus sum	*be born*
nītor	-ī	nīxus (nīsus) sum	*lean on, strive*
oblīvīscor	-ī	oblītus sum	*forget*
pacīscor	-ī	pactus sum	*bargain*
patior	-ī	passus sum	*suffer*
proficīscor	-ī	profectus sum	*set out*
queror	-ī	questus sum	*complain*
sequor	-ī	secūtus sum	*follow*
ulcīscor	-ī	ultus sum	*avenge*
vēscor	-ī	—	*feed on*
ūtor	-ī	ūsus sum	*use*

Note. The form -gressus is very rarely found except in Compounds. Morior has Future Participle moritūrus.

160   SEMI-DEPONENT:

fīdō	-ere	fīsus sum	*trust*

161   **Fourth Conjugation: I- Stems** (Perfect -ītus sum)

		Exceptions	
adsentior	-īrī	adsēnsus sum	*agree*
experior	-īrī	expertus sum	*try*
largior	-īrī	largītus sum	*bestow*
mētior	-īrī	mēnsus sum	*measure*
opperior	-īrī	oppertus sum	*wait for*
ōrdior	-īrī	ōrsus sum	*begin*
orior	-īrī	ortus sum	*arise*
potior	-īrī	potītus sum	*acquire*

Note. Orior has some forms like capior (133): oreris, oritur, orerer. Potior has potītur or potitur, potīmur or potimur, potīrer or poterer.

PARTICLES

Particles are the four Parts of Speech which do not have inflexion: Adverbs, Prepositions, Conjunctions, Interjections. They are, for the most part, cases of Substantives or Adjectives, which have become limited to special uses.

Adverbs originally limited or qualified the action expressed by the Verb, but their use was afterwards extended to qualify Adjectives, and sometimes other Adverbs.

Prepositions are Adverbs which have acquired the special use of standing before Nouns to express relations of place and time.

Many Conjunctions are also Adverbs which have come to be used merely as links between words or sentences.

ADVERBS (cf. 395-8)

163 Adverbs are formed either from cases of Substantives, Adjectives or Participles, or from Pronoun roots (**85a**). Those which are formed from Adjectives or Participles generally have comparison (**85b**). Those which are derived from Pronoun roots have no comparison.

In regard to meaning, they are divided chiefly into Adverbs of (1) Manner; (2) Degree; (3) Cause; (4) Place; (5) Time; (6) Order.

The following are a few of each class:

164 *Adverbs of Manner*:

lentē, *slowly*	**celeriter,** *quickly*
facile, *easily*	**sapienter,** *wisely*
falsō, *falsely*	**vehementer,** *strongly*
ultrō, *spontaneously*	
aequē, ⎫	**aliter,** ⎫ *otherwise*
perinde, ⎬ *in like manner*	**secus,** ⎭ *differently*
proinde, ⎭	**ita,** ⎫
similiter, ⎫ *in the same*	**sic,** ⎬ *so*
itidem, ⎭ *manner*	**tam,** ⎭
quam, *how?*	**adeō,** *so far*
	ut, *as, how*

165 *Adverbs of Degree*:

multum, *much*	**paulum,** *little*
quantum, *how much*	**tantum,** *so much*
satis, *enough*	**magis,** *more*
nimis, ⎫ *too much*	**potius,** *rather*
nimium, ⎭	**potissimum,** *by preference*
valdē, *very*	**parum,** *too little*
fermē, ⎫ *almost*	**magnopere,** *greatly*
ferē, ⎭	**vix, aegrē,** *scarcely*

166 *Adverbs of Cause*:

ideō, idcircō, proptereā, *on that account*

167   *Adverbs of Place*:

WHERE: ubi, *where?*   hīc, *here*
        ibi, ⎱   ibidem, *in the same place*
        illic, ⎰ *there*   alibi, *elsewhere*
        ūsquam, *anywhere*   nūsquam, *nowhere*
WHITHER: quō, *whither?*   hūc, *hither*
          eō, ⎱   eōdem, *to the same place*
          illūc, ⎰ *thither*   ūsque, *so far*
WHENCE: unde, *whence?*   hinc, *hence*
         inde, ⎱   indidem, *from the same place*
         illinc, ⎰ *thence*   hāc, *by this way*
         quā, *by what way?*   eā, illāc, *by that way*

168   *Adverbs of Time*:

WHEN: quandō, *when?*   tum, tunc, *then*
       nunc, modo, *now*   iam, *now, already*
       simul, *at the same time*   aliās, *at another time*
       umquam, *ever*   numquam, *never*
       semper, *always*   interdum, *now and then*
       ōlim, ⎱   mox, *by and by*
       quondam, ⎰ *at some time*   nūper, *lately*
       ante, *before*   post, *after*
       dēmum, *at length*   nōndum, *not yet*
HOW LONG: quam diū, *how long?*   tam diū, *so long*
           diū, *long*   ūsque, *continuously*
           iam diū, *long since*
HOW OFTEN: quotiēns, *how often?*   totiēns, *so often*
            semel, *once*   iterum, *a second time*
            saepe, *often*   rārō, *seldom*
            crēbrō, *frequently*   identidem, *repeatedly*

169   *Adverbs of Order*:

       prīmum, *first*   prīmō, *in the beginning*
       deinde, *in the next place*   praetereā, ⎱
       deinceps, *afterwards*   īnsuper, ⎰ *moreover*
       tertiō, *thirdly*   dēnique, ⎱
                                         postrēmō, ⎰ *lastly*

170 Sometimes an Adverb qualifies a sentence or phrase, rather than any particular word.

                           Adverbs of

AFFIRMATION: etiam, *also*; quidem, equidem, *indeed*; vērō, *but*; plānē, *quite*; sānē, *certainly*; profectō, omnīnō, certē, *surely, by all means*
LIMITATION: pariter, *alike*; simul, *together*; plērumque, *usually*; sōlum, tantum, modo, *only*; partim, *partly*.
NEGATION: nōn, haud, *not*; haudquāquam, neutiquam, *by no means*.
DOUBT: fortasse, forsan, forsitan, *perhaps*; forte, *by chance*.
QUESTION: cūr, quārē, quamobrem? *why?* quōmodo, quemadmodum, quam, ut? *how?*

PREPOSITIONS (*cf.* **284–7**)

Prepositions are used (*a*) as separate words, to indicate the relation between the case of a Noun, Adjective, or Pronoun and other words in a sentence; (*b*) compounded with Verbs, to modify the meaning of the simple verb.

The following Prepositions are used with the Accusative:

ad	*to, at*	iūxtā	*next to, beside*
adversus ⎱	⎰ *towards, against*	ob	*over against, on account of*
adversum ⎰	⎱ *opposite to*	penes	*in the power of*
ante	*before*	per	*through*
apud	*at, near, among*	pōne	*behind*
circum	*around*	post	*after, behind*
circā, circiter	*about*	praeter	*beside, past*
cis, citrā	*on this side of*	prope	*near*
clam (511 n.)	*unknown to*	propter	*near, on account of*
contrā	*against*	secundum	*next, along, according to*
ergā	*towards*	suprā	*above*
extrā	*outside of, without*	trāns	*across*
infrā	*below*	ultrā	*beyond*
inter	*between, amidst*	versus ⎱	*towards*
intrā	*within*	versum ⎰	

73 The following are used with the Ablative:

ā, ab, abs	*by, from*	palam (511 n.)	*in sight of*
absque	*without*	prae	*before, in front of*
cōram	*in the presence of*	prō	*before, for*
cum	*with*	sine	*without*
dē	*from, concerning*	tenus	*as far as, reaching to*
ex, ē	*out of, from*		

Note. Tenus is placed after the Noun, and is sometimes used with the Genitive.

174 The following take the Accusative when they denote motion towards, and the Ablative when they denote rest:

in	*into, against, in, on*	super	*over, upon*
sub	*up to, under*	subter	*under*

175 Prepositions used only in Verb compounds are:

ambi, amb-, am-, an-	*around*	ambiō	*go around*
dis-, dī-	*apart*	dissolvō,	*separate*; **dīrigō,** *direct*
red-, re-	*back, again*	red-eō,	*go back*; **referō,** *bring back*
sē-	*apart*	sēcēdō,	*step apart*

CONJUNCTIONS

176 Conjunctions are: **I.** Co-ordinative (**400**); **II.** Subordinative (**421a–449**).

177 I. Co-ordinative Conjunctions are:

CONNECTIVE:	et, -que, atque ac, } *and*	neque, nec, } *nor* etiam, quoque, } *also* item,	
SEPARATIVE:	aut, vel, } *or, either* ve-,	sīve, seu, } *whether, or*	
ADVERSATIVE:	sed, at (ast), } *but* atquī, *but yet* at enim, *but it will be said* tamen, { *yet, however,* *nevertheless*	autem, *but, however* cēterum, vērum, } *but, moreover* vērō attamen, } *but never-* vērumtamen, } *theless*	
CAUSAL:	nam, namque, enim, etenim, } *for*	enimvērō, *for indeed*	
CONCLUSIVE:	ergō, itaque, } *therefore* igitur,	quārē, quamobrem, quāpropter, } *wherefore* quōcircā,	

Note. For the Interrogative particles see **405, 406**.

---

178 II. Subordinative Conjunctions are:

CONSECUTIVE:	ut, *so that* ut nōn, *so that not*	quin, { *that not* *but that*	

FINAL:	ut, *in order that*
	nēve, neu, { *and that not*
	          and lest
	quō, { *whereby*
	       in order that
		nē, *lest*
		
		quōminus, } *whereby not*
		           in order that
		           not	

CAUSAL:	quod, *because* cum, *since* quippe, { *for as much as,* *seeing that*	quia, *because* quoniam, quandōquidem, } *since* sīquidem, sī quidem, } *inasmuch as*	

TEMPORAL:	cum, *when*	quandō, *when*
	ut, *when*	ubi, *when*
	dum, dōnec, quoad, } *while / so long as*	dum, dōnec, quoad, } *until*
		quātenus, *how long*
	antequam, priusquam, } *before that*	postquam, *after that*
	simul ac, *as soon as*	quotiēns, *as often as*
CONDITIONAL:	sī, *if*	sīn, *but if*
	sīve, seu, } *whether / or if*	nisi, nī, *unless*
		sī nōn, *if not*
	sī modo, *if only*	modo, tantum, } *only*
	modo, dummodo, *provided that*	
CONCESSIVE:	etsī, etiamsī, } *even if, although*	tametsī, *although*
	quamquam, utut, } *however, although*	quamvīs, { *although / however much*
	cum, *whereas, although*	
	ut, licet, *granting that, although*	
COMPARATIVE:	ut, utī, velut, veluti, sicut, sīcuti, ceu, } *as*	quōmodo, quemadmodum, } *as, how*
		quam, *than, as*
	utpote, *as being*	
	quasi (quam sī), ut sī (velut sī), } *as if*	ceu, tamquam, } *as though*

179 The following pairs are often used as Correlatives:

et . . . et -que . . . -que -que . . . et }	*both . . . and*	sīve . . . sīve seu . . . seu }	*whether . . . or*
aut . . . aut vel . . . vel }	*either . . . or*	sīc . . . ut,	*so . . . as*
		ut . . . ita,	*as . . . so*
neque . . . neque nec . . . nec nēve . . . nēve }	*neither . . . nor*	ita . . . ut,	*so . . . that*
		adeō . . . ut,	*so far . . . that*

INTERJECTIONS

180 An Interjection is an exclamatory word, used either to draw attention or to express feeling. The most usual are:

Ō, O! *oh!*	prŏ *or* prōh, *forbid it!*
Ā *or* āh, *alas!*	vae, *woe!*
ēheu, heu, ei, *alas!*	ēn, ecce, *lo! behold!*
ehem, *well!*	heus, *ho there!*
iō, euoe, *o joy!*	

In this book the sign - is used to indicate that a *vowel* is pronounced long, as in mēnsa; it is not used to show the length of a *syllable*.

(See §§ 4b, 8b, 471, and p. 42.*)

INTRODUCTORY OUTLINE

SYNTAX treats of the use of words in the structure of Sentences. Sentences are either **Simple, Compound,** or **Complex.**

A **Simple Sentence** is one which contains only one Finite Verb (or its equivalent, a Historic Infinitive).

A **Compound Sentence** is a combination of two or more Simple Sentences linked together generally by one or more Co-ordinative Conjunctions (**177**).

1 A **Complex Sentence** consists of a Simple Sentence (called the Principal Sentence) on which another Sentence (called a Subordinate Clause) is grammatically and logically dependent. The Principal Sentence and the Subordinate Clause or Clauses are generally linked by Subordinative Conjunctions (**178**).

2 A Simple Sentence has two parts:

1. The Subject: indicating that which performs the action or is in the state referred to by the Predicate;
2. The Predicate: indicating the action or state of the Subject.

83 1. The **Subject** is generally a **Substantive,** or some word or words taking the place of a Substantive:

A **Substantive**: lēx, *the law*; satis temporis, *enough time*;

A **Pronoun**: ego, *I*; nōs, *we*;

An **Adjective, Participle,** or **Adjectival Pronoun**: Rōmānus, *a Roman*; īrātus, *an angry man*; ille, *that (man)*;

A **Verb Noun Infinitive**: nāvigāre, *to sail,* or *sailing.*

184 2. The **Predicate,** since it indicates an action or state, is either a **Verb** or contains a Verb.

185
EXAMPLES OF THE SIMPLE SENTENCE

Subject	Predicate	Subject	Predicate
Lēx	iubet	Nāvigāre	dēlectat
Law	*commands*	*Sailing*	*delights*
Nōs	pārēmus	Satis temporis	datur
We	*obey*	*Enough time*	*is given*

Note. When the Subject is a Personal Pronoun, it is omitted in classical Latin unless it is emphatic. Hence, a single Verb may be a sentence. Vēnī, vīdī, vīcī, *I came, I saw, I conquered*, comprises three sentences.

186 Some Verbs cannot by themselves form complete Predicates. The Verb **sum** is a complete Predicate only when it means *I exist*:

Seges	est	ubi	Troia	fuit	OVID.
Corn	*is*	*where*	*Troy*	*was*	

More often **sum** links the Subject with the **Complement,** which defines the action, state, or quality of the Subject.

187 Verbs which link a Subject and Complement are called **Copulative Verbs.** Others besides **sum** are:

appāreō, *appear*;   audiō, *am called*; maneō, *remain*;
ēvādō, exsistō, *turn out*;   videor, *seem*

The Passives of Verbs of *making, saying, thinking, choosing, showing* (**Factitive** Verbs*) are also used as Copulative Verbs (*cf.* **206**):

fīō, *become* or *am made*;   feror, *am reported*;
appellor, *am called*;   legor, *am chosen*;
creor, *am created*;   putor, *am thought*;
dēclāror, *am declared*;   vocor, *am called*

188 The Complement is in the same case as the Subject.

189 The Complement may be an Adjective or a Substantive.

	Subject	Copulative Verb	Complement
	Subject	*Predicate*	
1.	Leō	est	validus
	The lion	*is*	*strong*
2.	Illī	appellantur	philosophī
	They	*are called*	*philosophers*

* These Verbs are called Factitive (from facere, *to make*), because they contain the idea of making.

Many Verbs usually require as their object another Verb in the Infinitive to make a complete Predicate; such are: soleō, *am wont*; possum, *am able*.

Solet legere	Possum īre
He is wont to read	*I am able to go*

The Infinitive following such Verbs is sometimes called **Prolative**, because it carries on (prōfert) their construction.   See **369–370** for a list of such Verbs.

The **Subject** may be qualified by Adjectives or Pronouns in Agreement, or may have words in Apposition (**194**) added to it.

The **Verb** may be qualified by Adverbs or Adverbial phrases; it may have a Preposition with a Case, or some part of the Verb Infinite depending on it; if Transitive, it has a Direct Object and may have also an Indirect Object; if Intransitive, it may have an Indirect Object in the Dative.

The **Complement** may be qualified by an Adjective or an Adverb, or by a Case of a Noun, or a Preposition with a Case.

b Simple Sentences may be classified as:

(1) Statements (including Exclamations): Caesar venit, *Caesar comes*; quam bonus est! *How good he is!*

(2) Commands (including Prohibitions): īte! *Go!* nē trānsierīs, *do not cross!*

(3) Wishes: dī prohibeant! *May the gods forbid!*

(4) Questions: quis venit? *Who comes?*

AGREEMENT

192 I. A Verb agrees with its Subject in Number and Person:

> Tempus fugit.   Nōs amāmur.
> *Time flies.*   *We are loved.*

193 II. An Adjective or Participle agrees in Gender, Number, and Case with the Substantive it qualifies:

> Vir bonus bonam uxōrem habet.
> *The good man has a good wife.*

> Vērae amīcitiae sempiternae sunt.   CICERO.
> *True friendships are everlasting.*

194 III. When a Substantive or Pronoun is followed by another Substantive, so that the second explains or describes the first, and has the same relation to the rest of the sentence, the second Noun agrees in Case with the first, and is said to be in Apposition to it:

> Nōs līberī patrem Lollium imitābimur.
> *We children shall imitate our father Lollius.*

> Procās, rēx Albānōrum, duōs fīliōs, Numitōrem et Amūlium, habuit. LIVY.
> *Procas, king of the Albans, had two sons, Numitor and Amulius.*

195 IV. The Relative **quī, quae, quod,** agrees with its Antecedent in Gender, Number, and Person; in Case it takes its construction from its own clause (*cf.* **330**):

> Amō tē, māter, quae mē amās.
> *I love you, mother, who love me.*

> Quis hic est homō quem ante aedēs videō?   PLAUTUS.
> *Who is this man whom I see before the house?*

> Arborēs multās serit agricola, quārum frūctūs nōn adspiciet.   CICERO.
> *The farmer plants many trees, of which he will not see the fruit.*

Notes on the Concords

I. 1. The Verb *est, sunt,* is often understood, not expressed:

Nihil bonum nisi quod honestum. CICERO.
Nothing is good except what is virtuous.

2. A Copulative Verb occasionally agrees in number with the Complement rather than with the Subject:

Amantium īrae amōris integrātiō est. TERENCE.
The quarrels of lovers are the renewal of love.

II. 1. An adjective which qualifies more than one noun but does not form part of a predicate with a copulative verb, agrees with the nearest noun:

Vir et cōnsilī magnī et virtūtis. CAESAR.
A man of great wisdom and courage.

2. For the number and gender of an adjective which qualifies more than one noun and forms part of a predicate, see **198**, 1, 3, 4.

III. 1. A Noun in apposition agrees, if possible (*cf.* **31d**), in Number and Gender with the Noun to which it is in apposition:

Stilus, optimus et praestantissimus dīcendī magister. CICERO.
The pen, best and chief teacher of oratory.

Philosophia, vītae magistra. CICERO.
Philosophy, the mistress of life.

2. A Noun may be in apposition to a Personal Pronoun understood:
Hannibal petō pācem (LIVY), *I, Hannibal, sue for peace.*

COMPOSITE SUBJECT AND PREDICATE

198 **1.** When the Subject consists of two or more Nouns, the Verb and Predicative Adjectives are usually in the Plural:

Aetās, metus, magister eum cohibēbant. TERENCE.
Age, fear, and a tutor were restraining him.

Venēnō absūmptī sunt Hannibal et Philopoemēn. LIVY.
Hannibal and Philopoemen were cut off by poison.

2. If a Composite Subject comprises different Persons, the Verb agrees with the First Person rather than the Second or Third; with the Second rather than the Third:

Sī tū et Tullia valētis, ego et Cicerō valēmus. CICERO.
If you and Tullia are well, I and Cicero are well.

3. When the Nouns of the Subject differ in Gender, an Adjective in the Predicate agrees with the Masculine rather than with the Feminine:

> Rēx rēgiaque classis ūnā profectī. LIVY.
> *The king and the royal fleet set out together.*

4. If the Subject refers to inanimate things, an Adjective in the Predicate is generally Neuter:

> Rēgna, honōrēs, dīvitiae, cadūca et incerta sunt. CICERO.
> *Kingdoms, honours, riches, are frail and fickle things.*

199 Notes on the Composite Subject and Predicate

SINGULAR FOR PLURAL

1. When several Subjects of the Third Person are united, the Verb is often found in the Singular, agreeing with the nearest singular subject:

> Nunc mihi nihil librī, nihil litterae, nihil doctrīna prōdest. CICERO.
> *Now neither do books avail me, nor letters, nor does learning.*

2. If the Nouns of a Composite Subject form a single notion, the Verb is usually Singular:

> Senātus populusque Rōmānus intellegit. CICERO.
> *The Roman senate and people understand.*

PLURAL FOR SINGULAR

Sometimes when a Collective Noun is the Subject, although it is Singular in form, the Verb and Predicative Adjectives are Plural:

> Pars mīlitum captī, pars occīsī sunt. LIVY.
> *Part of the soldiers were taken captive, part were slain.*

This construction, however, is not used unless the neighbouring words or the general sense suggest a plural.

Observe that the Adjectives agree in Gender with the individuals to which the Collective Noun refers.

THE CASES

The Subject of a Finite Verb is in the Nominative Case:

Annī fugiunt.   Lābitur aetās.   OVID.
Years flee.   *Time glides away.*

Note. When an Infinitive, called Historic, is used for a past tense of a Finite Verb, the Nominative remains as the Subject (372):

Tum pius Aenēās umerīs abscindere vestem.   VIRGIL.
Then the pious Aeneas rent his garment from his shoulders.

The Complement (**186**) of a Finite Copulative Verb is in the Nominative Case:

Cicerō dēclārātus est cōnsul.   CICERO.
Cicero was declared consul.

The Vocative stands apart from the construction of the sentence, with or without an Interjection (**404**):

Ō sōl pulcher, ō laudande!   HORACE.
O beauteous sun, worthy of praise!

Pompēī, meōrum prīme sodālium!   HORACE.
O Pompeius, earliest of my comrades!

Note. The Nominative sometimes takes the place of the Vocative:

Audī, tū, populus Albānus.   LIVY.
Hear, thou, people of Alba.

---

03 The Accusative Case is used to express:

A. The Direct Object of the Verb.
B. Place to which there is motion, and Extent in Time and Space.
C. The idea contained in the Verb (Cognate Accusative).
D. Adverbial Relations.

A. Accusative of Direct Object

204   1. The Direct Object of a Transitive Verb is in the Accusative Case:

> Haec studia adulēscentiam alunt, senectūtem oblēctant.   CICERO.
> *These studies nurture youth, and delight old age.*

205   *Note 1.*   Intransitive Verbs often become transitive when compounded with Prepositions (especially with: circum, praeter, trāns; less frequently with: ad, in, ob, per, sub; *cf.* **220**):

> Antōnius oppugnat Brūtum, Mutinam circumsedet.   CICERO.
> *Antonius is making war on Brutus, and besieging Mutina.*

Note 2.   Verbs compounded with trāns often take two Accusatives, one the Object of the Verb, the other depending on the Preposition:

> Caesar equitēs flūmen trānsiēcit.   CAESAR.
> *Caesar threw his cavalry across the river.*

Compare the Passive.

> Mīlitēs flūmen trādūcēbantur.   CAESAR.
> *The soldiers were being led across the river.*

206   2. Factitive Verbs (verbs of *making, saying, thinking, choosing, showing,* **187**) have a second Accusative (Predicative) in agreement with the Object:

> Sōcratēs tōtīus sē mundī cīvem arbitrābātur.   CICERO.
> *Socrates used to consider himself a citizen of the whole world.*

207   *Note.*   The Accusative is used as the Subject of an Infinitive to form a Substantival Clause which may be the Subject of Impersonal Verbs or the Object of verbs of *saying, thinking,* and *perceiving,* &c. (**414**).

> Sōlem fulgēre vidēmus; *We see that the sun shines.*

208   3. Some Verbs of *teaching, asking, concealing* (doceō, *teach*; flāgitō, postulō, poscō, *demand*; rogō, *ask*; ōrō, *pray*; cēlō, *conceal*), take two Accusatives: one of the Person, the other of the Thing:

> Racilius prīmum mē sententiam rogāvit.   CICERO.
> *Racilius asked me my opinion first.*

Antigonus iter omnēs cēlat. NEPOS.
Antigonus conceals from all his line of march.

Note 1. In the Passive, the Accusative of the Thing is occasionally kept:
Prīmus ā Raciliō sententiam rogātus sum.
I was the first to be asked my opinion by Racilius.

Note 2. Quaerō, petō, take Ablative of the Person with ā or ab (instead of the Accus. of the Person): hoc ā tē petō, *this I ask of you.*

Note 3. Moneō, *advise,* accūsō, arguō, *accuse,* cōgō, *compel* take Acc. of the Thing if it is a Neuter Pronoun:
Hoc tē moneō: *I give you this advice.*

Note 4. Intransitive Verbs which express feeling sometimes take an Accusative of the Object which excites the feeling:

Nōn omnia quae dolēmus querī possumus. CICERO.
We cannot complain of all things for which we grieve.

Virgās ac secūrēs dictātōris horrent et tremunt. LIVY.
They shudder and tremble at the rods and axes of the dictator.

Note 5. An Accusative Noun or Pronoun (generally accompanied by an adjective) is used in exclamations, with or without an Interjection (**404**): Mē miserum, *O wretched me!* Ō fragilem fortūnam! *O fickle fortune!*

Note 6. Some Passive Verbs in poetry take an Accusative, when used semi-reflexively. Such verbs are: induor, *dress oneself,* exuor, *undress oneself,* cingor, *gird oneself:*

Inūtile ferrum cingitur. VIRGIL.
He girds on the useless steel.

Exuitur cornua. OVID.
She puts off her horns.

Virginēs longam indūtae vestem canentēs ībant. LIVY.
Virgins marched singing, arrayed in long robes.

Nāscuntur flōrēs īnscrīptī nōmina rēgum. VIRGIL.
Flowers spring up inscribed with names of kings.

This construction is analogous to that of the Greek Middle Voice; and the Accus. is a Direct Object, not an Accus. of Respect (**213**).

---

211 B. **Place to which Motion** is directed is in the Accusative: eō Rōmam, *I go to Rome* (**270, 275**).

Note. Similar are the phrases: pessum īre, *to go to the bad;* īnfitiās īre, *to deny;* suppetiās īre, *to march in aid;* vēnum īre, *to be sold.*

For the Accusative of Extent in Time and Space, see **278–283**.

5

C. Cognate Accusative

212   Many Verbs, which are otherwise Intransitive, take an Accusative containing the same idea as the Verb and often etymologically connected with it:

> Fortūna lūdum īnsolentem lūdit.   HORACE.
> *Fortune plays an insolent game.*

> Itque reditque viam totiēns.   VIRGIL.
> *He goes and returns the same way so many times.*

Note. The Cognate Accusative limits the idea contained in the Verb, either by an Adjective or by implication in the Noun itself: lūdum īnsolentem lūdere, *to play an insolent game*; dicta dīcere, *to say witty sayings.*

D. Adverbial Accusative

213   The **Accusative of Respect** is used with Verbs and Adjectives:

> Tremit artūs.   VIRGIL.   Nūdae lacertōs.   TACITUS.
> *He trembles in his limbs.*   *Bare as to the arms.*

> Omnia Mercuriō similis vōcemque colōremque.   VIRGIL.
> *In all points like Mercury, both in voice and complexion.*

Note 1.   This type of Accusative (*a*) when used with Verbs is not a Direct Object, (*b*) usually refers to a part of the body, (*c*) is found chiefly in poetry.   Contrast 235.

Note 2.   The following Adverbial Accusatives are often used: multum, *much*; aliquid, *in some degree*; quid? *to what extent?*; cētera, *in other respects*; id temporis, *at that time*; maximam partem, *for the most part.*   So: multum amāre, *to love much*; quid rēfert? *what does it matter?*   Notice also: hominēs id genus, *men of that kind.*

Note 3.   Neuter Adjectives and Pronouns are used in the Accusative by poets as Adverbs:

> Dulce rīdēre.   Lūcidum fulgēre.   HORACE.
> *To smile sweetly.*   *To shine brightly.*

> Dulce rīdentem Lalagēn amābō, dulce loquentem.   HORACE.
> *I will love the sweetly smiling, sweetly speaking Lalage.*

THE DATIVE CASE

The Dative expresses relations which in English are generally indicated by the prepositions *to* and *for*:

- A. The person or thing *to* whom or which something is done: Dative of the Indirect Object.
- B. The person or thing *for* whom or which something is done: Dative of Advantage or Reference.
- C. Special uses are: (*a*) Dative of Agent, (*b*) Ethic Dative, (*c*) Dative of Possessor, (*d*) Predicative Dative, (*e*) Dative of Purpose, (*f*) Dative of Direction.

A. Dative of the Indirect Object

15 The Dative of the Indirect Object is used:

1. With Transitive Verbs of *giving*, *telling*, *showing*, *saying*, *promising*, which take also an Accusative of the Direct Object:

> Tibi librum sollicitō damus aut fessō.   HORACE.
> *We give you a book when you are anxious or weary.*

> Saepe tibi meum somnium nārrāvī.   CICERO.
> *I have often told you my dream.*

16 2. With some verbs which are Intransitive in Latin, although their English equivalents are transitive. Such verbs have the Dative as their only Object. The chief are:

auxilior, *help*; **crēdō**, *believe*; **faveō**, *favour*; **fīdō**, *trust*; **ignōscō**, *pardon*; **imperō*, *command*; **indulgeō**, *indulge*; **īrāscor**, *be angry with*; **medeor**, *heal*; **minor**, *threaten*; **moderor**, *control*; **noceō**, *harm*; **nūbō**, *marry a husband*; **placeō**, *please*; **pāreō**, *obey*; **serviō**, *serve*; **studeō**, *study*; **suādeō**, *advise*; **temperō**, *control*; †**vacō**, *have leisure for*; and a number of impersonal verbs (**290**). These verbs contain the idea of *being helpful to, favourable to*, &c.

> Victrīx causa deīs placuit.   LUCAN.
> *The conquering cause pleased the gods.*

> Imperat aut servit collēcta pecūnia cuique.   HORACE.
> *Money amassed rules or serves every man.*

* See also 220, n.   † See also 229.

217 *Note 1.* The compounds of many of these verbs are also intransitive: cōnfīdō, *trust*; diffīdō, *distrust*; persuădeō, *persuade*; inserviō, *serve*.

Note 2. Some of the verbs given in **216** (especially: crēdō, fīdō, minor, suădeō) are sometimes used transitively and then have an Accus. of the Direct Object, as well as a Dative:

> Perfidīs sē crēdidit hostibus. HORACE.
> *He trusted himself to treacherous enemies.*

> Eī Lȳsimachus rēx crucem minātus est.
> *King Lysimachus threatened him with death.*

Note 3. Temperō, moderor, *control, restrain*, sometimes take an Accus. instead of a Dative:

> Hic moderātur equōs quī nōn moderābitur īrae.
> *This man controls horses who will not restrain his anger.*

Note 4. Some verbs similar in meaning to those given in **216** are transitive in Latin, and therefore take an Accusative. They are:

> adūlor, *favour, flatter*; cūrō, *heal*; dēlectō, *please*; gubernō, regō, *govern, control*; hortor, *advise*; iubeō, *command*; iuvō, *help*; laedō, *harm*.

Note 5. The poets use pugnō, *fight*, certō, *strive* with a Dative, whereas prose writers use an Ablative with cum.

Note 6. The verbs given in **216**, since they are intransitive, are used in the Passive only in an Impersonal construction (**302**):

> Tibi parcitur.   Mihi imperātum est.
> *You are pardoned.*   *I was commanded.*

218 3. With Adjectives implying *nearness, fitness, likeness, help, kindness, trust, obedience*, or any opposite idea:

> Hortus ubi et tēctō vīcīnus iūgis aquae fōns. HORACE.
> *Where is a garden, and near to the house a fount of flowing water.*
> Hominī fidēlissimī sunt equus et canis. PLINY.
> *The horse and dog are most faithful to man.*
> Turba gravis pācī, placidaeque inimīca quiētī. LUCAN.
> *The crowd hostile to peace, unfriendly to tranquil rest.*

Note 1. The English equivalents of such adjectives are generally followed by *to* or *for*.
Note 2. The following take Genitive *or* Dative: commūnis, *common*, proprius, *proper*. Adfīnis, *akin*, aliēnus, *foreign*, pār, *equal*, sacer, *sacred*, superstes, *surviving*, take usually Dative, sometimes Genitive. Similis, *like*, usually takes Genitive, sometimes Dative. Adjectives of fitness, as aptus, sometimes take Accusative with ad.

4. More rarely with Substantives or Adverbs in which a verbal notion is prominent:

> Iūstitia est obtemperātiō lēgibus. CICERO.
> *Justice is obedience to laws.*

> Congruenter nātūrae vīvendum est. CICERO.
> *We must live agreeably to nature.*

5. When compounded with any preposition (except per, praeter, trāns), or with re-, or with the adverbs bene, male, satis (*cf.* **205,** n. 1):

(*a*) Many intransitive verbs which took neither the Accusative of the Direct Object, nor the Dative of the Indirect Object, now take a Dative of the Indirect Object:

> Subvēnistī hominī iam perditō. CICERO.
> *You have come to the help of a man already lost.*

> Nūllus in orbe sinus Baiīs praelūcet amoenīs. HORACE.
> *No bay in the world outshines the pleasant Baiae.*

(*b*) Many transitive verbs which took only an Accusative of the Direct Object now may take also a Dative of the Indirect Object:

> Mūnītiōnī Labiēnum praefēcit. CAESAR.
> *He put Labienus in charge of the fortification.*

Note. Imperō (*cf.* **216**), being a compound of the transitive parō, often takes both Dat. and Accus.:

> Prōvinciae tōtī mīlitēs imperat. CAESAR.
> *He makes demands for soldiers on the whole province.*

B. Dative of Advantage or Reference

21 The person (or thing) for whose advantage or disadvantage something is done, or in reference to whom something happens, is indicated by the Dative Case:

> Sīc vōs nōn vōbīs mellificātis, apēs! VIRGIL.
> *Thus ye make honey not for yourselves, O bees!*

> Nōn sōlum nōbīs dīvitēs esse volumus. CICERO.
> *We do not wish to be rich for ourselves alone.*

> Illī sevēritās amōrem nōn dēminuit. TACITUS.
> *In his case, severity did not diminish love.*

C. Special Uses of the Dative

222   (a) A Dative, commonly called the **Dative of the Agent**, is often
used with the Gerundive (381), and occasionally with Passive
Participles and with Adjectives in -bilis, instead of the Ablative of
the Agent with ā:

> Ut tibi ambulandum, sīc mihi dormiendum est.   CICERO.
> *As you have to walk, I have to sleep.*

> Magnus cīvis obīt et formīdātus Othōnī.   JUVENAL.
> *A great citizen and one dreaded by Otho has died.*

> Multīs ille bonīs flēbilis occidit.   HORACE.
> *He died a cause of weeping to many good men.*

Note.   Rarely, in poetry, such a Dative is used with other passive forms:
Nōn intellegor ūllī.   OVID.
I am understood by none.

---

223   (b) A Dative of a Personal Pronoun, called the **Ethic Dative**, is
used, in familiar talk or writing, to mark interest or call attention:

> Quid mihi Celsus agit?   HORACE.
> *Tell me, what is Celsus about?*

> Haec vōbīs per bīduum eōrum mīlitia fuit.   LIVY.
> *This, mind you, was their style of fighting for two days.*

Note.   The person indicated by this Dative derives no advantage from the
action, nor is he in any way involved in it.

---

224   (c) The **Dative of the Possessor,** with esse, is used when emphasis
is laid on the thing possessed, not on the possessor:

> Est mihī plēnus Albānī cadus.   HORACE.
> *I have a jar full of Alban wine.*

> Fōns cui nōmen Arethūsa fuit.   CICERO.
> *A fountain of which the name was Arethusa.*

Note.   With such phrases as 'cui nōmen est' a second Dative is sometimes
joined by attraction: Volitāns cui nōmen asīlō Rōmānum est (VIRGIL), *an insect
of which the Roman name is 'asilus'*.   A like attraction occurs with other factitive
and copulative verbs: Huic ego diēī nōmen Trinummō faciam (PLAUTUS), *I will
give to this day the name Trinummus*.   Analogous to these is the attraction of an
adjective after licet: Mihi nōn licet esse neglegentī (CICERO), *I must not be
negligent.*

(*d*) The **Predicative Dative,** accompanied by a Dative of Reference
(221) is used instead of the Nominative or Accusative of a Noun or
Adjective in the Predicate after (1) sum, *I am, I serve as,* (2) verbs
like habeō, dūcō, meaning *I consider as, reckon as*:

Exitiō est avidum mare nautīs. HORACE.
The greedy sea is a destruction to sailors.

Habēre quaestuī rem pūblicam turpe est. CICERO.
It is base to treat the state as one's source of gain.

L. Cassius quaerere solēbat 'cui bonō fuisset'. CICERO.
Lucius Cassius used to ask 'to whom had it been an advantage?'

Note 1. The Dative of Reference is sometimes not expressed:

Nimia fīdūcia calamitātī solet esse. NEPOS.
Too great confidence is wont to be a calamity (to men).

Exemplō est magnī formīca labōris. HORACE.
The ant is an example of great industry.

Note 2. The Predicative Dative is never qualified except by an adjective of
quantity.

26 (*e*) The **Dative of Purpose** expresses the end in view:

Equitātum auxiliō Caesarī mīsērunt. CAESAR.
They sent the cavalry as a help to Caesar.

Hōs tibi mūnerī mīsit. NEPOS.
He sent these to you as a present.

Vercingetorix locum castrīs dēligit. CAESAR.
Vercingetorix chooses a place for the camp.

Note 1. Observe the phrases, receptuī canere, *to give the signal for retreat*;
alimentō serere, *to sow for food*; laudī vertere alicui, *to turn to the praise of someone*;
vitiō vertere alicui, *to impute as a fault to someone.*

Note 2. For the Dative of the Gerundive in this construction, see **380,** n. 5.

227 (*f*) The **Dative of Direction** is used in poetry for the place towards
which there is motion (*cf.* **270**):

It clāmor caelō. VIRGIL.   *A shout ascends towards heaven.*

THE ABLATIVE CASE

228 The Ablative Case expresses relations which in English are generally indicated by the Prepositions, *from, with, by, in.*

Its uses may be divided into:

A. Ablative of Separation (*from, of*).
B. Ablative of Association (*with*).
C. Instrumental Ablative (*by, with*).
D. Ablative of 'Place and Time' (Locative, *in, at*).

A. Pure Ablatives

229 1. The **Ablative of Separation** is used (*a*) with Verbs meaning *to keep away from, free from, deprive, lack* (as abstineō, pellō; līberō, solvō, levō; prīvō, spoliō; egeō, careō, vacō); (*b*) with Adjectives of similar meaning (līber, vacuus, nūdus); (*c*) with the Adverb procul, *far from*:

> Populus Athēniēnsis Phōciōnem patriā pepulit. NEPOS.
> *The Athenian people drove Phocion from his country.*
>
> Procul negōtiīs, solūtus omnī faenore. HORACE.
> *Far from business, freed from all usury.*

Note 1. The Abl. with ā, ab is often used with līberō, and generally with compounds of dis-, sē- (dissentiō, sēcernō).

Note 2. Indigeō generally takes a Genitive (**253**).

Note 3. For an Abl. of Separation denoting **'Place Whence'**, see **269, 274**.

---

230 2. ·The **Ablative of Origin** is used with Verbs, chiefly Participles, implying descent or origin:

> Atreus, Tantalō prōgnātus, Pelope nātus. CICERO.
> *Atreus, descended from Tantalus, and son of Pelops.*

231 3. The **Ablative of Comparison** is used with Comparative Adjectives and Adverbs instead of quam (*than*) with a Nominative or Accusative:

> Nihil est amābilius virtūte. CICERO.
> *Nothing is more worthy of love than virtue.*

Note 1. The Ablative expresses the point 'from which' the comparison begins: *starting with virtue,* &c.

Note 2. If other cases than the Nom. or Accus. are involved in the comparison, the quam construction *must* be used:

> Nihilō amīcior est Phaedriae quam Antiphōnī. TERENCE.
> *He is in no degree more friendly to Phaedria than to Antipho.*

B. Ablatives of Association

Note. These include some uses of a lost Instrumental Case (30 n.), which expressed the circumstances associated with the Subject or the action of the Sentence.

1. The **Ablative of Association** is used with Verbs and Adjectives denoting *plenty, fulness, possession* (*cf.* **253**):

> Vīlla abundat gallīnā, lacte, cāseō, melle. CICERO.
> *The farm abounds in poultry, milk, cheese, honey.*

> Iuvenem praestantī mūnere dōnat. VIRGIL.
> *He presents the youth with a noble gift.*

Note. Dōnō also takes Accusative of the thing with Dative of Person: Caesar praedam mīlitibus dōnat, *Caesar gives the booty to the soldiers.*

2. The **Ablative of Quality** is used with an Adjective in agreement (*cf.* **255**):

> Senex prōmissā barbā, horrentī capillō. PLINY.
> *An old man with long beard and rough hair.*

> Habuit frātrem Dumnorigem summā audāciā. CAESAR.
> *He had a brother Dumnorix of supreme audacity.*

Note. Generally an Abl. of Quality does not depend on a proper name but on the word vir, or fēmina, placed in apposition: Philippus, vir summā nōbilitāte.

35   3. **Ablative of Respect or Specification:**

> Et corde et genibus tremit. HORACE.
> *It trembles both in heart and knees.*

> Ennius, ingeniō maximus, arte rudis. OVID.
> *Ennius, mighty in genius, in art (is) rude.*

Note 1. In the phrases nātū maior, *older*, nātū minor, *younger*, nātū is an Ablative of Respect.

Note 2. Dignus, *worthy*, indignus, *unworthy*, dignor, *deem worthy*, are followed by an Abl. of Respect:

> Dignum laude virum Mūsa vetat morī. HORACE.
> *A man worthy of praise the Muse forbids to die.*

236   4. The **Ablative of the Manner** in which something happens or is done has an Adjective in agreement with it; *or* it follows the Preposition **cum**, *with*:

> Iam veniet tacitō curva senecta pede. OVID.
> *Presently bent old age will come with silent foot.*

5*

Magnā cum cūrā atque dīligentiā scrīpsit. CICERO.
He wrote with great care and attention.

Note 1. A few Ablatives of Manner are used without an adjective or cum fraude, *deceitfully,* silentiō, *in silence,* mōre maiōrum, *in the fashion of our ancestors,* iūre, *by right,* iniūriā, *wrongfully,* ratiōne, *on principle.*
Note 2. Observe: eā condiciōne, *on those terms;* meā (tuā, suā) sponte, *voluntarily;* pāce tuā, *by your leave.*

---

237   5. The **Ablative Absolute** is a phrase, consisting of a Noun in the Ablative Case and a Participle (or another Noun or Adjective) in agreement with it:

Rēgibus exāctīs cōnsulēs creātī sunt. LIVY.
Kings having been abolished, consuls were elected.

Pereunte obsequiō imperium intercidit. TACITUS.
Obedience failing, government falls to pieces.

Caesare ventūrō, Phōsphore, redde diem. MARTIAL.
Caesar being on his way, star of morn, restore the day.

Nīl dēspērandum Teucrō duce. HORACE.
There must be no despair, Teucer being leader.

Nātus est Augustus cōnsulibus Cicerōne et Antōniō. SUETONIUS.
Augustus was born when Cicero and Antonius were consuls.

Note 1. The Ablative Abs. defines some circumstance which is connected with the action of the Sentence. It is called Absolute (absolūtus, *set free*) because the Noun and Participle are independent of the rest of the Sentence in construction. A dependent clause joined to the Sentence by a Conjunction may be used instead of an Ablative Absolute construction. In the first example 'Rēgibus exāctīs' might be replaced by 'Cum rēgēs exāctī essent', *when kings had been driven out* (392).
Note 2. This construction is not used if the Noun would represent either the Subject or Object of the sentence.

C. Instrumental Ablatives

238 *Note.* These include other uses of the old Instrumental Case (30 n.).

---

239 The **Ablative of the Agent** indicates the *person* by whom something is done, and it is accompanied by the Preposition **ā, ab.** See **296, 300, 303.**

240   1. The **Ablative of Instrument or Means** indicates the *instrument* by which something is done, and it is not accompanied by a preposition:

Hī iaculīs, illī certant dēfendere saxīs. VIRGIL.
These strive to defend with javelins, those with stones.

Dente lupus, cornū taurus petit. HORACE.
The wolf attacks with his teeth, the bull with his horns.

Note. The road by which one goes is in the Ablative.
Ībam forte Viā Sacrā. HORACE.
I was going by chance along the Sacred Way.

The Deponent Verbs **fungor**, *perform*, **fruor**, *enjoy*, **vēscor**, *feed on*, **ūtor**, *use*, **potior**, *possess oneself of*, unlike their English equivalents, are Intransitive and take an Ablative of Instrument:

Hannibal cum victōriā posset ūtī fruī māluit. LIVY.
Hannibal, when he could use his victory, preferred to enjoy it.

Numidae ferīnā carne vēscēbantur. SALLUST.
The Numidians used to feed on the flesh of wild animals.

Note 1. Potior sometimes takes a genitive (253).
Note 2. Ūtor, fungor, fruor, are sometimes used in early Latin as transitive verbs and take an Accusative. See also: 302, n.; 383, n. 1.

---

242 An Ablative of Instrument is used with **frētus (sum)**, **nītor**, *I support myself, lean on*, **opus**, **ūsus (est)**, *there is need*, **cōnsistō**, *consist of*:

Iuvenis quī nītitur hastā. VIRGIL.
A youth who leans on a spear.

Mortālī cōnsistit corpore mundus. LUCRETIUS.
The universe consists of mortal substance.

Ubi rēs adsunt, quid opus est verbīs? SALLUST.
When the facts are at hand, what is the need of words?

243 2. The **Ablative of the Cause** is used with Adjectives, Passive Participles, and Verbs (especially those denoting a mental state):

Coeptīs immānibus effera Dīdō. VIRGIL.
Dido driven wild by her horrible designs.

Ōdērunt peccāre malī formīdine poenae. HORACE.
The bad hate to sin through fear of punishment.

244 3. An **Ablative of the Measure** of difference is used with Comparatives and Superlatives and, rarely, with Verbs:

Sōl multīs partibus maior est quam lūna. CICERO.
The sun is a great deal larger than the moon.

Especially the Ablatives:

hōc, eō, quō,	dīmidiō, quantō, tantō,
nihilō and nimiō	paulō, multō, aliquantō.

Quō plūs habent, eō plūs cupiunt.
The more they have, the more they desire.

Hibernia dīmidiō minor est quam Britannia.   CAESAR.
Ireland is smaller by half than Britain.

Note.   For difference in Time and Space, see **279, 280, 282.**

---

245   4. The **Ablative of Price** is used with Verbs and Adjectives of *buying* and *selling*:

Servum quadrāgintā minīs ēmit.
He bought a slave for (with) forty minae.

Multōrum sanguine victōria stetit.   LIVY.
The victory cost (literally stood at) the blood of many.

Note 1.   Ablatives of price are: magnō, *at a high price*; parvō, minimō, vīlī, *at a low price*:

Parvō famēs cōnstat, magnō fastīdium.   SENECA.
Hunger costs little, daintiness much.

Note 2.   For the genitive of value, see **257.**

D. The Ablative of Place and Time; the Locative Case

246 The **Ablative of Time and Place** includes the uses of the old Locative case which expressed the place where, or the time at which, an action occurred.

For the Ablative indicating 'Place Where', see **268.**
For the Ablative indicating 'Time at Which', see **276–7.**

The true **Locative Case** is used:

(*a*) In the singular of names of towns and small islands of the First and Second Declensions (and occasionally of the Third):

Rōmae; Corcȳrae; Corinthī; Carthāginī.

(*b*) In some special forms:

domī; bellī; mīlitiae; rūrī; humī; vesperī.

Note 1.   The word animī in such phrases as anxius animī, *anxious*, pendēre animī, *to waver in mind*, is probably Locative.
Note 2.   In Early Latin, Locatives like diē septimī, *on the seventh day*, are found.

THE GENITIVE CASE

The Genitive is used to define or complete the meaning of another Noun on which it depends. It is also used with certain Verbs and Adjectives.

The uses of the Genitive may be divided into:

A. Genitives of Definition
B. Possessive Genitive.
C. Genitive of Quality.
D. Genitive of the Whole or Partitive Genitive.

E. Subjective and Objective Genitive.
F. Genitive with Verbs.

A. Genitives of Definition

248 1. The **Appositional Genitive** depends on another noun which it qualifies like a noun in apposition:

Vōx voluptātis.	Nōmen rēgis.	Ars scrībendī.
The word pleasure.	*The name of king.*	*The art of writing.*

Note. But the name of a city is always placed in Apposition: urbs Rōma, *the city of Rome.*

249 2. The **Attributive** or **Descriptive Genitive** defines the Noun on which it depends by mentioning its content or material:

Acervus frūmentī.   Obtortī circulus aurī.
A pile of corn.   *A chain of twisted gold.*

250 3. The **Genitive of the Author**:

Ea statua dīcēbātur esse Myrōnis.   CICERO.
That statue was said to be Myro's.

Legendī sunt vōbīs Platōnis librī.   CICERO.
You should read the works of Plato (i.e. '*written by*', not '*belonging to*', cf. **254**).

251 4. The **Genitive of Characteristic** is used in an Impersonal construction with a Copulative Verb and an Infinitive, where in English a word such as *nature, part, characteristic,* or *mark,* must be supplied to complete the meaning:

Cuiusvīs hominis est errāre.   CICERO.
It is (the nature) of any man to err.

Est adulēscentis maiōrēs nātū verērī. CICERO.
It is a young man's (part) to reverence his elders.

Temporī cēdere habētur sapientis. CICERO.
To yield to occasion is considered (the mark) of a wise man.

Sapientis est proprium nihil quod paenitēre possit facere. CICERO.
It is the characteristic of a wise man to do nothing of which he may repent.

252 5. Verbs and Adjectives of *accusing, condemning, convicting,* or *acquitting* take a Genitive of the fault or crime:

Alter latrōciniī reus, alter caedis convictus est. CICERO.
The one was accused of robbery, the other was convicted of murder.

Miltiadēs capitis absolūtus pecūniā multātus est. NEPOS.
Miltiades, acquitted of capital crime, was fined.

Note 1. Sometimes the Ablatives nōmine, *on the ground of,* crīmine, *on the charge of,* are used (with a dependent genitive):

Themistoclēs crīmine prōditiōnis absēns damnātus est. NEPOS.
Themistocles was convicted while absent on the charge of treason.

Note 2. The penalty is expressed by an Ablative of Instrument (240).

253 6. Verbs and Adjectives implying *want* and *fulness,* especially egeō, indigeō, *want,* impleō, *fill,* potior, *get possession of,* plēnus, *full,* often take a Genitive (*cf.* 229, 233, 241):

Virtūs plūrimae exercitātiōnis indiget. CICERO.
Virtue needs very much practice.

Hanc iuventūtem speī animōrumque implēvēre. LIVY.
They filled these youths with hope and spirit.

Rōmānī sīgnōrum et armōrum potītī sunt. SALLUST.
The Romans got possession of standards and arms.

254 ### B. Possessive Genitive

Rēgis cōpiae. CICERO.
The king's forces.

Contempsī Catilīnae gladiōs. CICERO.
I have braved the swords of Catiline.

Singulōrum opēs dīvitiae sunt cīvitātis. CICERO.
The means of individuals are the state's riches.

Sometimes the Genitive depends on a Noun understood:

Hectoris Andromachē. VIRGIL.
Hector's (wife) Andromache.

Ventum erat ad Vestae. HORACE.
We had come to Vesta's (temple).

Note 1. Of a similar origin are the genitives dependent on grātiā, causā, *for the sake of.*

Note 2. A Possessive Genitive is sometimes used in conjunction with a Possessive Adjective:

Rēspūblica meā ūnīus operā salva est. CICERO.
The state was saved by my own unaided effort.

C. Genitive of Quality

55 1. The **Genitive of Quality** has an Adjective in agreement:

Ingenuī vultūs puer ingenuīque pudōris. JUVENAL.
A boy of noble countenance and noble modesty.

Memoriae fēlīciōris est nōmen Appiī. LIVY.
The name of Appius is of happier memory.

56 2. Number, age, and size are expressed by such a Genitive:

Classis septuāgintā nāvium.   Puer annōrum novem.
A fleet of seventy ships.   *A boy of nine years.*

Fossa quīndecim pedum: *a trench fifteen feet deep.*

257 3. **Genitives of Value,** magnī, parvī, plūrimī, minimī, nihilī, are used with Verbs of *valuing*; the Genitives tantī, quantī, plūris, minōris, are also used with Verbs of *buying* and *selling*, but not to express a definite price (*cf.* **245**):

Voluptātem sapiēns minimī facit.
The wise man accounts pleasure of very little value.

Ēmit hortōs tantī, quantī Pȳthius voluit. CICERO.
He bought the gardens for as much as Pythius wished.

Nūlla possessiō plūris quam virtūs aestimanda est. CICERO.
No possession is to be regarded as more precious than virtue.

Note. The Genitives floccī, naucī were used in the popular speech to express worthlessness, corresponding to the English expressions, *not worth a straw, a nut,* &c.

Iūdicēs rempūblicam floccī nōn faciunt. CICERO.
The judges do not care a straw for the republic.

D. Genitive of the Whole, or Partitive Genitive

258 The Genitive of a Noun of which a part is mentioned is called a Genitive of the Whole, or a Partitive Genitive.

259 1. Such a genitive may depend on any word denoting a part:

(a) Substantives:

> Sic partem maiōrem cōpiārum Antōnius āmīsit.   CICERO.
> *Thus Antony lost the greater part of his forces.*

> Nēmō mortālium omnibus hōrīs sapit.   PLINY.
> *No one of mortals is wise at all times.*

(b) Pronouns or Pronominal Adjectives:

> Elephantō bēluārum nūlla est prūdentior.   CICERO.
> *Of animals none is more sagacious than the elephant.*

Note. 1.   Nostrum and vestrum are used as Partitive Genitives (*cf.* **92a**, n. 2).

> Incertum est quam longa nostrum cuiusque vīta futōra sit.
> *It is uncertain how long the life of each one of us will be.*

Note 2.   Quīdam, *a certain one*, is generally constructed with the Abl. of Separation and ex: quīdam ex amīcīs, *a certain one of his friends.*

(c) Numerals and Adjectives of number:

> Sulla centum vīgintī suōrum āmīsit.   EUTROPIUS.
> *Sulla lost a hundred and twenty of his men.*

> Multae hārum arborum meā manū sunt satae.   CICERO.
> *Many of these trees were planted by my hand.*

Note 3.   Cardinal Numerals are often constructed with an Abl. of Separation and ex: ūnus ex amīcīs, *one of his friends.*   For the use of mīlle, see **89, 311**.

(d) Comparatives and Superlatives:

> Maior Nerōnum.   HORACE.
> *The elder of the Neros.*

> Hoc ad tē minimē omnium pertinet.   CICERO.
> *This belongs to you least of all men.*

> Tōtīus Graeciae Platō doctissimus erat.   CICERO.
> *Plato was the most learned man of all Greece.*

Note 4. In poetry, the word (*e.g.* ūnus) on which a Partitive Genitive depends is sometimes omitted:

Scrībe tuī gregis hunc. HORACE.
Enlist this man in your train.

Fīēs nōbilium tū quoque fontium. HORACE.
Thou too shalt become a famous fountain.

2. A Partitive Genitive may depend on the Nominative or Accusative Singular Neuter of a Pronoun denoting quantity, and on the Adverbs satis, nimis, parum used Substantively:

Aliquid prīstinī rōboris cōnservat. CICERO.
He keeps somewhat of his old strength.

Catilīnae erat satis ēloquentiae, sapientiae parum. SALLUST.
Catiline had plenty of eloquence, of wisdom too little.

Note 1. The Partitive Genitives: gentium, *of nations,* terrārum, *of countries,* depend on such Adverbs of Place as: ubi, *where,* eō, *thither,* quō, *whither,* longē, *far:*

Ubinam gentium sumus? CICERO.
Where in the world are we?

Migrandum aliquō terrārum arbitror. CICERO.
I think we must migrate to some part of the world.

Note 2. The genitive in: prīdiē (postrīdiē) eius diēī, *on the day before (after) that,* is partitive in origin.

E. The Subjective and Objective Genitive

61 The terms Subjective and Objective Genitive refer primarily to two different relations of the Genitive to a Noun on which it depends. The Subjective Genitive represents what would be the subject of a verb corresponding to the noun on which the Genitive depends: the Objective Genitive represents the object of such a verb. Thus amor patris, *the love of a father,* may mean either 'the love felt by a father' (where patris is a Subjective Genitive, *cf.* pater amat), or 'the love felt for a father' (where patris is an Objective Genitive, *cf.* amō patrem).

262 An Objective Genitive is used with Substantives and Adjectives (especially those in -āx) in which a verbal notion is prominent, and with Participles which have the meaning of *love, desire, hope, fear, care, knowledge, ignorance, skill, power.*

(*a*) With Substantives:

> Erat īnsitus mentī cognitiōnis amor. CICERO.
> *Love of knowledge had been implanted in the mind.*

> Difficilis est cūra rērum aliēnārum. CICERO.
> *The care of other people's affairs is difficult.*

(*b*) With Adjectives:

> Avida est perīculī virtūs. SENECA.
> *Valour is greedy of danger.*

> Cōnscia mēns rēctī fāmae mendācia rīsit. OVID.
> *The mind conscious of right smiled at the lies of rumour.*

> Homō multārum rērum perītus. CICERO.
> *A man skilled in many things.*

> Vir prōpositī tenāx. HORACE.
> *A man holding to his purpose.*

(*c*) With Participles:

> Semper appetentēs glōriae fuistis. CICERO.
> *You were always desirous of glory.*

> Quis famulus amantior dominī quam canis? COLUMELLA.
> *What servant is fonder of his master than the dog is?*

63 Meī, *of me*, tuī, *of thee*, suī, *of him, her, them*, nostrī, *of us*, vestrī, *of you* (*cf.* **92a**, n̄. 2), are Objective Genitives:

> Nīciās tuā suī memoriā dēlectātur. CICERO.
> *Nicias is delighted by your recollection of him.*

> Sī tibi cūra meī, sit tibi cūra tuī. OVID.
> *If you care for me, take care of yourself.*

F. Genitive with Verbs

64 1. Most Verbs of *remembering, forgetting,* **meminī, reminīscor,** oblīvīscor, usually take a Genitive:

> Animus meminīt praeteritōrum. CICERO.
> *The mind remembers past things.*

> Epicūrī nōn licet oblīvīscī. CICERO.
> *We must not forget Epicurus.*

Note 1. The phrase mihi venit in mentem takes the genitive like meminī.

Note 2. The Accus. is sometimes used instead of the Gen. with these verbs.

Nam modo vōs animō dulcēs reminīscor, amīcī. OVID.
For now I remember you, O friends, dear to my soul.

Note 3. Recordor, *I remember*, almost always takes the Accus.

The Adjectives corresponding to these Verbs, **memor, immemor,** always take a Genitive.

Omnēs immemorem beneficī ōdērunt. CICERO.
All hate one who is forgetful of a kindness.

2. Verbs of Reminding, **admoneō, commoneō, commonefaciō,** take an Accusative of the person reminded and a Genitive of the thing:

Admonēbat alium egestātis, alium cupiditātis. SALLUST.
He reminded one of his poverty, another of his desires.

Tē veteris amīcitiae commonefēcit. CICERO.
He reminded you of your old friendship.

Note. If the Thing is expressed by a Neut. Pronoun, it also is in the Accus.:
Hoc mē admonet, *He reminds me of this.*

3. Two Verbs of *pitying*, **misereor, miserēscō,** take a Genitive:

Arcadiī, quaesō, miserēscite rēgis. VIRGIL.
Take pity, I entreat, on the Arcadian king.

Nīl nostrī miserēre. VIRGIL.
You pity me not at all.

Miseror, commiseror take an Accusative.

67 For the Genitive with Impersonal Verbs, see **288, 291–2.**

Note. Verbs of *refraining* and *ceasing* and some Adjectives are used by poets with a Genitive in imitation of the Greek use; especially by Horace: Abstinētō īrārum, *Refrain from angry words.*

PLACE, TIME AND SPACE

Place

268 **Place where** anything is or happens is generally expressed by the Ablative Case (246) with the Preposition **in**; sometimes (especially in poetry), when an Adjective qualifies the Substantive, the Preposition is omitted:

> Castra sunt in Italiā contrā rempūblicam conlocāta. CICERO.
> *A camp has been set up in Italy against the republic.*

> Celsā sedet Aeolus arce. VIRGIL.
> *Aeolus is seated on his high citadel.*

269 **Place whence** there is motion is expressed by the Ablative (229) with **ā, ab, ex,** or **dē:**

> Ex Asiā trānsīs in Eurōpam. CURTIUS.
> *Out of Asia you cross into Europe.*

> Ruunt dē montibus amnēs. VIRGIL.
> *The rivers rush down from the mountains.*

270 **Place whither** is expressed by the Accusative (211) with a Preposition; but in poetry the Preposition is sometimes omitted:

> Caesar in Italiam magnīs itineribus contendit. CAESAR.
> *Caesar hastened by long marches into Italy.*

> Ītaliam fātō profugus Lāvīnaque vēnit lītora. VIRGIL.
> *Driven by fate he came to Italy and the Lavinian shores.*

271 In names of **towns** and **small islands,** also in **domus** and **rūs, Place where, whence,** or **whither** is expressed by a Case without a Preposition:

272   (*a*) **Place where,** by the Locative (246):

> Quid Rōmae faciam? JUVENAL. | Is habitat Mīlētī. TERENCE.
> *What am I to do at Rome?* | *He lives at Miletus.*

> Philippus Neāpolī est, Lentulus Puteolīs. CICERO.
> *Philip is at Naples, Lentulus at Puteoli.*

> Sī domī sum, forīs est animus; sīn forīs sum, animus est domī. PLAUTUS.
> *If I am at home, my mind is abroad; if I am abroad, my mind is at home.*

Note. The Locative domī is used with a Genitive of the Possessor; domī Caesaris, *at the house of Caesar*; or with the Locative of a Possessive Adjective: domī meae, *at my house.*

(*b*) **Place whence,** by the Ablative:

Dēmarātus fūgit Tarquiniōs Corinthō. CICERO.
Demaratus fled from Corinth to Tarquinii.

With names of towns, **ab** is used to mean *from the neighbourhood of*: ā Gergoviā discessit. CAESAR.

'5 (*c*) **Place whither,** by the Accusative:

Rēgulus Carthāginem rediit. CICERO.
Regulus returned to Carthage.

With names of towns, **ad** is used to mean *to the neighbourhood of*: ventum est ad Cannās. LIVY.

Time

76 Time **at** which, in answer to the question When? is expressed by the Ablative (**246**): hieme, *in winter*; sōlis occāsū, *at sunset*:

Ego Capuam vēnī eō ipsō diē. CICERO.
I came to Capua on that very day.

277 Time **within** which, by the Ablative:

Quicquid est, bīduō sciēmus. CICERO.
Whatever it is, we shall know in two days.

Note. In is sometimes added: in hōrā, *within an hour.*

278 Time **during** which, by the Accusative (**211**):

Rōmulus septem et trīgintā rēgnāvit annōs. LIVY.
Romulus reigned thirty-seven years.

Note 1. Per is sometimes added: per trīduum, *for three days.*
Note 2. Age is expressed by the participle nātus, *born*, used with the Accusative, sometimes with the Ablative:
Catō quīnque et octōgintā annōs nātus excessit ē vītā. CICERO.
Cato died aged eighty-five years.
Note 3. Occasionally an Abl. is used instead of an Accus. to express duration of time:
Nostrī quīnque hōrīs proelium sustinuērunt. CAESAR.
Our men sustained the battle for five hours.

279 How long ago, is expressed by the Accusative (**211**), or (less frequently) by the Ablative (**244**) with **abhinc**:

> Hoc factum est fermē abhinc biennium. PLAUTUS.
> *This was done about two years ago.*

> Comitia iam abhinc diēbus trīgintā habita. CICERO.
> *The assembly was held thirty days ago.*

280 How long before, How long after, are expressed by **ante,** *before,* **post,** *after,* with the Ablative (**244**):

> Pecūnia reciperāta est multīs post annīs. CAESAR.
> *The money was recovered many years afterwards.*

Quam is used when a comparison is expressed:

> Numa annīs permultīs ante fuit quam Pȳthagorās. CICERO.
> *Numa lived very many years before Pythagoras.*

Space

281 Space traversed, is expressed by the Accusative (**211**):

> Mīlia tum prānsī tria rēpimus. HORACE.
> *Then having had luncheon we crawl three miles.*

282 Space which lies between, is expressed by the Accusative (**211**) or the Ablative (**244**):

> Reliquae legiōnēs magnum spatium aberant. CAESAR.
> *The rest of the legions were at a long distance.*

> Hic locus aequō ferē spatiō ab castrīs Ariovistī et Caesaris aberat. CAESAR.
> *This place was at a nearly equal distance from the camps of Ariovistus and Caesar.*

283 Space of measurement, answering the questions *how high? how deep? how broad? how long?* is generally expressed by the Accusative (**211**):

> Erant mūrī Babylōnis ducēnōs pedēs altī. PLINY.
> *The walls of Babylon were two hundred feet high.*

PREPOSITIONS

Prepositions, in conjunction with the case-endings, shew the relations of Nouns, Adjectives, and Pronouns to other words, and they are used where these relations cannot be clearly expressed by the case-endings alone. All Prepositions except **tenus** take the Accusative or the Ablative case; they are usually placed before the Noun.

Prepositions with Accusative

Ad, *to, towards* (with Accusative of Motion), *at*: ad urbem īre, *to go to the city*; ad summam senectūtem, *to extreme old age*; ad octingentōs caesī, *there were slain to the number of* 800; pugna ad Alliam, *the battle at the Allia*; ad prīmam lūcem, *at daybreak*; ad hoc, *moreover*; ad tempus, *for a time*; ad verbum, *word for word*; nihil ad Atticum, *nothing to (in comparison with) Atticus*; nihil ad rem, *nothing to the purpose.*

Adversus, Adversum, *towards, against, opposite to*; adversum Antipolim, *opposite to Antipolis*; reverentia adversus senēs, *respect towards the aged.*

Apud, *at, near* (used chiefly with persons, rarely with places): apud mē, *at my house*; apud veterēs, *among the ancients*; apud Homērum, *in Homer's works*; but in Īliade Homērī, *in Homer's Iliad.*

Ante, *before*:
Post, *behind, after*:
$\left\{ \begin{array}{l} \text{ante oculōs, } \textit{before one's eyes}\text{; ante merīdiem, } \textit{before noon}\text{;} \\ \text{ante aliquem esse, } \textit{to surpass someone}\text{; post terga, } \textit{behind} \\ \textit{the back}\text{; post mortem, } \textit{after death.} \end{array} \right.$

Pōne, *behind*: pōne nōs, *behind us.*

Circum, Circā, *around, about* (in Place):

Circā, Circiter, *about* (in Time, Number):
Circum caput, *round the head*; circā forum, *around the forum.*
Circā prīmam lūcem, *about daybreak*; circā, circiter trīgintā, *about thirty.*

Cis, Citrā, *on this side of*: cis Alpēs, *on this side of the Alps.*

Trāns, *across*: trāns Rhēnum dūcere, *to lead across the Rhine*; trāns Alpēs, *on the further side of the Alps.*

Ultrā, *beyond*: ultrā Euphrātem, *beyond the Euphrates*; ultrā vīrēs, *beyond their powers.*

Contrā, *against, opposite to*: contrā hostem, *against the enemy*; contrā arcem, *opposite to the citadel.*

Ergā, *towards* (not used of Place): ergā aliquem benevolus, *feeling kindly towards someone.*

Extrā, *outside of, without*: extrā mūrōs, *outside the walls*; extrā culpam, *free from blame.*

Intrā, *within*: intrā mūros, *within the walls*; intrā vīgintī diēs, *within twenty days.*

Inter, *between* (in Place); *during* (in Time), *among*: inter urbem et Tiberim, *between the city and the Tiber*; inter silvās, *among the woods*; inter cēnandum, *during dinner*; cōnstat inter omnēs, *all are agreed*; inter nōs, *between ourselves*; inter sē amant, *they love each other.*

Infrā, *under, beneath*: īnfrā caelum, *under the sky*; īnfrā dignitātem, *beneath one's dignity*.

Suprā, *over, above*: suprā terram, *above the ground*; suprā mīlia vīgintī, *more than twenty thousand*; suprā vīrēs, *beyond one's strength*.

Iūxtā, *adjoining to, beside*: iūxtā viam, *adjoining the road*; iūxtā deōs, *next to the gods*.

Ob, *over against, on account of*: mihi ob oculōs, *before my eyes*; quam ob rem, *wherefore*.

Penes, *in the power of*: penes mē, *in my power*; penes tē es? *are you in your senses?*

Per, *through (by)*: per viās, *through the streets*; per vim, *by force*; per mē licet, *I give leave*; per tē deōs ōrō, *I pray you by the gods*; per explōrātōrēs certior fīō, *I ascertain through scouts*.

Praeter, *beside, past, along*: praeter rīpam, *along the bank*; praeter omnēs, *beyond all others*; praeter mē, *except me*; praeter opīnōnem, *contrary to expectation*.

Prope, *near*: prope amnem, *near the river*; prope lucem, *towards daybreak*.

Propter, *on account of* (rarely of Place, *near, close to*): propter hoc, *on this account;* propter aquam, *close to the water's edge*.

Secundum, *next, along, according to (following)*: secundum vōs, *next to (behind) you*; secundum lītus, *along the shore*; secundum lēgem, *in accordance with the law*; secundum nōs, *in our favour*.

Versus, *towards* (following the Noun): Italiam versus, *towards Italy*.

Clam, *unknown to* (much more frequently used as an adverb): clam nostrōs, *unknown to our men*. An Abl. is occasionally found instead of an Accus.

286 Prepositions with Ablative

Ā, ab, *from, by*: ab eō locō, *from that place*; ab ortū ad occāsum, *from East to West*; procul ā patriā, *far from one's country*; prope abesse ab, *to be near*; ā tergō, *in the rear*; ā senātū stetit, *he took the side of the senate*; hoc ā mē est, *this is in my favour*; ab urbe conditā, *from the foundation of Rome*; servus ab epistulīs, *secretary*; nōn ab rē fuerit, *it will not be irrelevant*; ab īrā facere, *to do in anger*.

Absque, *without* (rare): absque vōbis esset, *if it were not for you*.

Palam, *in sight of*: palam omnibus, *in sight of all* (511 n.).

Cōram, *in the presence of*: cōram populō, *in the presence of the people*.

Cum, *with*: cum aliquō congruere, certāre, *to agree, strive with someone*; magnō cum perīculō, *with great danger*; with mē, tē, nōbīs, vōbīs, often with quō, quibus, cum follows the Pronoun; mēcum, *with me*.

Sine, *without*: sine rēgibus, *without kings*; sine dubiō, *without doubt*.

Dē, *from (down from), concerning*: dē monte, *down from the mountain*; dē diē, *in the daytime*; dē diē in diem, *from day to day*; ūnus dē multīs, *one of many*; dē pāce, *concerning peace*; quid dē nōbīs fīet, *what will become of us?* dē industriā, *on purpose*; dē mōre, *according to custom*; dē integrō, *anew*.

Ex, Ē, *out of, from*: ex urbe, *out of the city*; ē longinquō, *from far*; ex equīs pugnant, *they fight on horseback*; diem ex diē, *from day to day*; ex eō audīvī, *I heard it from him*; ūnus ex illīs, *one of those*; ex quō, *from the time when*; ē rēpūblicā, *for the good of the State*; ex sententiā, *satisfactorily*; ex occultō, *secretly*; ex marmore sīgnum, *a marble bust*.

Prae, *before, in front of (for)* (Place rarely, chiefly used in idioms): prae sē fert speciem virī bonī, *he wears the semblance of a good man*; prae nōbīs beātus es, *you are happy compared with us*; prae gaudiō ubi sim nescio, *I do not know where I am for joy*.

Prō, *before, for*: prō foribus, *before the door*; prō patriā morī, *to die for one's country* (in defence of); mihi prō parente fuit, *he was in the place of a parent to me*; prō certō hoc habuī, *I held this for certain*; prō ratā parte, *in proportion*; prō rē, *according to circumstances*.

Note. **Prae** means *in advance of*; **prō,** *standing for, defending*.

Tenus, *as far as* (generally follows the Noun): verbō tenus, *so far as the word goes*. Sometimes with Genitive: Corcȳrae tenus, *as far as Corcyra*; especially with a plural Noun: crūrum tenus, *as far as the legs*.

Prepositions with Accusative or Ablative

In, *into, to, towards, against*; with Accusative: ībō in Pīraeum, *I will go into the Piraeus*; in orbem īre, *to go round*; līberālis in mīlitēs, *liberal towards the troops*; Cicerō in Verrem dīxit, *Cicero spoke against Verres*; in aeternum, *for ever*; in vicem, *in turn*; in poenam dare, *to deliver to punishment*; venīre in cōnspectum, *to come into sight*; in diēs, *daily*.

In, *in, among, on*; with Ablative: in urbe Rōmā, *in the city of Rome*; in oculīs esse, *to be before one's eyes*; in tempore, *at the right time*; in dīcendō, *while speaking*; in bonīs habēre, *to count among blessings*; in Ganymēde, *in the case of Ganymede*; in eō reprehendere quod, *to blame on the score that*.

Sub, *up to*; with Accusative: sub montem venīre, *to come close to the foot of the mountain*; sub lūcem, *towards daybreak*; sub noctem, *at nightfall*; sub haec dicta, *just after these things were said*.

Sub, *under*; with Ablative; sub terrā, *underground*; sub monte esse, *to be beneath the mountain*; sub poenā, *under penalty of*.

Subter, *underneath*: with Acc., subter mūrum venīre, *to come close to the wall*. Abl., subter lītore esse, *to be close to the shore*.

Super, *over*; with Accusative: super terram, *over the ground*; super omnia, *above all*.

Super, *upon*; with Ablative: super focō, *on the hearth*; super Hectore, *about Hector*.

IMPERSONAL VERBS

CASE CONSTRUCTION

288 The following verbs of *feeling* take an Accusative of the person with a Genitive of the cause: **miseret, piget, paenitet, pudet, taedet** (*cf.* **266**):

> Miseret tē aliōrum, tuī tē nec miseret nec pudet. PLAUTUS.
> *You pity others, for yourself you have neither pity nor shame.*
> Mē cīvitātis mōrum piget taedetque. SALLUST.
> *I am sick and weary of the morals of the state.*

289 **Decet, dēdecet, iuvat** take an Accusative of the person with an Infinitive as the Impersonal Subject (*cf.* **366**):

> Ōrātōrem īrāscī minimē decet, simulāre nōn dēdecet. CICERO.
> *It by no means becomes an orator to feel anger, it is not unbecoming to feign it.*
> Sī mē gemmantia dextrā scēptra tenēre decet. OVID.
> *If it befits me to hold in my right hand the jewelled sceptre.*

Note. Fallit, fugit, praeterit, when used impersonally with meaning *it escapes notice*, take this construction.

---

290 **Libet, licet, liquet, contingit, convenit, ēvenit, expedit,** take a Dative (sometimes with an Infinitive as the Impersonal Subject; *cf.* **366**):

> Nē libeat tibi quod nōn licet. CICERO.
> *Let not that please you which is not lawful.*
> Licet nēminī contrā patriam dūcere exercitum. CICERO.
> *It is not lawful for anyone to lead an army against his country.*

291 With **rēfert**, *it concerns, it matters*, the person concerned is expressed by the feminine Ablative singular of a Possessive Adjective (meā, tuā, &c.); the degree of concern by adverbs of degree (magnopere, &c.) or by a Genitive of value (parvī, &c.), or by an Adverbial Accusative (multum, plūs, quid, &c.):

> Quid meā rēfert cui serviam? PHAEDRUS.
> *How much does it matter to me whom I serve?*
> Hoc nōn plūris rēfert quam sī imbrem in crībrum gerās. PLAUTUS.
> *This matters no more than if you should pour rain-water into a sieve.*

Note 1. Rē- in rēfert was regarded as an Abl.; hence meā, tuā.
Note 2. Cicero and Caesar prefer to use interest rather than rēfert.

Interest, *it concerns, it is of importance,* has the same constructions as rēfert; in addition, it may take a Genitive of the person or thing concerned:

> Interest omnium rēctē facere.   CICERO.
> *It is for the good of all to do right.*
>
> Et tuā et meā interest tē valēre.   CICERO.
> *It is of importance to you and to me that you should be well.*
>
> Illud meā magnī interest ut tē videam.   CICERO.
> *It is of great importance to me that I should see you.*

Note 1.   The use of meā, tuā with interest is due to the analogy of rēfert.
Note 2.   A Gen. of the person concerned is rare with rēfert.

---

3 Pertinet, attinet take an Accusative with **ad**:

> Nihil ad mē attinet.   TERENCE.
> *It does not concern me at all.*

4 Oportet is used with an Accusative and Infinitive clause, or with the Subjunctive alone; rarely with the Infinitive alone:

> Lēgem brevem esse oportet.   CICERO.
> *A law ought to be brief.*
>
> Mē ipsum amēs oportet, nōn mea.   CICERO.
> *You ought to love me, not my possessions.*
>
> Vīvere nātūrae sī convenienter oportet.   HORACE.
> *If one ought to live agreeably to nature.*

---

295 *Note.*   Coepit, dēbet, dēsinit, potest, solet are used impersonally with an Impersonal Infinitive:

> Pervenīrī ad summa sine industriā nōn potest.   QUINTILIAN.
> *One cannot reach the highest without industry.*

PASSIVE CONSTRUCTION

296 When a sentence is changed from the Active to the Passive form:
(*a*) The Object of a Transitive Verb becomes the Subject; the Subject becomes the Agent in the Ablative with the Preposition **ā** or **ab** (239):

> { Numa lēgēs dedit.   CICERO.   *Numa gave laws.*
> { Lēgēs ā Numā datae sunt.   *Laws were given by Numa.*

297   (*b*) Factitive Verbs and Verbs of *saying* and *thinking* become
          Copulative (**187**):

   Clōdium plēbs tribūnum   *The plebs elected Clodius tribune.*
   creāvit.

   Clōdius ā plēbe tribūnus   *Clodius was elected tribune by the*
   creātus est.   *plebs.*

298   (*c*) Transitive Verbs which have two Objects in the Accusative
          (*i.e.* the Person and the Thing, **208**), keep the Accusative of
          the Thing in the Passive form:

   Mē sententiam rogās.   *You ask me my opinion.*
   Ā tē sententiam rogor.   *I am asked my opinion by you.*

299 Intransitive Verbs are used in the Passive only in an Impersonal
        construction:

300   (*a*) The Personal Subject of an Intransitive Verb (1) becomes the
          Agent (**239**):

   Nōs currimus: Ā nōbīs curritur: *We run.*

301   or (2) is not referred to at all:

   Conclāmātum 'ad arma', concursumque ad mūrōs est. LIVY.
   They raised the shout 'To arms', and rushed to the walls.

302   (*b*) The Dative of the Indirect Object which is used with some
          Intransitive verbs (**216, 220**) is retained in the Impersonal
          Passive construction:

   Nihil facile persuādētur invītīs. QUINTILIAN.
   The unwilling are not easily persuaded of anything.

Note. Intransitive verbs which take an Abl. (**241**) are all deponent. Their
gerunds are used impersonally:

   Num argūmentīs ūtendum in rē eius modī? CICERO.
   Are we to use proofs in a matter of this kind?

Their Gerundives, which alone have a Passive sense, are used as if the verbs
were transitive (*cf.* **383**, n. 1):

   Iūstitiae fruendae causā. CICERO.
   For the sake of enjoying justice.

---

303 The Ablative of the Agent is used with Quasi-Passive Verbs (**128**):

   Mālō ā cīve spoliārī quam ab hoste vēnīre. QUINTILIAN.
   I would rather be despoiled by a citizen than be sold by a foe.

ADJECTIVES

Some Adjectives are used as Substantives to express persons or things: sapiēns, *a wise man*; bonī, *the good*; Rōmānī, *the Romans*; superī, *the gods*; omnia, *all things*; multa, *many things*; bona, *goods*.

> Bonōs bonī dīligunt. CICERO.
> *The good love the good.*

> Aiunt multum legendum esse, nōn multa. CICERO.
> *They say that much should be read, not many things.*

Neuter Adjectives are used for Abstract Substantives: vērum or vēra, *the truth*.

> Omne tulit pūnctum quī miscuit ūtile dulcī. HORACE.
> *He who has combined the useful with the pleasing has won every vote.*

Some Adjectives, when used as Substantives, can be qualified by other Adjectives: amīcus, *friend*; vīcīnus, *neighbour*; dextra, *right hand*; maiōrēs, *ancestors*.

> Vetus vīcīnus ac necessārius. CICERO.
> *An old neighbour and intimate acquaintance.*

7 Medius, *middle*, and superlatives, as summus, īmus, prīmus, ultimus, are used to express relative position in place and time; ad īmam quercum, *at the foot of the oak*:

> Mediō sedet īnsula pontō. OVID.
> *The island lies in mid-ocean.*

> Prīmā lūce summus mōns ā Labiēnō tenēbātur. CAESAR.
> *At dawn of day the mountain top was held by Labienus.*

Note. The singular forms of cēterī, *the rest* (of which the masc. nom. sing. is wanting), are similarly used with collective nouns: cētera turba, *the rest of the crowd*; ā cēterō exercitū, *by the rest of the army*.

---

08 Adjectives are often used where in English the meaning is expressed by an Adverb:

> Sōcratēs laetus venēnum hausit. SENECA.
> *Socrates drank the poison cheerfully.*

> Mātūtīnus arā. VIRGIL. | Vespertīnus pete tēctum. HORACE.
> *Plough at morn.* | *At eventide go home.*

Hannibal prīmus in proelium ībat, ultimus excēdēbat. Livy.
Hannibal used to be first to go into battle, last to withdraw.

COMPARATIVE AND SUPERLATIVE ADJECTIVES

309 Comparatives may express a certain degree, without special comparison: longior, *rather long*; senior, *elderly*. After a Comparative with quam, a second Comparative is often found where English prefers a Positive:

Aemiliī cōntiō fuit vērior quam grātior populō. Livy.
The harangue of Aemilius was more truthful than popular.

310 Superlatives often express a very high degree, and not the highest:

Ego sum miserior quam tū, quae es miserrima. Cicero.
I am more wretched than you, who are very wretched.

Note. Comparatives and Superlatives are often strengthened by adverbs and adverbial phrases: multō cārior, *much dearer*; longē eārissimus, *far dearest*; quam maximus, *the greatest possible*.

NUMERAL ADJECTIVES

311 Cardinals: Ūnus is often used only to give emphasis, *the one of all others*:

Dēmosthenēs ūnus ēminet inter omnēs ōrātōrēs. Cicero.
Demosthenes is pre-eminent among all orators.

Mīlle is generally used as an indeclinable Adjective; rarely as a Substantive taking the Genitive after it. Mīlia is used as a Substantive, followed by a Genitive:

Mīlle gregēs illī. Ovid.　　Mīlle annōrum. Plautus.
He had a thousand flocks.　　*A thousand years.*

Quattuor mīlia hominum Capitōlium occupāvēre. Livy.
Four thousand men seized the Capitol.

Note. If a smaller number is added to mīlia, the compound number becomes adjectival: tria mīlia et sescentī hominēs, *three thousand six hundred men.*

312 Ordinals are used in expressing position in a series:

Octāvus annus est ex quō Britanniam vīcistis. Tacitus.
It is the eighth year since you conquered Britain.

Note 1. In compound numbers, ūnus is used for prīmus: ūnō et octōgēnsimō annō, *in the eighty-first year.*

Note 2. Ūnus, alter, tertius, &c., are used for *a first, a second, a third,* where the order is of no importance, as distinguished from the regular ordinals, prīmus, secundus, tertius, which can only mean *the first, the second,* &c.

Distributives express *how many each* or *at a time*:

> Mīlitibus quīnī et vīcēnī dēnāriī datī sunt. LIVY.
> *Twenty-five denarii were given to each soldier.*

Note 1. With a Substantive which is plural in form but singular in meaning Distributives are used in place of Cardinals, as: bīna castra, *two camps*; but the plural of ūnus is used with such Substantives instead of singulī:

> Ūna castra iam facta ex bīnīs vidēbantur. CAESAR.
> *One camp now seemed to have been formed from two.*

Note 2. Bīnī is also used for a pair:
> Pamphilus bīnōs habēbat scyphōs sigillātōs. CICERO.
> *Pamphilus had in use a pair of embossed cups.*

Note 3. Distributives are also used in expressions of multiplication: bis bīna sunt quattuor, *twice two are four.*

Quam is often omitted before Numerals when **plūs, amplius,** or **minus** precedes:

> Rōmānī paulō plūs sescentī cecidērunt. LIVY.
> *Rather more than six hundred Romans fell.*

PRONOUNS AND PRONOMINAL ADJECTIVES

5 The Personal Pronouns as the Subjects of Verbs are generally not expressed; but they are sometimes added for emphasis:

> Ego rēgēs ēiēcī, vōs tyrannōs intrōdūcitis. CICERO.
> *I expelled kings, you are bringing in tyrants.*

Note. Nōs is often used for ego, and noster for meus; but vōs is not used for tū, nor vester for tuus.

---

16 The Reflexive Pronoun, Sē, is used to refer:

    (*a*) to the subject of the Simple Sentence or Subordinate Clause in which it stands;

    (*b*) to the subject of a Principal Sentence, if the Subordinate Clause in which it stands represents something in the mind of that subject;

    (*c*) to the subject of a Verb of *saying* which introduces Oratio Obliqua (**458–467**):

(a) Fūr tēlō sē dēfendit. CICERO.
The thief defends himself with a weapon.

Īra suī impotēns est. SENECA.
Anger is not master of itself.

(b) Impetrat ā senātū ut diēs sibi prōrogārētur. CICERO.
He prevailed upon the senate to postpone the date for himself.

(c) Ariovistus respondit: nōn oportēre sēsē impedīrī. CAESAR.
Ariovistus replied that he ought not to be hindered.

Note 1. There is no Reciprocal Pronoun (= *each other*) in Latin; but **nōs, vōs, sē,** with **inter** are used reciprocally: inter sē amant, *they love each other.*

Note 2. Reflexives of the First and Second Persons are supplied by the oblique cases of ego and tū.

317 The Possessive Adjective **suus** is used like **sē**:

Sentit animus sē vī suā, nōn aliēnā movērī. CICERO.
The mind feels that it moves by its own force, not by that of another.

Note 1. Sometimes, when no ambiguity is likely, suus refers in a Simple Sentence to something other than the grammatical subject:

Suīs flammīs dēlēte Fīdēnās. LIVY.
With its own flames destroy Fidenae.

Note 2. Suus is often used as a Possessive in reference to the Indefinite **quisque** even though quisque is not the subject:

Suus cuique erat locus attribūtus. CAESAR.
To each man his own place had been assigned.

Sua quemque fraus et suus terror vexat. CICERO.
His own sin and his own alarm harass a man.

318 Eius, *his,* never refers to the Subject of the Sentence:

Chīlius tē rogat, et ego eius rogātū. CICERO.
Chilius asks you, and I at his request.

Note. The Possessive Adjectives are often omitted when the meaning is clear without them: frātrem amat, *he loves his brother.*

319 Hic and **ille** are often used in contrast:

Quōcumque adspiciō, nihil est nisi pontus et āēr,
   flūctibus hic tumidus, nūbibus ille mināx. OVID.

Whithersoever I look, there is nought but sea and sky,
   the one heaped with clouds, the other threatening with billows.

Note. Iste is sometimes contemptuous: quid sibi istī miserī volunt? *What do those wretched ones want?* Ille may imply respect: philosophus ille, *that famous philosopher.* Is often is the antecedent to quī: is cuius, *he whose*; eum cui, *him to whom.* Hic, ... ille often mean *the latter ... the former,* but not invariably.

Ipse, *self,* is of all the three Persons, with or without a Personal Pronoun: ipse ībō, *I shall go myself.*

Note. **Ipse** sometimes means *of one's own accord:* ipsī veniunt, *they come of their own accord.* Ipse, ipsa, also stand for an important person (master, mistress): Ipse dīxit, *The master himself* (i.e. *Pythagoras*) *said it.* Sometimes a superlative is formed: ipsissima verba, *the very exact words.*

Īdem, *the same,* is of all the three Persons.

Note 1. Īdem is often used in conjunction with the Relative quī to mean *the same . . . as:*

Cīmōn incidit in eandem invidiam quam pater suus. NEPOS.
Cimon fell into the same odium as his father.

Note 2. When each of two attributes of a noun is stressed, īdem precedes the second:

Avunculus meus, vir innocentissimus īdemque doctissimus. CICERO.
My uncle, a man most guiltless and also most learned.

2 Of the Indefinite Pronouns and Adjectives, the most definite is **quīdam,** the least so **quis.**

Quīdam means *a certain one* (often known, but not named):

Accurrit quīdam, nōtus mihi nōmine tantum. HORACE.
A certain man runs up, known to me only by name.

Diē quōdam nātus sum; aliquō moriar.
I was born on a certain day; I shall die some day or other.

Quis, *any,* cannot begin a sentence, and generally follows sī, nisi, num, nē:

Sī mala condiderit in quem quis carmina iūs est. HORACE.
If anyone has composed malicious verses on another, there is a remedy at law.

Sī quid tē volam, ubi eris? PLAUTUS.
If I want anything of you, where will you be?

Aliquis means *some one:* dīcat aliquis, *suppose some one to say;* sī vīs esse aliquis, *if you wish to be somebody.*

Nescio quis, *some one or other* (*I know not who*), used as if one word, forms an Indefinite Pronoun:

Nescio quid mihi animus praesāgit malī. TERENCE.
My mind forbodes I know not what evil.

6

323 Quisquam (Substantive), **Ūllus** (Adjective), *any at all*, are generally used after a negative word, or a question expecting a negative answer:

> Nec vērō necesse est ā mē quemquam nōminārī. CICERO.
> *Nor indeed is it necessary for anyone to be named by me.*

> Nōn ūllus arātrō dignus honōs. VIRGIL.
> *Not any due honour (is given) to the plough.*

Note. Quisquam and ūllus are used after sī when negation is implied, or with comparatives:

> Aut nēmō aut, sī quisquam, Catō sapiēns fuit. CICERO.
> *Either no man was wise, or, if any, Cato was.*

---

324 Quīvīs, quīlibet, *any you like*:

> Quīvīs homō potest quemvīs dē quōlibet rūmōrem prōferre.
> *Any man can put forth any report of anybody.* CICERO.

> Nōn cuivīs hominī contingit adīre Corinthum. HORACE.
> *It does not happen to every man to go to Corinth.*

325 Quisque, *each* (severally), is often used with sē, suus (**317,** n. 2):

> Sibi quisque habeant quod suum est. PLAUTUS.
> *Let them have each for himself what is his own.*

With Superlatives it expresses *every, all*:

> Epicūrēōs doctissimus quisque contemnit. CICERO.
> *All the most learned men despise the Epicureans.*

It also distributes Ordinal numbers:

> Quīntō quōque annō Sicilia tōta cēnsētur. CICERO.
> *A census of all Sicily is taken every fifth year.*

3 26 Uterque, *each* (of two), can be used with the Genitive of Pronouns; but with Substantives it agrees in case:

> Uterque parēns. OVID.   Utrōque vestrum dēlēctor. CICERO.
> *Both father and mother.*   *I am delighted with each of you.*

Note. Uterque treats of two individuals separately: **ambō** treats of them together.

---

327 Uter, *which?* (of two), is Interrogative:

> Uter utrī īnsidiās fēcit? CICERO.
> *Which of the two laid an ambush for the other?*

Note. Utrī, plural, is used for *which of two parties?*, utrīque for *both parties* So alterī ... alterī, *one party, the other party.*

Alter, *the one, the other* (of two), *the second,* is the Demonstrative of iter: alter ego, *a second self.*

> Quicquid negat alter, et alter; adfirmant pariter. HORACE.
> *Whatever the one denies, so does the other; they affirm alike.*

Alius, *another* (of any number), *different*:

> Fortūna nunc mihi, nunc aliī benigna. HORACE.
> *Fortune, kind now to me, now to another.*

Alius, alius, *one . . . another*; **aliī, aliī** (plural), *some . . . others*:

> Aliud est maledīcere, aliud accūsāre. CICERO.
> *It is one thing to speak evil, another to accuse.*
> Aliī Dēmosthenem laudant, aliī Cicerōnem.
> *Some praise Demosthenes, others Cicero.*

Note 1. Alius repeated in different cases in the same sentence, or with one of its derived adverbs, has an idiomatic use:

> Aliī alia sentiunt.
> *Some think one thing, some another.*
> Illī aliās aliud īsdem dē rēbus iūdicant. CICERO.
> *They judge differently, at different times, about the same things.*

Note 2. Alius expresses comparison and difference: nīl aliud quam, *nothing else than*; alius Lȳsippō, HORACE, *other than Lysippus.*

The Relative **quī, quae, quod,** connects a Noun or Pronoun (called the Antecedent) with a descriptive or qualifying clause (called Relative; *cf.* **450–7**). It agrees in number and gender with the Antecedent, but its case is determined by the construction of the clause in which it stands:

> Animum rege quī, nisi pāret, imperat. HORACE.
> *Rule the temper, which, unless it obeys, commands.*
> Dēmus igitur imperium Caesarī, sine quō rēs mīlitāris administrārī nōn potest. CICERO.
> *Let us, then, give the command to Caesar, without which military affairs cannot be conducted.*
> Pācis vērō quae potest esse cum eō ratiō, in quō est nūlla fidēs? CICERO.
> *What kind of peace can there be with him, in whom there is no loyalty?*

a The Antecedent is sometimes omitted:

> Sunt quibus in satirā videor nimis ācer. HORACE.
> *There are some to whom I seem too keen in satire.*

331b The logical Antecedent is sometimes incorporated in the Relativ
clause:

> Sīc tibi dent nymphae quae levet unda sitim. OVID.
> *So may the nymphs give thee water to assuage thirst.*

Note. Hence arise idiomatic expressions like: quā es prūdentiā, *such is you*
prudence.

331c The Antecedent is sometimes repeated in the Relative clause:

> Erant itinera duo, quibus itineribus exīre possent. CAESAR.
> *There were two roads by which they might go forth.*

332 *Note 1.* If the Relative is the Subject of a Copulative Verb, it often agrees in
Gender and Number with the Complement:

> Thēbae, quod Boeōtiae caput est. LIVY.
> *Thebes, which is the capital of Boeotia.*

Note 2. When an Adjective which logically qualifies the Antecedent is emphatic,
as ūnus, sōlus, or is a Superlative, it is often attracted to the Clause of the
Relative, agreeing with it in Case:

> Sī veniat Caesar cum cōpiīs quās habet firmissimās. CICERO.
> *Should Caesar come with the very strong forces that he has.*

Note 3. If the Antecedent consists of two or more Nouns, or is a Collective
Noun, the rules for the Agreement of the Relative in number and gender are the
same as for the Agreement of Adjectives with the Composite Subject (**198, 199**).

Note 4. The Antecedent is sometimes a Neut. Pronoun (expressed or understood) standing in apposition to a sentence:

> Diem cōnsūmī volēbat, id quod est factum. CICERO.
> *He was wishing the day to be wasted, which came to pass.*

Note 5. The Relative clause sometimes comes first:

> Quam quisque nōrit artem, in hāc sē exerceat. CICERO.
> *Let everyone practise the art which he knows.*

CORRELATION

333 Pronouns and Pronominal Adverbs are said to be Correlatives when
they correspond to one another as Antecedent and Relative (**102**).

334 The Pronoun Antecedent to **quī** is usually the Demonstrative **is**;
sometimes hic, ille, īdem:

> Is minimō eget quī minimum cupit. PUBLILIUS SYRUS.
> *He wants least who desires least.*

Tālis ... quālis, *of such a kind ... as*; tantus ... quantus, *as much (great) ... as*; tot ... quot, *as many ... as*:

> Tālis est quālem tū eum esse scrīpsistī. CICERO.
> *He is such as you wrote word that he was.*

Note. A pair of comparatives is correlated by eō ... quō, or tantō ... quantō:
Tantō brevius omne quantō fēlīcius tempus. PLINY.
The happier any occasion is, so much the shorter is it.

Tam ... quam, *so (as) ... as*; ut ... ita, *as ... so*:

> Tam ego ante fuī līber quam gnātus tuus. PLAUTUS.
> *I was formerly as free as your son.*
>
> Ut optāstī, ita est (CICERO), *As you wished, so it is.*

THE VERB

TENSES OF THE INDICATIVE (*cf.* 105a)

336 The **Present** expresses:

(1) What happens at the present moment: iaciō, *I throw.*

(2) What is going on at the present time and may continue in the future: scrībō, *I am writing.*

Note. The Pres. Tense is also used to express general truths which are not confined to the past and are assumed as valid for the future: quod semper movētur aeternum est, CICERO, *that which is always in motion is eternal.*

---

337 A Present (called Historic) is used for a Past by orators, historians, and poets, to give variety or vividness:

> Decemvirī prōdeunt in cōntiōnem abdicantque sē magistrātū. LIVY.
> *The decemvirs went forth to the assembled people and resigned office.*

338 For the use of Dum with the Historic Pres., see 430.
For the idiomatic use of iam diū, &c., with the Pres., see 105a, n. 1.

339 The **Perfect** expresses:

(1) What, from the point of view of the present moment, has been completed: scrīpsī, *I have written.* This tense is called the Present Perfect, and is Primary (105a).

Note. The Present Perfect is used in poetry to express past existence which has ceased: Fuimus Trōes; fuit Īlium (VIRGIL), *We have been Trojans* (*i.e.* are no longer); *Troy has been* (exists no longer).

(2) What is simply a past action: scrīpsī, *I wrote.* This Tense is called the Historic Perfect (*cf.* **105a**).

340 The **Imperfect** expresses what was continued or repeated in past time, as opposed to the completed or momentary past:

> Aequī sē in oppida recēpērunt mūrīsque sē tenēbant. LIVY.
> *The Aequi retreated into their towns and continued to remain within their walls.*

Note. The Imperfect is sometimes used to express something attempted or intended:

> Hostēs nostrōs prōgredī prohibēbant. CAESAR.
> *The enemy tried to prevent our men from advancing.*

341 The **Pluperfect** expresses that which, from the point of view of the past, was completed:

> Massiliēnsēs portās Caesarī clauserant. CAESAR.
> *The Massilians had closed their gates against Caesar.*

Note. The Romans, in writing letters, often speak of the time of writing in a Past Tense, because it would be past when a letter was received:

> Rēs, cum haec scrībēbam, erat in extrēmum adducta discrīmen. CICERO.
> *At the time I write, the affair has been brought to a crisis.*

Tenses so used are called **Epistolary**. The Imperf. and Perf. are used for the Pres.; the Pluperf. for the Perf.; the Fut. Participle with eram for the Future.

342 The **Future Simple** expresses what will happen in the future:

> Ut volēs mē esse, ita erō. PLAUTUS.
> *As you wish me to be, so I shall be.*

Note. Latin often uses a Fut. where English uses a Pres. with future meaning.

343 The **Future Perfect** expresses that which will be complete in the future; if two future actions are spoken of, one of which will take place before the other, the prior one is in the Future Perfect:

> Ut sēmentem fēceris, ita metēs. CICERO.
> *As you sow, so will you reap.*

Note. Latin often uses a Fut. Perf. where English idiom uses a Present. *Cf.* fēceris in the example above.

MOODS (*cf.* **106**)

The **Indicative** is the Mood which makes a statement or enquiry about a fact, or something which will be a fact in the future.

Note. For a use of the Indic., instead of the Subjunctive, see **441**.

6 The **Imperative** is the Mood of positive command or direct request and entreaty:

I, sequere Italiam. VIRGIL.
Go, seek Italy.

Pergite, adulēscentēs. CICERO.
Proceed, youths.

7 *Note 1.* For commands expressed by the Subjunctive, see 353.

Note 2. The forms in -tō, -tōte are specially used in laws:

Rēgiō imperiō duo suntō, iīque cōnsulēs appellantor. CICERO.
Let there be two with royal power, and let them be called consuls.

48 *Note 3.* **Fac** and **cūrā**, *see to it,* with a dependent Subjunctive (sometimes connected by ut) are used to express commands. **Mementō**, *remember,* is used similarly with either the Subjunctive or Infinitive:

Magnum fac animum habeās. CICERO.
Mind you have a lofty spirit.

Note 4. For a courteous command the Future Indicative is often used: faciēs ut sciam, CICERO, *you will please let me know.*

349 Prohibitions (negative Commands) in the second person are expressed in prose by **nōlī, nōlīte** with the Infinitive:

Nōlīte id velle quod fierī nōn potest. CICERO.
Do not wish what cannot be.

350 *Note 1.* Prohibitions are also expressed by **nē** and the Subjunctive, Perfect for the 2nd pers., and Pres. for the 3rd pers.:

Nē fēcerīs quod dubitās. PLINY.
Do not do anything about which you are doubtful.

Note 2. **Fac nē** and **cavē nē** are also used: cavē nē eās, *beware of going, don't go.*

Note 3. In poetry **nē** with the Imperative is used for Prohibitions:

Equō nē crēdite, Teucrī. VIRGIL.
Do not trust the horse, Trojans.

Note 4. In poetry fuge, mitte, parce, are also used with the Infinitive to express Prohibition: Rosam mitte sectārī, *do not seek out the rose.*

351 The **Subjunctive Mood** expresses a verbal activity as willed, desired, conditional, or prospective.

Note. The Latin Subjunctive represents two moods: an old Subjunctive expressing will (and futurity) and an old Optative expressing desire (and futurity).

The Subjunctive is used (A) in Simple or Principal Sentences, and (B) in Subordinate Clauses.

352 A. In **Independent sentences** the Subjunctive expresses will, desire, or conditioned futurity:

The Subjunctive of Will (Volitive) expresses:

353   (1) Commands (Jussive use; Pres. or Perf. tenses):

Sit sermō lēnis. CICERO.   Vīlicus nē sit ambulātor. CATO.
Let speech be calm.   *Let not a steward be a loiterer.*
Nē trānsierīs Hibērum. LIVY.
Do not cross the Ebro.

354   (2) Exhortation (Hortative use; generally Pres. tense):

Amēmus patriam, pāreāmus senātuī. CICERO.
Let us love our country, let us obey the senate.

355   (3) Concessions or Suppositions (Concessive use; Pres. or Perf. tense, rarely Imperf.):

Haec sint falsa sānē. CICERO.   Fuerit malus cīvis. CICERO.
Granting this to be quite untrue.   *Suppose he was a bad citizen.*

356   (4) What ought to be done as a matter of propriety or duty (Pres. and Imperf. tenses; sometimes Pluperf.):

Quid faciam? inveniās argentum. TERENCE.
What am I to do? You are to find the money.
At tū dictīs, Albāne, manērēs. VIRGIL.
But you should have kept your word, man of Alba.

When used in a question, this Subjunctive is called **Deliberative**.

Note. Nē is the negative used with types (1), (2), and (3); nōn is used with (4).

357 The Subjunctive of Desire (Optative use; negative, nē) expresses a wish or prayer. The Present and Perfect express a wish for the future; the Imperfect a wish that something were so now; the Pluperfect a wish that something had been so in the past. Such wishes are often introduced by utinam:

Sīs fēlīx. HORACE.   Utinam potuissem.
May you be happy.   *Would that I had been able.*
Adsīs placidusque iuvēs. VIRGIL.
Mayst thou be with us and help us with thy favour.

The Subjunctive of Conditioned Futurity (negative, nōn) expresses one verbal activity as being dependent on the fulfilment of another. (For the use of tenses, see **439, 440**.)

(Sī foret in terrīs) rīdēret Dēmocritus. HORACE.
(If he were upon earth) Democritus would be laughing.

Note. The condition necessary to fulfilment is often not expressed:

Crēderēs victōs. LIVY.
You would think (have thought) them conquered (if you had seen them).

Migrantēs cernās. VIRGIL.
One would see them leaving (if one were there).

Fortūnam facilius reperiās quam retineās. CICERO.
One would find Fortune more easily than one would keep it (if one were to try).

Especially common are: dīcat fortasse aliquis; velim; nōlim.

---

60   B. In **Subordinate Clauses** the Subjunctive is used:

(*a*) In expressions of Will and Desire or Conditioned Futurity which are dependent on another sentence:

Imperō ut veniās.	Cupiō ut impetret.
I command you to come.	*I wish him to gain it.*

Nōn dubium est quīn Dēmocritus rīdēret, sī hīc esset.
There is no doubt that Democritus would be laughing if he were here.

361   (*b*) To represent something, not as a fact, but as anticipated (**Prospective** use):

Exspectāre dum hostium cōpiae augeantur summae dēmentiae est. CAESAR.
To wait until the enemy's forces are increased is the height of madness.

362   (*c*) With meaning so weakened that it represents actual facts:

Ita est mulcātus ut vītam āmīserit. CICERO.
He was so maltreated that he lost his life.

Note 1. In Ōrātiō Oblīqua (**458–67**) the verbs of Subordinate Clauses are Subjunctives even though they were Indicatives in Direct Speech. For exceptions, see **461**, nn. 2–3.

363 *Note 2.* The Subjunctive cannot *of itself* express such ideas as may (= may possibly), may (= am permitted), can (= am able). 'He may (possibly) come' is expressed in Latin by fortasse veniet, forsitan veniat, or fierī potest ut veniat 'He may (is permitted to) come', by eī venīre licet; 'He can (is able to) come' by venīre potest.

6*

THE VERB INFINITE

364 The parts of the Verb Infinite have some of the uses of Verbs and some of the uses of Nouns.

THE INFINITIVE

365 The **Infinitive** as a Verb has Voices (Active and Passive) and Tenses (Present, Past, and Future), it governs cases, and is qualified by Adverbs; as a Noun it is neuter and indeclinable, used only as Nominative or Accusative.

Note 1. The Pres. Infin. indicates a time contemporaneous with that of the verb on which it depends; the Perf. Infin. refers to a prior time, the Fut. Infin. to a subsequent time. *Cf.* **412.**·

Note 2. The Accus. case is used as the Subject of an Infin. See **207, 414.**

Note 3. When an Infin. depends on possum, dēbeō, oportet, the idea of past time is expressed by the past tenses of these verbs but not, as in English, by the Infinitive: poteram vidēre, *I could have seen.*

Note 4. For the Fut. Infin. of verbs which have no Participial-stem, see **412,** n. 1.

366 The **Infinitive** as a Nominative may be the Subject of Impersonal Verbs, or of verbs used impersonally (*cf.* **289–290**):

> Iuvat īre et Dōrica castra vidēre.   VIRGIL.
> *It is pleasant to go and view the Doric camp.*
>
> Dulce et decōrum est prō patriā morī.   HORACE.
> *To die for one's country is sweet and seemly.*

Note. Occasionally the Infinitive is a Complement (**186**):
Homō cui vīvere est cōgitāre.   CICERO.
Man to whom to live is to think.

367 The **Infinitive** is often one of the two Accusatives depending on Factitive verbs (**206**):

> Errāre, nescīre, dēcipī et malum et turpe dūcimus.   CICERO.
> *To err, to be ignorant, to be deceived, we deem both unfortunate and disgraceful.*

368 *Note.* Sometimes, though rarely, an Infinitive is a simple Object:

> Hoc rīdēre meum nūllā tibi vēndō Īliade.   PERSIUS.
> *This laughter of mine I won't sell you for an Iliad.*

The **Prolative Infinitive** (so called, *cf.* **190**) is used as the Direct Object of:

Verbs of *possibility*, *duty*, *habit*: possum, queō, nequeō; dēbeō; soleō, cōnsuēvī.

Verbs of *wishing*, *purposing*, *daring*: vōlō, nōlō, mālō, cupiō, optō; statuō, cōnstituō; audeō.

Verbs of *beginning*, *ceasing*, *endeavouring*, *continuing*, *hastening*, *hesitating*: incipiō, coepī; dēsinō, dēsistō; cōnor; pergō, persevērō; festīnō, properō, mātūrō; moror, dubitō.

Verbs of *knowing how*, *learning*, *teaching*: sciō; discō, doceō.

Ego plūs quam fēcī facere nōn possum. CICERO.
I cannot do more than I have done.

Solent diū cōgitāre quī magna volunt gerere. CICERO.
They are wont to reflect long who wish to do great things.

Praecēdere coepit. HORACE.   Sapere audē. HORACE.
He began to walk on.   *Dare to be wise.*

Note. The **Infinitive** of a Copulative Verb (**187**) used Prolatively is followed by a Complement in the Nominative:

Sōcratēs parēns philosophiae iūre dīcī potest. CICERO.
Socrates may rightly be called the parent of philosophy.

---

70 The **Prolative Infinitive** is also used with the Passives of Verbs of *saying* and *thinking*:

Barbara nārrātur vēnisse venēfica tēcum. OVID.
A barbarian sorceress is said to have come with you.

Aristīdēs ūnus omnium iūstissimus fuisse trāditur. CICERO.
Aristides is recorded to have been the one man of all most just.

Note. This personal construction, sometimes called the Nominative with Infinitive, is used with most Passive Verbs of *saying* and *thinking*. A few, however, such as nārror, nūntior, trādor, are used Impersonally—always when in the Perfect, and often when in the Present and Imperfect:

Galbam et Āfricānum doctōs fuisse trāditum est. CICERO.
It has been handed down that Galba and Africanus were learned.

---

371 In this construction esse is often omitted:

> Pōns in Hibērō prope effectus nūntiābātur. CAESAR.
> *The bridge over the Ebro was announced to be nearly finished.*
>
> Titus Manlius ita locūtus fertur. LIVY.
> *Titus Manlius is reported to have thus spoken.*

372 The **Historic** Infinitive is the Present Infinitive used in vivid description for an Imperfect Indicative:

> Multī sequī, fugere, occīdī, capī. SALLUST.
> *Many were following, fleeing, being slain, being captured.*

Note. The action is of more importance here than the indication of time.

---

373 In poetry and late prose an Infinitive often follows an Adjective:

> Audāx omnia perpetī. HORACE.   Īnsuētus vincī. LIVY.
> *Bold to endure all things.*   *Unused to be conquered.*
>
> Fīgere doctus erat sed tendere doctior arcūs. OVID.
> *He was skilled in piercing (with a dart), but more skilled in bending the bow.*

Note. An Infin. is occasionally used (in poetry) after a verb of motion to express purpose: veniō vīsere, *I come to look around.*

GERUND AND GERUNDIVE

374 The Gerund is a Verbal Noun, active in meaning; it has no plural. The Gerundive is a Verbal Adjective, passive in meaning.

375 The **Accusative** of the Gerund follows some Prepositions, usually ad, sometimes ob, inter:

> Ad bene vīvendum breve tempus satis est longum. CICERO.
> *For living well a short time is long enough.*
>
> Mōrēs puerōrum sē inter lūdendum dētegunt. QUINTILIAN.
> *The characters of boys show themselves in their play.*

376 The **Genitive** of the Gerund depends on some Abstract Substantives, and on Adjectives which take a Genitive:

> Ars scrībendī discitur.   Cupidus tē audiendī sum. CICERO.
> *The art of writing is learnt.*   *I am desirous of hearing you.*

The **Dative** of the Gerund is used with a few Verbs, Adjectives, and Substantives, implying *help, use, fitness*:

Pār est disserendō. CICERO.	Operam legendō dat.
He is equal to arguing.	*He gives attention to reading.*

Note. Observe the phrase: solvendō nōn est, *he is insolvent.*

The **Ablative** of the Gerund expresses Instrument or Cause; or it follows one of the Prepositions in, ab, dē, ex:

Fugiendō vincimus.	Dē pugnandō dēlīberant.
We conquer by fleeing.	*They deliberate about fighting.*

If a verb is transitive its **Gerundive** is used in preference to its Gerund with an accusative:

Ad pācem petendam vēnērunt. LIVY.
They came to seek peace.

Brūtus in līberandā patriā est interfectus. CICERO.
Brutus was slain in freeing his country.

Note 1. The Gerundive is passive: 'ad pācem petendam' properly means 'for peace which is to be sought'; but it is equivalent in meaning to the active 'for seeking peace'.

Note 2. The Gerundive construction is used especially to avoid a Direct Object with the Dat. of the Gerund, or with the Accus. or Abl. of the Gerund and a preposition.

Note 3. The Gerund construction, however, is preferred (1) if its object is a neuter pronoun or adjective; (2) if the Gerundive construction involves Gen. plurals.

Note 4. The genitives meī, tuī, suī, nostrī, vestrī are used in the Gerundive construction without reference to Number or Gender, since they are regarded as neuter singulars: nostrī servandī causā, *for the sake of saving us.*

Note 5. The Dative of the Gerundive is used to show purpose (226):

Comitia rēgī creandō. LIVY.
An assembly for electing a king.

Trēsvirī agrīs dīvidendīs. FLORUS.
Three commissioners for dividing lands.

381 The Gerundive is also used to express that something *must* or *ought to be done*, the Dative of the Agent being expressed or understood (222):

382 (a) If a Verb is Intransitive the nominative neuter of its Gerundive is used with a tense of esse in an impersonal passive construction (*cf.* 299):

> Eundum est. | Mihi eundum est.
> *One must go.* | *I must go.*
>
> Suō cuique iūdiciō est ūtendum. CICERO.
> *Each must use his own judgment.*

Note. If an Intransitive Verb has an Indirect Object in the Dative, the Agent is in the Ablative with the preposition ā or ab: patriae est ā tē cōnsulendum, *you must take thought for your country.*

383 (b) If a Verb is Transitive its Gerundive is used as a predicative adjective:

> Caesarī omnia ūnō tempore erant agenda. CAESAR.
> *All things had to be done by Caesar at one time.*
>
> Prīncipiō sēdēs apibus statiōque petenda. VIRGIL.
> *First of all a home and habitation must be sought for the bees.*

Note 1. Ūtor, fruor, fungor, potior are sometimes regarded as Transitive Verbs (*cf.* 241, n. 2) and their Gerundives are then used as predicative adjectives (*cf.* 302, n.).

384 *Note 2.* After some Verbs, as dō, trādō, cūrō, the Gerundive is used in agreement with the Object to indicate that something is caused to be done:

> Caesar pontem faciendum cūrat. CAESAR.
> *Caesar causes a bridge to be made.*

SUPINES

385 The Supines in -um and -ū are the Accusative and Dative (or Ablative) cases of a Verbal Noun.

386 The Supine in **-um** is used after Verbs of motion, expressing purpose:

> Lūsum it Maecēnās, dormītum ego. HORACE.
> *Maecenas goes to play, I to sleep.*

387 With the Infinitive **īrī**, used impersonally, it forms a Future Passive Infinitive:

> Aiunt urbem captum īrī.
> *They say that the city will be taken.*

Note. Literally, *they say there is a going to take the city.*

The **Supine** in **-ū** is used with some Adjectives, such as facilis, dulcis, turpis, and the Substantives fās, nefās:

> Hoc fās est dictū. Lībertās, dulce audītū nōmen. LIVY.
> *It is lawful to say this.* *Freedom, a name sweet to hear.*

> Nec vīsū facilis, nec dictū adfābilis ūllī. VIRGIL.
> *One not easy for any to gaze on, or to address.*

Note. The Supine in -ū does not take an Accusative.

PARTICIPLES

The Present Participle represents a time contemporaneous with that of the verb with which it is constructed; the Perfect Participle refers to a prior time, the Future Participle to a subsequent time.

Note 1. The Present and Perfect Participles of some Verbs are used as Adjectives:

> Homō frūgī ac dīligēns. CICERO. | Odōrāta cedrus. VIRGIL.
> *A thrifty and industrious man.* | *The fragrant cedar.*

Note 2. Most Participles which can be used as Adjectives have Comparison: pietāte praestantior, *more excellent in piety*; nocentissima victōria, *a very hurtful victory.*

A Participle, agreeing with a Noun in any Case, often expresses within one sentence what might be expressed by a dependent or a co-ordinate clause:

> Aquilifer fortissimē pugnāns occīditur. CAESAR.
> *The eagle-bearer falls while fighting most bravely.*

> Elephantēs, amnem trānsitūrī, minimōs praemittunt. PLINY.
> *Elephants, intending to cross a river, send forward the smallest ones.*

> Tīmotheus ā patre acceptam glōriam multīs auxit virtūtibus. NEPOS.
> *Timotheus increased by many virtues the glory which he had received from his father.*

> Sacrās iaculātus arcēs terruit urbem. HORACE.
> *He has smitten the sacred towers and terrified the city.*

> Caesar mīlitēs hortātus castra mōvit. CAESAR.
> *Caesar encouraged the soldiers, and moved his camp.*

392 *Note 1.* Most Latin verbs lack a Perfect Participle which is active in meaning. Consequently where English uses a Perfect Active Part., Latin uses either the Ablative Absolute construction (237) or a Subordinate Temporal Clause (427-36):

Hostēs $\begin{cases} \text{armīs abiectīs} \\ \text{cum arma abiēcissent} \end{cases}$ terga vertērunt.
The enemy, having thrown away their arms, fled.

A Subordinate Clause is the only possible construction if the verb is intransitive.

Deponent Verbs have a Perfect Participle with Active meaning:

Omnia expertī, Gallī cōnsilium cēpērunt ex oppidō profugere. CAESAR.
The Gauls, having tried every expedient, decided to flee from the town.

393 *Note 2.* Sometimes a Substantive and a Perfect Participle in agreement with it must be rendered in English by two Substantives, connected by *of*: ante urbem conditam, *before the foundation of the city*.

Terra mūtāta nōn mūtat mōrēs. LIVY.
Change of country does not change character.

CASE CONSTRUCTIONS WITH THE VERB INFINITE

394 The Infinitive, the Gerund, the Supine in -um and the Participles take the same Cases as the Finite Verbs to which they belong.

Ingenuās didicisse fidēliter artēs ēmollit mōrēs. OVID.
To have truly learned the liberal arts refines the character.

Cupiō satisfacere reīpūblicae. CICERO.
I desire to do my duty to the republic.

Rōmae prīvātīs iūs nōn erat vocandī senātum. LIVY.
At Rome private persons had not the right of summoning the senate.

Ast ego nōn Graiīs servītum mātribus ībō. VIRGIL.
But I shall not go to be a slave to Greek matrons.

Castrīs hostium potītus. CAESAR.
Having taken the enemy's camp.

ADVERBS

395 **Adverbs** show how, when, or where the action of the Verb takes place; they also qualify Adjectives or other Adverbs: rēctē facere, *to do rightly*; hūc nunc venīre, *to come hither now*; facile prīmus, *easily first*.

Many words are both Adverbs and Prepositions, as ante, *before*, post, *after*:

as Adverbs: multō ante, *long before*; paulō post, *shortly after.*
as Prepositions: ante oculōs, *before one's eyes*; post tergum, *behind one's back.*

The **Negative Adverbs** are **nōn, haud, nē.**

Nōn, *not,* simply denies:

> Nivēs in altō marī nōn cadunt.   PLINY.
> *No snow falls on the high seas.*

Haud, *not,* negatives other Adverbs, Adjectives, and a few Verbs of *knowing* and *thinking*:

> haud aliter, haud secus, *not otherwise*; rēs haud dubia, *no doubtful matter*; haud scio an vērum sit, *I am inclined to think it is true.*

Nē negatives the Imperative and (generally) Subjunctives of Will and Desire (*cf.* **353–7**):

> Tū nē cēde malīs, *Do not yield to misfortunes*; Nē trānsierīs Hibērum, *Do not cross the Ebro*; Nē vīvam, sī scio, *May I not live, if I know.*

▶7 Two Negatives make an Affirmative, as in English:

> Nōn sum nescius, *I am not unaware,* that is, *I am aware.*   Nōn nēmō means *somebody*; nēmō nōn, *everybody*; nōn nihil, *something*; nihil nōn, *everything.*
>
> > In ipsā cūriā nōn nēmō hostis est.   CICERO.
> > *In the very senate-house there is some enemy.*
> >
> > Nēmō Arpīnās nōn Planciō studuit.   CICERO.
> > *Every citizen of Arpinum was zealous for Plancius.*

Note 1.   **Neque, nec,** *nor* (Conjunction) is used for et nōn:

> Rapimur in errōrem, neque vēra cernimus.   CICERO.
> *We are hurried into error, and do not perceive truth.*

Observe also:

and no one,	nec quisquam, nec ūllus;
and nothing,	nec quidquam (quicquam);
and never, nowhere,	nec umquam, nec ūsquam.

Note 2.   **Nēve** or **neu,** *nor,* is used for et nē:

> Aenēās adveniat, vultūs nēve exhorrēscat amīcōs.   VIRGIL.
> *Let Aeneas approach and let him not shrink from friendly faces.*

398 *Note 3.* Nē is used with **quidem** to express *not even*, and the word or words on which emphasis is laid must come between them:

> Nē ad Catōnem quidem prōvocābō. CICERO.
> *Not to Cato even shall I appeal.*

'*Not only not* . . ., *but not even*' is nōn modo nōn . . ., sed nē . . . quidem:

> Nōn modo tibi nōn īrāscor, sed nē reprehendō quidem factum tuum. CICERO.
> *I am not only not angry with you, but I do not even blame your act.*

If the predicate of both clauses is the same, it is often expressed only in the second clause with nē . . . quidem, and the negative in the first clause is omitted— *i.e.* nōn modo is used rather than nōn modo nōn.

> Adsentātiō nōn modo amīcō, sed nē līberō quidem digna est. CICERO.
> *Flattering is unworthy, not only of a friend, but even of a free man.*

CONJUNCTIONS

399 Conjunctions connect words, sentences, and clauses.

400 (1) **Co-ordinative** Conjunctions (**177**) connect two or more Nouns in the same case:

> Mīrātur portās strepitumque et strāta viārum. VIRGIL.
> *He marvels at the gates and the noise and the pavements.*

> Sine imperiō nec domus ūlla nec cīvitās stāre potest. CICERO.
> *Without government neither any house nor any State can be stable.*

Or they connect two or more Simple Sentences (**402**).

Note 1. **Aut** . . . **aut** are used when the alternatives exclude one another; **vel** . . . **vel** where the distinction is of little importance:

> Aut Caesar aut nūllus. | Vel magna, vel potius maxima. CICERO
> *Either Caesar or nobody.* | *Great, or rather very great.*

Note 2. **Sed** distinguishes with more or less opposition, or passes to a fresh point; **autem** corrects slightly, continues, or explains:

> Nōn scholae sed vītae discimus. SENECA.
> *We learn not for the school but for life.*

> Rūmōribus mēcum pugnās, ego autem ā tē ratiōnēs requīrō. CICERO.
> *You fight me with rumours, whereas I seek reasons from you.*

Note 3. **Autem, enim, vērŏ,** never begin a sentence:

Neque enim tū is es quī quid sīs nesciās. CICERO.
For you are not the man to be ignorant of your own nature.

(2) **Subordinative** Conjunctions **(178)** join Dependent Clauses to the Principal Sentence. (See Complex Sentence.)

CO-ORDINATION

2 Two or more Sentences joined together by Co-ordinative Conjunctions are said to be **Co-ordinate Sentences,** and each is independent of the other in construction.

Gȳgēs ā nūllō vidēbātur, ipse autem omnia vidēbat. CICERO.
Gyges was seen by no one, but he himself saw all things.

Caesar properāns noctem diēī coniūnxerat neque iter intermīserat. CAESAR.
Caesar in his haste had joined night to day and had not broken his march.

03 The Relative Pronoun with a Verb in the Indicative is often equivalent to a Co-ordinate Sentence:

Rēs loquitur ipsa, quae semper valet plūrimum. CICERO.
The fact itself speaks, and this always avails most.

INTERJECTIONS

404 Interjections are apart from the construction of the sentence:

O fōrmōse puer, nimium nē crēde colōrī. VIRGIL.
O beautiful boy, trust not too much to complexion.

Ŏ fortūnātam Rōmam! CICERO.
O fortunate Rome!

Ēn ego vester Ascanius! VIRGIL.
Lo here am I your Ascanius!

Ei miserŏ mihi! | Vae victīs! LIVY.
Alas! wretched me. | *Woe to the vanquished!*

Note. The sentence in which an Interjection occurs often contains a Vocative **(202),** or Accus. (of Exclamation, **209**), or Dative (of Reference, **221**).

QUESTION AND ANSWER

405 Direct Questions are simple sentences.

Indirect Questions are Dependent Clauses and have their Verb in the Subjunctive (**420**).

(*a*) Direct Single Questions are introduced by:

> nōnne, implying the answer *yes*;
> num,   ,,   ,,   *no*;
> -ne, with no implication.

Canis nōnne similis lupō est? CICERO.
Is not a dog like a wolf?

Num negāre audēs? CICERO. | Potesne dīcere? CICERO.
Do you venture to deny? | *Can you say?*

Note 1. Questions are also introduced by Interrogative Pronouns (**98, 100, 102, 327**) and Adverbs (**167, 168, 170**).

Note 2. An sometimes introduces a Single Direct Question and expresses surprise:

> An tū mē tristem esse putās? *Do you think I am sad?*

Note 3. A single question sometimes depends only on an inflexion of the voice:
Īnfēlīx est Fabricius quod rūs suum fodit? SENECA.
Is Fabricius unhappy because he digs his land?

(*b*) Direct Alternative Questions are introduced by:

> utrum ⎫
> -ne   ⎬ ... an, anne (*or*), an nōn (*or not*).
> ‾‾‾‾ ⎭

Haec utrum abundantis an egentis sīgna sunt? CICERO.
Are these the tokens of one who abounds or lacks?

Rōmamne veniō, an hīc maneō, an Arpīnum fugiō? CICERO.
Do I come to Rome, or stay here, or flee to Arpinum?

Isne est quem quaerō an nōn? TERENCE.
Is he the man wl.om I am seeking or not?

406   (*c*) Indirect Single Questions are introduced in the same way as Direct Single Questions:

> Fac mē certiōrem quandō adfutūrus sīs. CICERO.
> *Let me know when you will be here.*

Note 1. Num and -ne are used without distinction of meaning; nōnne is used only after the verb quaerō.

Note 2. After verbs of *expectation* and *endeavour* (exspectō, cōnor) sī (*in case that, in the hope that*) is used:

> Cōnantur sī perrumpere possint. CICERO.
> *They try in the hope that they can break through.*

(d) Indirect Alternative Questions are introduced like Direct Alternative Questions, except that anne is rare, and **necne** is used instead of an nōn:

Sitque memor nostrī necne, referte mihi.   OVID.
Tell me whether she is mindful of me or not.

Deliberative Questions, whether Direct or Indirect, are expressed by the Subjunctive (356):

Quid faciam? roger anne rogem?   OVID.
What am I to do?   Am I to be asked or ask?

Note. Context is the sole guide in sentences like 'rogās quid faciam', *You ask what I am doing,* or *You ask what I am to do.*

---

8 Affirmative Answer is expressed:

(a) By repeating the emphatic word of the question, sometimes with vērō, sānē, inquam.

Estne? ... Est. LIVY.	Dāsne? ... Dō sānē. CICERO.
Is it? ... It is.	*Do you grant? I grant indeed.*

(b) By ita, ita est, etiam, sānē, sānē quidem ...:

Vīsne potiōra tantum interrogem? ... Sānē.   CICERO.
Would you have me ask only the principal matters? ... Certainly.

09 Negative Answer is expressed:

(a) By repeating the emphatic Verb with nōn.

Estne frāter intus? ... Nōn est.   TERENCE.
Is my brother within? ... No.

(b) By nōn, nōn ita, minimē, minimē vērō:

Vēnitne? .   .   .   . Nōn.   PLAUTUS.
Did he come? .   .   . *No.*

Nōn pudet vānitātis? .   .   . .   . Minimē.
Are you not ashamed of your folly? .   . *Not at all.*

Note. **Immō,** *nay rather, yes even,* is used in answers to correct or modify, either by contradicting or by strengthening:

Ubi fuit Sulla, num Rōmae?   .   . Immō longē āfuit.   CICERO.
Where was Sulla? at Rome? .   .   . *Nay, he was far away from it.*

Tenāxne est? .   .   . Immō pertināx.   PLAUTUS.
Is he tenacious? .   . *Yes, even pertinacious.*

THE COMPLEX SENTENCE

410 A **Complex Sentence** consists of a Principal Sentence with one or more Subordinate Clauses.

Subordinate Clauses are divided into:

I. Substantival.   **II. Adverbial.**   **III. Adjectival.**

I. A Substantival Clause stands, like a Substantive, in some case-relation to a Verb.

II. An Adverbial Clause qualifies the Principal Sentence like an Adverb, answering the questions *how? why? when?* Adverbial Clauses are introduced by Subordinative Conjunctions, and are (1) Consecutive (*so that*); (2) Final (*in order that*); (3) Causal (*because, since*); (4) Temporal (*when, while, until*); (5) Conditional (*if, unless*); (6) Concessive (*although, even if*); (7) Clauses of Proviso (*provided that*); (8) Comparisons (*as, as if, as though*).

III. An Adjectival Clause qualifies the Principal Sentence like an Adjective. It is introduced by the Relative quī or by a Relative Particle, as ubi (*where*), unde (*whence*), quō (*whither*).

SEQUENCE OF TENSES

411 The general rule for the Sequence of Tenses is that a Primary Tense (**105a, b**) in the Principal Sentence is followed in the Subordinate Clause by a Primary Tense, a Historic Tense (**105a, b**) by a Historic Tense.

In Subordinate Clauses the Present and Imperfect Subjunctive are used to represent incomplete action, the Perfect aṇd Pluperfect to represent completed action.

PRIMARY

Simple Pres.	rogō *I ask*	*Act.* quid agās	} *what you are doing*
Pres. Perf.	rogāvī *I have asked*	*Pass.* quid ā tē agātur	
		Act. quid ēgerīs	} *what you have done*
Simple Fut.	rogābō	*Pass.* quid ā tē āctum sit	
Fut. Perf.	rogāverō	*Act.* quid āctūrus sīs	*what you are going to do*

HISTORIC

Imperf.	rogābam	*Act.* quid agerēs	} *what you were doing*
Perf.	rogāvī *I asked*	*Pass.* quid ā tē agerētur	
		Act. quid ēgissēs	} *what you had done*
Pluperf.	rogāveram	*Pass.* quid ā tē āctum esset	
		Act. quid āctūrus essēs	*what you were going to do*

Note 1. The Historic Present (**337**) and Historic Infinitive (**372**) are generally used with Historic Sequence. The Primary Perfect Indicative has Primary Sequence in most writers, but Cicero often gives it Historic Sequence.

Note 2. For exceptions to the Sequence of Tenses, see **422**, n. 2, **443**, n. 7, **467**.

TENSES OF THE INFINITIVE IN ŌRĀTIŌ OBLĪQUA

412 The principles governing the use of a dependent Infinitive are given in **365**, n. 1. Hence, in Ōrātiō Oblīqua (**458**) we find these sequences:

Dīcō *I say*	{ eum amāre *that he is loving*	amāvisse *has loved*	amātūrum esse *will love*
	cōpiās mittī *that forces are being sent*	missās esse *have been sent*	missum īrī *will be sent*
Dīxī *I said*	{ eum amāre *that he was loving*	amāvisse *had loved*	amātūrum esse *would love*
	cōpiās mittī *that forces were being sent*	missās esse *had been sent*	missum īrī *would be sent*

Note 1. When a verb has no Participial- or Supine-stem, Future Infinitives (Active and Passive) are formed periphrastically by **fore ut** or **futūrum esse ut** with the (active or passive) Subjunctive; and such a periphrasis is sometimes used even when a verb has a Supine-stem.

Note 2. For the use of the Infin. to represent the Apodosis of Conditional Sentences, see **467**.

I. SUBSTANTIVAL CLAUSES

413 A **Substantival Clause** is an Indirect Statement, Command, Wish, or Question standing, like a noun, in some case-relation (generally that of Nominative or Accusative) to the Verb of the Principal Sentence.

1. Indirect Statement

414 I. An **Infinitive with Subject Accusative** is the most usual form of Indirect Statement. It may stand:

(a) As the Subject of an Impersonal Verb, or of est with an Abstract Substantive or Neuter Adjective:

> Cōnstat lēgēs ad salūtem cīvium inventās esse. CICERO.
> *It is agreed that laws were devised for the safety of citizens.*

> Rem tē valdē bene gessisse rūmor erat. CICERO.
> *There was a report that you had conducted the affair very well.*

> Vērum est amīcitiam nisi inter bonōs esse nōn posse. CICERO.
> *It is true that friendship cannot exist except between the good.*

(b) As Object, after Verbs of *saying, thinking, feeling, perceiving, knowing, believing, denying*:

> Dēmocritus dīcit innumerābilēs esse mundōs. CICERO.
> *Democritus says that there are countless worlds.*

> Pompeiōs dēsēdisse terrae mōtū audīvimus. SENECA.
> *We have heard that Pompeii has perished in an earthquake.*

Note 1. An Accus. and Infin. may also be the object of (1) iubeō, vetō, patior, sinō; (2) volō, mālō, nōlō, cupiō, when the Subject of the Infin. is different from that of the Main Verb; (3) verbs of *rejoicing* and *grieving* (*cf.* **416,** n.).

Note 2. Verbs of *hoping, promising, swearing, threatening*, generally require the Accus. with Future Infin.:

> Spērābam id mē adsecūtūrum. CICERO.
> *I was hoping to attain this.*

> Pollicēbātur pecūniam sē esse redditūrum. CICERO.
> *He used to promise that he would return the money.*

415a II. A Clause introduced by **ut** and having its verb in the **Subjunctive** is used (a) as Subject with Impersonal Verbs or phrases which express fact or occurrence; (b) as the Object of faciō and its compounds:

(a) Fit ut nēmō esse possit beātus. CICERO.
It is the case that no one can be happy.

Extrēmum illud est ut tē obsecrem. CICERO.
The last thing is for me to beseech you.

(b) Quae rēs ut commeātus portārī posset efficiēbat. CAESAR.
And this had the result that provisions could be brought.

Note. This type of Substantival Clause is analogous to Adverbial Clauses of Result (**421a**).

▶ III. A Clause introduced by **quīn** and having its verb in the **Subjunctive** is used as the Subject or Object of negative and interrogative expressions of doubt (**nōn, dubium est, nōn dubitō, quis dubitat?**):

Nōn dubium erat quīn plūrimum Helvētiī possent. CAESAR.
There was no doubt that the Helvetii were the most powerful.

Quis dubitet quīn in virtūte dīvitiae positae sint? CICERO.
Who would doubt that riches consist in virtue?

16 IV. A Clause introduced by **quod** (*the fact that*) and having its verb in the **Indicative** is used (a) as the Subject of Impersonal Verbs or phrases where a fact is stressed, (b) as the Object of verbs like **addō, mittō, omittō, praetereō,** and verbs of *rejoicing* and *grieving*; (c) in apposition to a preceding demonstrative:

Bene mihi ēvenit quod mittor ad mortem. CICERO.
It is well for me that I am sent to death.

Adde quod īdem nōn hōram tēcum esse potes. HORACE.
Besides, you cannot keep your own company for an hour.

Gaudē quod spectant oculī tē mīlle loquentem. HORACE.
Rejoice that a thousand eyes behold you speaking.

Hōc praestāmus maximē ferīs, quod loquimur. CICERO.
We excel beasts most in this respect, that we speak.

Note. With Verbs of *rejoicing* and *grieving*, either a quod-Clause or an Accus. and Infin. Clause may be used: 'I rejoice that you arrive in health' is either Salvum tē advenīre gaudeō, or Gaudeō quod salvus advenīs (*cf.* **414,** n. 1).

---

2. Indirect Command or Prohibition

417 Indirect Commands or Prohibitions are Substantival Clauses which correspond to simple sentences in which the Imperative (346–50) or the Subjunctive of Will (353–6) is used. The conjunctions are **ut** (positive) and **nē** (negative). Here belong clauses depending on verbs *implying an act of the will*, as:

1. *Command, entreat*: imperō, mandō, praecipiō, oportet, necesse est, rogō, ōrō, petō, postulō, obsecrō, precor;

2. *exhort, urge*: hortor, suādeō, moneō;

3. *persuade, induce*: persuādeō, impetrō, impellō;

4. *resolve*: cēnseō, dēcernō, cōnstituō;

5. *take care*: cūrō, videō, caveō;

6. *permit*: permittō, concēdō, licet.

    (1) Etiam atque etiam tē rogō atque ōrō ut eum iuvēs. CICERO.
    I urgently beg and pray you to help him.

    (2) Hortātur eōs nē animō dēficiant. CAESAR.
    He exhorts them not to lose courage.

    (3) Helvētiīs persuāsit ut exīrent. CAESAR.
    He persuaded the Helvetii to depart.

    (4) Dēcrēvit senātus ut Opīmius vidēret. CICERO.
    The senate decreed that Opimius should see.

    (5) Cūrā et prōvidē ut nē quid eī dēsit. CICERO.
    Take care and see that he lack nothing.

    (6) Cōnsulī permissum est ut duās legiōnēs scrīberet. LIVY.
    The consul was permitted to enrol two legions.

Note 1. With many of these verbs (especially rogō, moneō, suādeō, imperō, cūrō, oportet, necesse est, licet) the Subjunctive is often used without the conjunction ut:

    Haec omnia praetermittās licet. CICERO.
    It is allowable for you to omit all these things.

Note 2. Cavē is often used without nē.

Note 3. Ut nē is sometimes used for nē (*cf.* (5) above).

Note 4. Iubeō, *command*, sinō, patior, *permit*, regularly take an Accus. and Infin. clause (*cf.* **414,** n. 1).

Note 5. Some of these verbs, as moneō, persuādeō, are used also as verbs of *saying*; and then they take an Accus. and Infin. Clause (**414** (b)).

The Conjunction with Verbs of *hindering*, *preventing*, and *forbidding* (prohibeō, impediō, dēterreō, retineō, obstō, obsistō, interdīcō, recūsō) is **nē, quōminus** (*whereby the less*), or **quīn** (*whereby not*):

> Per Afrānium stetit quōminus proelium dīmicārētur. CAESAR.
> *It was owing to Afranius that no battle was fought.*

> Atticus, nē qua sibi statua pōnerētur, restitit. NEPOS.
> *Atticus opposed having any statue raised to him.*

> Nihil abest quīn sim miserrimus. CICERO.
> *Nothing is wanting to my being most miserable.*

Note 1. Quīn is used only when the main verb is negative or virtually negative.
Note 2. Vetō (regularly) and prohibeō (often) take an Accus. and Infin. clause (*cf.* **414**, n. 1).

3. Indirect Wishes

Clauses dependent on verbs of *wishing* (cupiō, optō, volō, nōlō, mālō) may have their verb in the Subjunctive (*cf.* **357**). The conjunctions are **ut** and **nē**:

> Volō utī mihi respondeās. CICERO.
> *I wish you to reply to me.*

Note 1. Frequently the conjunction ut is not used:

> Velim exīstimēs nēminem cāriōrem fuisse. CICERO.
> *I should wish you to consider that no one was more dear.*

Note 2. Cupiō, volō, nōlō, mālō often take an Accus. and Infin. clause; see **414**, n. 1.

9b A dependent clause of wish is found after verbs of *fearing*. The Principal Sentence fears the reverse of the wish. Hence: metuō ut faciat (*May he do it! I fear he will not*) is equivalent to 'I fear he will not do it'; and metuō nē faciat (*May he not do it! I fear he will*) is equivalent to 'I fear he will do it'. Sometimes nē nōn is used for ut:

> Timeō ut sustineās labōrēs. CICERO.
> *I fear that you will not hold out under your toils.*

> Timeō nē tibi nihil praeter lacrimās queam reddere. CICERO.
> *I am afraid that I can give you nothing but tears in return.*

> Vereor nē exercitum firmum habēre non possit. CICERO.
> *I fear he cannot have a strong army.*

4. Indirect Question

420 An Indirect Question is a Substantival Clause dependent upon a verb of *asking, enquiring, telling, knowing,* or the like. It is introduced by an Interrogative Pronoun or Particle (**406**), and its verb is Subjunctive:

> Quaesīvit salvusne esset clipeus. CICERO.
> *He asked whether his shield was safe.*

> Oculīs iūdicārī nōn potest in utram partem fluat Arar. CAESAR.
> *It cannot be determined by the eye in which direction the Arar flows.*

> Fac mē certiōrem quandō adfutūrus sīs. CICERO.
> *Let me know when you will be here.*

> Haud scio an quae dīxit sint vēra omnia. TERENCE.
> *I am inclined to think that all he has said is the truth.*

> Ipse quis sit, utrum sit, an nōn sit, id quoque nescit. CATULLUS.
> *He knows not even this, who he himself is, whether he is or not.*

II. ADVERBIAL CLAUSES

1. Consecutive Clauses

421a Consecutive Clauses define the consequence of what is stated in the Principal Sentence. They are introduced by **ut**, *so that,* and their Verb is in the Subjunctive. The negative adverb is **nōn**.

A Consecutive Clause often has reference to a Demonstrative (**adeō, eō, ita, tam, sīc, tantus, tālis, tot**) in the Principal Sentence:

> Nōn sum ita hebes ut istud dīcam. CICERO.
> *I am not so stupid as to say that.*

> Quis tam dēmēns est ut suā voluntāte maereat? CICERO.
> *Who is so mad as to mourn of his own free will?*

> Nēmō adeō ferus est ut nōn mītēscere possit. HORACE.
> *No one is so savage that he cannot soften.*

Note. Sometimes no Demonstrative precedes the Subordinate Clause:

Arboribus cōnsita Italia est, ut tōta pōmārium videātur. VARRO.
Italy is planted with trees, so as to seem one orchard.

Clārē, et ut audiat hospes. PERSIUS.
Aloud, and so that a bystander may hear.

After **ita,** a Consecutive Clause is sometimes restrictive:

Litterārum ita studiōsus erat ut poētās omnīnō neglegeret.
He was fond of literature, with the reservation that he cared nothing for poetry. CICERO.

A Consecutive Clause sometimes follows **quam** with a Comparative:

Isocratēs maiōre ingeniō est quam ut cum Lysiā comparētur. CICERO.
Isocrates is too great a genius to be compared with Lysias.

Note 1. The impersonal phrase tantum abest, whose subject is a Substantiva Clause introduced by ut (**415a**), has a Consecutive Clause dependent on it:

Tantum abest ut nostra mīrēmur, ut nōbīs nōn satisfaciat ipse Dēmosthenēs. CICERO.

So far am I from admiring my own productions, that Demosthenes himself does not satisfy me.

Note 2. The verb in a Consecutive Clause violates the rule for sequence of tenses (**411**) after a Historic in the Principal sentence:

(*a*) If the result is regarded as a completed action:

Nōn adeō virtūtum sterile erat saeculum ut nōn et bona exempla prōdiderit.
TACITUS.
The age was not so barren of virtues that it has not also provided some good examples.

Tantum āfuit ab īnsolentiā ut commiserātus sit fortūnam Graeciae.
NEPOS.
So far was he from insolence that he pitied the misfortune of Greece.

(*b*) To avoid ambiguity:

Verrēs Siciliam ita perdidit ut ea restituī nōn possit. CICERO.
Verres so ruined Sicily that it cannot now be restored.

Note 3. For Consecutive Clauses introduced by Quī, see **452.**

Note 4. For Consecutive Substantival Clauses, see **415a.**

2. Final Clauses

423 Final Clauses express the aim or purpose of the action of the Principal Sentence. They are introduced by **ut,** *in order that* (if negative, by **nē, ut nē**) and the Verb is Present or Imperfect Subjunctive:

Veniō ut videam.   Abiī nē vidērem.
I come that I may see.   *I went away that I might not see.*

Ut iugulent hominem surgunt dē nocte latrōnēs.   HORACE.
Robbers rise by night that they may kill a man.

Scīpiō rūs abiit nē ad causam dīcendam adesset.   CICERO.
Scipio went into the country that he might not be present to defend his cause.

Final Clauses often have reference to a Demonstrative (**eō, ideō, idcircō, punctereā, ob eam rem**) in the Principal Sentence:

Lēgum idcircō servī sumus ut līberī esse possīmus.   CICERO.
We are the bondmen of the law in order that we may be free.

Note 1. A Final Clause with **ut** or **nē** is used parenthetically in such phrases as: ut ita dīcam, *so to say*; nē longus sim, *not to be tedious*.

Note 2. The purpose of action may be expressed in many ways, all equivalent to a Final Clause. *He sent ambassadors to seek peace* may be rendered:

Lēgātōs mīsit ut pācem peterent.
    ,,   ,, quī pācem peterent (**453**).
    ,,   ,, ad pācem petendam (**379, 285**).
    ,,   ,, pācis petendae causā (**379, 254,** n. 1).
    ,,   ,, pācem petītum (**386**).

Note 3. The Sequence of Tenses in Final Clauses always follows the general rule.

Note 4. For Final Clauses introduced by the Relative Quī, see **453**.

---

3. Causal Clauses

424 Causal Clauses assign a reason for the statement made in the Principal Sentence.

When the speaker vouches for the reason, **quod, quia, quoniam, quandō**, are used with the Indicative;* otherwise the verb is Subjunctive.

> Adsunt proptereā quod officium sequuntur; tacent quia perīculum metuunt. CICERO.
> *They are present because they follow duty; they are silent because they fear danger.*

> Gerāmus, dīs bene iuvantibus, quandō ita vidētur, bellum. LIVY.
> *Let us wage war, the gods helping us, since so it seems good.*

Note 1. **Quod, quia, quoniam** often have reference to **eō, īdeō, idcircō, proptereā**, in the Principal Sentence:

> Quia nātūra mūtārī nōn potest, idcircō vērae amīcitiae sempiternae sunt. CICERO.
> *Because nature cannot be changed, on that account true friendships are everlasting.*

Note 2. **Nōn quod, nōn quia**, generally refer to a cause not vouched for, and introduce a Subjunctive clause; a further clause, introduced by **sed**, with the Indicative, gives the true reason:

> Nōn quia salvōs vellet, sed quia perīre causā indictā nōlēbat. LIVY.
> *Not because he wished them to be saved, but because he did not wish them to die without trial.*

---

26 A Causal Clause introduced by **cum**, *since*, has its verb in the Subjunctive even though the reason is vouched for:

> Quae cum ita sint, ab Iove pācem ac veniam petō. CICERO.
> *Since these things are so, I ask of Jupiter peace and pardon.*

Note 1. After grātulor, laudō, gaudeō, doleō, **cum**, *for the reason that*, sometimes introduces an Indicative Clause:

> Grātulor tibi cum tantum valēs apud Dolābellam. CICERO.
> *I congratulate you that you have so much weight with Dolabella.*

Note 2. For Causal Clauses introduced by the Relative Quī, see **454**.

---

* Clauses in Ōrātiō Oblīqua must be understood to be excepted from this and
all following rules for the use of the Indicative.

4. Temporal Clauses

427 Temporal Clauses define the time when anything has happened, is happening, or will happen.

The Mood of a Temporal Clause is Indicative if its Connexion with the Principal Sentence is one of time only; but if the connexion involves any other idea, or if the action is merely anticipated, the Mood of the Clause is Subjunctive.

428 Ubi, ut, *when,* **postquam,** *after,* **simulac, cum prīmum,** *as soon as,* **quotiēns,** *whenever,* are generally used with the Indicative:

> Olea ubi mātūra erit quam prīmum cōgī oportet. CATO.
> *When the olive is ripe, it must be gathered in as soon as possible.*

> Ut Hostus cecidit, cōnfestim Rōmāna inclīnātur aciēs. LIVY.
> *When Hostus fell, immediately the Roman line gave way.*

> Eō postquam Caesar pervēnit, obsidēs, arma poposcit. CAESAR.
> *After Caesar had arrived there, he demanded hostages and arms.*

Note. In such clauses Latin uses the Fut. (or Perf.) where English idiom generally prefers the Pres. (or Pluperf.).

---

429 Dum, dōnec, quoad, quam, diū, *while, as long as,* are used with the Indicative:

> Hominēs dum docent discunt. SENECA.
> *Men learn while they teach.*

> Dum haec Veiīs agēbantur, interim Capitōlium in ingentī perīculō fuit. LIVY.
> *While these things were being done at Veii, the Capitol was meanwhile in dire peril.*

> Catō, quoad vīxit, virtūtum laude crēvit. NEPOS.
> *Cato increased in the renown of virtue as long as he lived.*

430 Dum, *while,* is regularly used with the Historic Present (*cf.* **337**) to denote a period of time in the course of which something else happens:

> Dum haec in conloquiō geruntur, Caesarī nūntiātum est equitēs accēdere. CAESAR.
> *While this parley was being carried on, it was announced to Caesar that the cavalry were approaching.*

Dum, dōnec, quoad, *until,* and **antequam, priusquam,** *before that,* are used with the Indicative when the only idea conveyed is that of time:

Milō in senātū fuit eō diē, quoad senātus dīmissus est. CICERO.
On that day Milo was in the Senate until the Senate was dismissed.

Priusquam respondeō, dē amīcitiā pauca dīcam. CICERO.
Before I answer, I shall say a few things about friendship.

But when the action is only expected or anticipated, the verb is Subjunctive (Prospective use **361**):

Exspectāte dum cōnsul aut dictātor fīat Caesō. LIVY.
Wait till Caeso become consul or dictator.

Caesar, priusquam sē hostēs ex terrōre reciperent, in fīnēs Suessiōnum exercitum dūxit. CAESAR.
Before the enemy should recover from their alarm, Caesar led the army into the territory of the Suessiones.

Cum, referring to a Present or Future action, is used with the Indicative:

Dē tē cum quiēscunt probant, cum tacent clāmant. CICERO.
Concerning you, when they are quiet, they approve; when they are silent, they cry aloud.

Cum vidēbis, tum sciēs (PLAUTUS), *When you see, you will know.*

Note. Observe expressions like:

Multī annī sunt cum Fabius in aere meō est. CICERO.
For many years past Fabius has been in my debt.

Cum, referring to a Past action, is used with the Indicative in the following cases only:

(*a*) If it expresses merely the time when something happened:

Cum Caesar in Galliam vēnit, alterīus factiōnis prīncipēs erant Aeduī, alterīus Sēquanī. CAESAR.
When Caesar came into Gaul, the Aedui were chiefs of one faction, the Sequani of the other.

Note 1. Such clauses often have reference to a Demonstrative in the Principal Sentence (tum, tunc, eō tempore):

Lituō Rōmulus regiōnēs dīrēxit tum cum urbem condidit. CICERO.
Romulus marked out the districts with a staff at the time when he founded the city.

(*b*) If it means *whenever*:

Cum rosam vīderat, incipere vēr arbitrābātur. CICERO.
Whenever he saw (had seen) a rose, he thought spring was commencing.

7

(c) If the cum-clause, though grammatically subordinate, contains the chief idea:

Iam vēr appetēbat cum Hannibal ex hībernīs mōvit. LIVY.
Spring was already approaching when Hannibal moved out of his winter quarters.

Commodum discesserat Hilarus cum vēnit tabellārius. CICERO.
Hilarus had just departed, when the letter-carrier came.

Note 2. Cum in such clauses is called **cum inversum,** since it belongs *logically* to what is the Principal Sentence.

(d) If the cum-clause merely indicates the identity of one act with another:

Dīxī omnia cum hominem nōmināvī. PLINY.
I have said everything when I have named the man.

435 Cum, referring to a Past action, is used with the Imperfect or Pluperfect Subjunctive except in the cases mentioned in **434.**

Note. The Imperfect is used for time contemporaneous with that of the Principal Sentence, the Pluperfect for prior time:

Cum trīgintā tyrannī oppressās tenērent Athēnās, Thrasybūlus hīs bellum indīxit. NEPOS.
When the thirty tyrants were oppressing Athens, Thrasybulus declared war against them.

Cum Pausaniās dē templō ēlātus esset, cōnfestim animam efflāvit. NEPOS.
When Pausanias had been carried down from the temple, he immediately expired.

Cum hostēs adessent, in urbem prō sē quisque ex agrīs dēmigrant. LIVY.
On the approach of the enemy, they move, each as he best can, from the country into the city.

436 In and after the Augustan age the Subjunctive is used in Temporal Clauses for repeated action:

Id fētiālis ubi dīxisset, hastam in fīnēs hostium mittēbat. LIVY.
As soon as a fetial had thus spoken, he used to fling a spear within the enemies' boundaries.

5. Conditional Clauses

Conditional Statements consist of (i) a Clause introduced by **sī** (*if*), **nisi** (*unless*), containing a preliminary condition, which is called the Protasis, and (ii) a Principal Sentence, containing the consequence, which is called the Apodosis.

The condition contained in the sī-clause may be represented as:

(1) one that is open, *i.e.* nothing is implied about the fulfilment or probability of fulfilment;
(2) one that is conceded only as a supposition and may not be fulfilled;
(3) one that is contrary to known facts.

Type I. The Indicative is used in the Protasis and generally in the Apodosis, if the condition is represented as open; if the condition is (was, or will be) true, the consequence is (was, or will be) true:

Sī valēs, bene est. CICERO.
If you are in good health, all is well.

Parvī sunt forīs arma, nisi est cōnsilium domī. CICERO.
Arms are of little avail abroad, unless there is counsel at home.

Sī fēceris id quod ostendis, magnam habēbō grātiam. CICERO.
If you do what you offer, I shall be very grateful.

Sī quod erat grande vās, laetī adferēbant. CICERO.
If there was any large vessel, they gladly produced it.

Sī licuit, patris pecūniam rēctē abstulit fīlius. CICERO.
If it was lawful, the son rightly took his father's money.

Note 1. When the sense demands it, the Apodosis may be an imperative or a Subjunctive of Will or Desire:

Sī mē amās, paullum hīc ades. HORACE.
If you love me, stand by me here a short time.

Causam investīgātō, sī poteris. CICERO.
Search out the cause, if you can.

Moriar, sī vēra nōn loquor. CICERO.
May I die, if I am not speaking the truth.

Note 2. The Protasis is sometimes in the Subjunctive if the Subject is an Indefinite Second Person:

Memoria minuitur, nisi eam exerceās. CICERO.
The memory is weakened, unless one exercises it.

439 Type II. The Present (or Perfect) Subjunctive is used in the Protasis and generally in the Apodosis, if the condition is conceded only as a supposition which may not be fulfilled:

> Hanc viam sī asperam esse negem, mentiar. CICERO.
> *If I were to deny that this road is rough, I should lie.*
>
> Sī ā corōnā relictus sim, nōn queam dīcere. CICERO.
> *If I were forsaken by my audience, I should not be able to speak.*
>
> Sī vir bonus habeat hanc vim, hāc vī nōn ūtātur. CICERO.
> *If a good man were to have this power, he would not use it.*
>
> Quibus ego sī mē restitisse dīcam, nimium mihi sūmam. CICERO.
> *If I should say that it was I that withstood them, I should be claiming too much.*

440 Type III. The Imperfect or Pluperfect Subjunctive is used in the Protasis and generally in the Apodosis if the condition is represented as contrary to known facts. The Imperfect expresses something continuing even into the present time; the Pluperfect something completed in the past.

(a) The Imperfect Subjunctive in both Protasis and Apodosis:

> Sī foret in terrīs, rīdēret Dēmocritus. HORACE.
> *If Democritus were on earth, he would be laughing.*
>
> Sapientia nōn expeterētur sī nihil efficeret. CICERO.
> *Wisdom would not be desired if it accomplished nothing.*
>
> Servī meī sī metuerent, domum relinquendam putārem.
> *If my slaves feared me, I should think I ought to leave home.*

(b) The Pluperfect Subjunctive in both Protasis and Apodosis:

> Sī ibi tē esse scīssem, ad tē ipse vēnissem. CICERO.
> *If I had known you were there, I should have come to you myself.*
>
> Violātus esset tribūnus, nī cōntiō omnis coorta asset. LIVY.
> *The tribune would have been maltreated, if the whole assembly had not arisen.*
>
> Hectora quis nōsset, fēlīx sī Troia fuisset? OVID.
> *Who would have learned of Hector, had Troy been fortunate?*

(c) Imperfect and Pluperfect combined:

> Sī ad centēnsimum annum vīxisset, senectūtis eum suae paenitēret? CICERO.
> *If he had lived to his hundredth year, would he be regretting his old age?*
>
> Sī nihil litterīs adiuvārentur, numquam sē ad eārum studium contulissent. CICERO.
> *If they were not helped by literature at all, they would never have applied themselves to it.*
>
> Nisi ante Rōmā profectus essēs, nunc eam certē relinquerēs.
> *If you had not left Rome before, you would certainly leave it now.*

Note 1. Instead of a Subjunctive of Conditioned Futurity (358) in the **Apodosis** of Types II and III, we frequently find:

(*a*) An Indicative expressing action begun or intended, but hindered by a condition stated in the Protasis:

> Pōns iter paene hostibus dedit, nisi ūnus vir fuisset. LIVY.
> *The bridge almost gave (and would have given) a passage to the enemy but for one man.*

Erat and fuit with a Future Participle are similarly used:

> Et factūra fuit, pactus nisi Juppiter esset ... OVID.
> *And she would have done it, if Jupiter had not agreed ...*

(*b*) An Indicative of a Verb of *duty* or *possibility*:

> Eum sī ūlla in tē pietās esset, colere dēbēbās. CICERO.
> *You ought to have honoured him if there were any piety in you.*

> Nōn potest iūcundē vīvī nisi cum virtūte vīvātur. CICERO.
> *It is impossible to live happily except by living virtuously.*

In these examples it is 'colere' and 'iūcundē vīvī', not the *duty* or *possibility*, which are conditional on the fulfilment of the Protasis.

Erat and fuit with a Gerundive (see **381-3**) are similarly used:

> Sī ūnum diem morātī essētis, moriendum omnibus fuit. LIVY.
> *If you had delayed a single day, you must all have died.*

Note 2. Sī is sometimes omitted: Ait quis, aiō; negat, negō (TERENCE), *If anyone affirms, I affirm; if anyone denies, I deny.*

Note 3. Nisi **forte, nisi vērō** are ironical.

Note 4. Sī **nōn** is used instead of nisi:

(*a*) when the Apodosis contains **at, tamen, or certē:**

> Dolōrem sī nōn potuerō frangere, tamen occultābō. CICERO.
> *If I cannot suppress my sorrow, yet I will hide it.*

(*b*) When the positive of the same verb precedes:

> Sī fēceris, habēbō grātiam; si nōn fēceris, ignōscam. CICERO.
> *If you do it, I shall thank you; if not, I shall pardon you.*

Note 5. Sīve ... sīve (seu), seu ... seu (sīve), *whether ... or (or if)* are used (chiefly in Type I) for alternative conditions:

> Sīve retractābis, sīve properābis.
> *Whether you delay or hasten (it).*

Note 6. When two conditions exclude each other and each has its own Apodosis, the first is introduced by sī, the second by sīn, *but if:*

> Sī domī sum, forīs est animus: sīn forīs sum, animus domī est. PLAUTUS.
> *If I am at home, my mind is abroad; but if I am abroad, my mind is at home.*

443 *Note 7.* When a Conditional Statement of Type III is itself a Result Clause, an Indirect Question, or dependent on nōn dubitō quīn, the tense of the Protasis remains unchanged (even in violation of the rule for sequence). In the Apodosis an Imperf. remains, but an Active Pluperf. becomes -ūrus fuerim:

> Dīc quidnam factūrus fuerīs sī eō tempore cēnsor fuissēs. LIVY.
> *Tell me what you would have done if you had been censor then.*

Note 8. For Conditional Statements in Ōrātiō Oblīqua, see **467**.

Note 9. For complete suppression of Protasis, see **359**.

---

6. Concessive Clauses

444 Concessive Clauses are introduced by **etsī, etiamsī, tametsī,** *even if*; **quamquam, quamvīs, licet,** *although*.

445 **Etsī, etiamsī, tametsī** take (*a*) the Indicative or (*b*) the Subjunctive, like sī-clauses (**437**):

> (*a*) Etiamsī tacent, satis dīcunt. CICERO.
> *Even if they are silent, they say enough.*

> (*b*) Etiamsī nōn is esset Caesar quī est, tamen ōrnandus vidērētur. CICERO.
> *Even if Caesar were not what he is, yet he would be considered worthy of honour.*

446 **Quamquam** is used with the Indicative:

> Quamquam festīnās, nōn est mora longa. HORACE.
> *Although you are in haste, the delay is not long.*

Quamvīs, licet are used with the Subjunctive:

> Quamvīs nōn fuerīs suāsor, approbātor fuistī. CICERO.
> *Although you did not make the suggestion, you have given your approval.*

---

447 *Note 1.* **Quamquam** is used by later writers with the Subjunctive, and **quamvīs** is often found in poets with the Indicative.

Note 2. **Ut, nē, cum** occasionally introduce Concessive clauses. The verb in such cases is Subjunctive:

> Nē sit summum malum dolor, malum certē est. CICERO.
> *Granted that pain be not the greatest evil, it surely is an evil.*

Note 3. The Conjunction is sometimes omitted:

> Nātūram expellās furcā, tamen ūsque recurret. HORACE.
> *Though you drive out Nature with a pitchfork, yet she will always come back.*

7. Clauses of Proviso

Clauses of Proviso are introduced by **dum, dummodo, modo,** *provided that.* The Verb is in the Subjunctive, and the negative **nē.**

> Magnō mē metū līberābis, dummodo mūrus intersit. CICERO.
> *You will free me from a great fear, provided a wall is between us.*

> Nīl obstat tibi dum nē sit tē dītior alter. HORACE.
> *Nothing is a hindrance to you provided your neighbour be not richer than you.*

8. Clauses of Comparison

In these Clauses the action or fact of the Principal Sentence is compared:

(i) with something asserted as a fact (Indicative);
(ii) with a supposed condition (Subjunctive).

For the Conjunctions, see **178**:

> (i) Ut brevissimē dīcī potuērunt, ita ā mē dicta sunt. CICERO.
> *These things have been said by me as briefly as possible.*

> (ii) Quid ego hīs testibus ūtor quasi rēs dubia sit? CICERO.
> *Why do I use these witnesses as if the matter were doubtful?*

> Tamquam dē rēgnō dīmicārētur ita concurrērunt. LIVY.
> *They joined battle as if it were a struggle for the kingdom.*

> Tamquam sī claudus sim, cum fūstī est ambulandum. PLAUTUS.
> *I must walk with a stick as if I were lame.*

> Eius negōtium sīc velim cūrēs, ut sī esset rēs mea. CICERO.
> *I would wish you to care for his business just as if it were my affair.*

Note 1. Such clauses often have reference to a Demonstrative (**ita, sic, perinde, proinde, aequē, similiter**) in the Principal Sentence.

Note 2. In sentences of type (ii), the tense of the Subj. is generally determined by the rule for Sequence (**411**), and not by the principles which apply to Conditional Clauses (**439–40**).

Note 3. For Consecutive Clauses of Comparison, *see* **421c**.

III. ADJECTIVAL CLAUSES

450 When the **Relative quī** introduces a clause which merely states a fact about the Antecedent, the verb is Indicative:

> Est in Britanniā flūmen quod appellātur Tamesis. CAESAR.
> *There is in Britain a river which is called the Thames.*
>
> Quis fuit horrendōs prīmus quī prōtulit ēnsēs? TIBULLUS.
> *Who was (the man) who first invented terrible swords?*

Note. This rule applies to Correlatives, quālis, quantus, quot, and to the Universals, quisquis, quīcumque, &c. (**102**):

Nōn sum quālis eram. HOR.	Quidquid erit, tibi erit. CICERO.
I am not what I was.	*Whatever there is will be for you.*

---

451 But when the Relative introduces a Consecutive, Final or Causal Clause, corresponding to the Adverbial Clauses with similar meaning, the verb is Subjunctive:

452 **Quī** often introduces a **Consecutive** Clause with the meaning *of such a kind that*; such a clause defines a **characteristic** of the Antecedent:

(*a*) After a Demonstrative:

> Nōn sum is quī hīs rēbus dēlēcter. CICERO.
> *I am not one to delight in these things.*
>
> Ea est Rōmāna gēns quae victa quiēscere nesciat. LIVY.
> *The Roman race is such that it knows not how to rest quiet under defeat.*
>
> Nihil tantī fuit quō vēnderēmus fidem nostram. CICERO.
> *Nothing was of such value that we should sell for it our faith.*

(*b*) After Indefinite and Interrogative Pronouns, and **nēmō, nihil, nūllus, ūnus, sōlus:**

> Est aliquid quod nōn oporteat, etiamsī licet. CICERO.
> *There is something which is not fitting, even if it is lawful.*
>
> Quis est cui nōn possit malum ēvenīre? CICERO.
> *Who is there to whom evil cannot happen?*
>
> Nihil est quod tam deceat quam cōnstantia. CICERO.
> *Nothing is so becoming as consistency.*

Note. **Quin** for **quī** (quae, quod) **nōn** is similarly used:

Nēmō est quīn audierit quemadmodum captae sint Syrācūsae.
There is no one who has not heard how Syracuse was taken.

(c) After **est, sunt,** used indefinitely:

Sunt quī duōs tantum in sacrō monte creātōs tribūnōs esse dīcant.   LIVY.
There are some who say that only two tribunes were elected on the sacred mount.

but est quī, sunt quī introduce an Indicative clause if they refer to Definite Antecedents:

Sunt item quae appellantur alcēs.   CAESAR.
There are also (some animals) which are called elks.

(d) After Comparatives with **quam** (*cf.* **421c**):

Maiōra dēlīquerant quam quibus ignōscī posset.   LIVY.
They had committed greater offences than could be pardoned.

(e) After **dignus, indignus**:

Dignus est quī imperet.   CICERO.
He is worthy to govern.

53 **Quī** often introduces a **Final** Clause, *in order that*:

Clūsīnī lēgātōs Rōmam, quī auxilium ā senātū peterent, mīsēre.   LIVY.
The Clusini sent ambassadors to Rome to seek aid from the senate.

Quō introduces a Final Clause that contains a **Comparative**.

Castella commūnit quō facilius eōs prohibēre possit.   CAESAR.
He strengthens the forts that he may keep them off more easily.

454 **Quī** introduces a **Causal** Clause, and the verb is usually Subjunctive:

Miseret tuī mē quī hunc faciās inimīcum tibi.   TERENCE.
I pity you for making this man your enemy.

Note 1.   Quī causal is sometimes strengthened by **quippe, ut, utpote.**

Note 2.   Nōn quō is sometimes used for nōn quod: nōn quō quemquam plūs amem, eō fēcī (TERENCE), *I have not done it because I love anyone more.*

Note 3.   Quī with the Indicative forms a Causal Clause as a parenthesis:

Quā es prūdentiā (*cf.* **331b**, n.), nihil tē fugiet.   CICERO.
Such is your prudence, nothing will escape you.

455 The rules for the use of quī with Indicative or Subjunctive apply also to the Relative particles **quō** (*whither*), **quā** (*where*), **ubi** (*where*), **unde** (*whence*).

> Locus, quō exercituī aditus nōn erat. CAESAR.
> *A place whither there was no approach for the army.*
> Quā dūcitis, adsum. VIRGIL.
> *Where you lead, I am present.*
> Nē illī sit cēra, ubi facere possit litterās. PLAUTUS.
> *Let him have no wax on which to write.*
> Antōnius quō sē verteret nōn habēbat. CICERO.
> *Antony had no place whither he could turn.*

456 *Note 1.* A Relative Clause with its verb in the Subjunctive sometimes has a restrictive sense (*cf.* **421b**): quod sciam, *so far as I know*; omnium quōs quidem cognōverim, *of all those at least whom I have known.*

457 *Note 2.* A Relative Clause or an Ablative Absolute formed with the Relative Pronoun, is often used at the beginning of a Principal Sentence to show the connexion with something which has gone before: quō factō, *this accomplished*; quā dē causā, *for which reason*; quod dīcis, *as to that which you say.*

ŌRĀTIŌ OBLĪQUA

458 In Latin, a speech or narrative is often not given in the actual words of the speaker, but is reported indirectly as the object of a verb of *saying*. A speech so reported is called Ōrātiō Oblīqua. Its Simple and Principal sentences become Substantival Clauses (**413–20**).

Note. The verb of *saying* is sometimes not expressed, but inferred from the context. Inquam and inquit (*cf.* **142b**) do not introduce Ōrātiō Oblīqua; they are used when a speaker's actual words are quoted, and are always parenthetic.

SIMPLE AND PRINCIPAL SENTENCES IN ŌRĀTIŌ OBLĪQUA

459 **Statements and Exclamations** are expressed by an Accusative and Infinitive (**414**):

Direct	*Indirect*
Rōmulus urbem condidit.	(Nārrant:) Rōmulum urbem condidisse.
Romulus founded a city.	

Commands, Prohibitions, and Wishes are expressed by the Subjunctive (**417, 419a**):

Direct	*Indirect*
Īte, inquit, creāte cōnsulēs ex plēbe.	(Hortātus est:) īrent, creārent cōnsulēs ex plēbe.
Go and elect consuls from the plebs.	

Note 1. Prohibitions like nōlī abīre (**349**) become nē abeat, nē abīret.

Real Questions (*i.e.* those to which an answer is expected) **are** expressed by the Subjunctive (**420**):

Quid agis? inquit.   Cūr nōn   Quid ageret?   Cūr nōn anteā pugnam
anteā pugnam commīsistī?   commīsisset?
What are you about?   *Why have you not joined battle before?*

Rhetorical Questions* (*i.e.* those which do not expect an answer) are expressed by an Accusative and Infinitive (**414**):

Cūr ego prō hominibus ignāvīs   Cūr sē prō hominibus ignāvīs sanguinem
sanguinem profūdī?   profūdisse?

Why have I shed my blood for cowards?

Note 2.   Questions in the 1st and 3rd persons are often rhetorical.

SUBORDINATE CLAUSES IN ŌRĀTIŌ OBLĪQUA

0 Substantival Clauses (413–20) which involve an Accusative and Infinitive (or a Subjunctive) retain the Accusative and Infinitive (or Subjunctive); but the Indicative of a quod-clause (**416**) becomes Subjunctive:

Ego prōmittō mē officium meum   (Dīxit:) sē prōmittere sē officium
praestātūrum esse.   suum praestātūrum esse.

I promise that I shall do my duty.

Hōc praestāmus maximē ferīs quod   (Dīxit:) hōc praestāre maximē ferīs
loquimur.   quod loquerentur.

We excel beasts most in this respect, that we speak.

61 Adverbial and Adjectival Clauses (421a–457) have their verbs in the Subjunctive:

Maiōrum quibus ortī estis reminīs-   (Dīxit:) maiōrum quibus ortī essent
ciminī.   reminīscerentur.

Remember the ancestors from whom you are sprung.

Note 1.   A Relative Clause which is inserted parenthetically as the remark of the narrator, has its verb in the Indicative:

Xerxem certiōrem fēcī id agī ut pōns, quem in Hellēspontō fēcerat, dissolverētur. NEPOS.
I sent Xerxes word that a plot was afoot that the bridge (which he had made over the Hellespont) should be broken down.

Note 2.   A Relative Clause which is logically the equivalent of a Co-ordinate Sentence (**403**) is represented by an Accus. and Infin.

Note 3.   The Pres. Indic. in a dum Clause (**430**) is often retained.

* Such Questions are really Statements put for rhetorical effect in an Interrogative form.   'Why have I shed my blood for cowards?' means, 'I have shed my blood for cowards—why?   I have shed my blood for cowards to no purpose.'

PRONOUNS AND ADVERBS IN ŌRĀTIŌ OBLĪQUA

462 When the verb of saying is Third Person (as usually is the case):

Ego, nōs; meus, noster	*become*	sē; suus
Tū, vōs; tuus, vester	*become*	ille, illī; illīus, illōrum
Hic	*becomes*	ille or is.

Direct	*Indirect*
Ego tē prō hoste habēbō; sociī quoque nostrī amīcitiam tuam exuent.	(Dīxit:) sē illum prō hoste habitūrum; sociōs quoque suōs illīus amīcitiam exūtūros.

I shall regard you as an enemy; our allies also will throw off your friendship.

463 Since the Reflexives **sē, suus** may refer to the subject of a verb other than the verb of *saying* (see **316**), ambiguity is possible unless the context is clear:

> Nerviōs hortātur nē suī līberandī occāsiōnem dīmittant. CAESAR.
> *He urges the Nervii not to lose the opportunity of freeing themselves.*

> Rēx supplicem monuit ut cōnsuleret sibi.
> *The king warned the suppliant to take heed for himself.*

464 Sometimes **ipse** makes the distinction clear:

> (Rogāvit:) quid tandem verērentur aut cūr dē suā virtūte aut dē ipsīus dīligentiā dēspērārent? CAESAR.
> *What cause had they to fear, or why did they despair either of their own bravery or of his carefulness?*

465 When the verb of *saying* is Past, Adverbs of Time and Place are accommodated to the sense:

nunc, hodiē, heri, crās;	hīc, hūc, hinc;
become:	*become:*
tunc, illō diē, prīdiē, posterō diē;	ibi, illūc, ex eō locō.

TENSES IN ŌRĀTIŌ OBLĪQUA

466 The Tenses of the **Infinitive** as used in Ōrātiō Oblīqua are given in **412**.

Observe that the Pres. Infin. represents a Pres. Indic.; the Perf. Infin. represents either an Imperf., Perf. or Pluperf. Indic.; the Fut. Infin. represents either a Fut. or Fut. Perf. Indic.

The Tenses of the **Subjunctive** follow the rule for sequence (**411**).

If the verb of *saying* is Present, the Pres. and Perf. Subjunctive are used; if Past, the Imperf. and Pluperf. Subjunctive are used.

Note. For vividness, the Pres. and Perf. Subjunctive are often used, even though the verb of *saying* is Past.

CONDITIONAL STATEMENTS IN ŌRĀTIŌ OBLĪQUA

Type I (438) presents no irregularity.

Note. Observe that a Fut. Perf. Indic. in the Protasis becomes a Pluperf. Subjunctive after a Main Verb in the Past:

Sī peccāverit, dolēbit;   (Dīxit:) illum, sī peccāvisset, dolitūrum esse.

Type II (439). The Subjunctive of the Protasis follows the rule for Sequence **(411)**; the Present Subjunctive of the Apodosis becomes a Future Infinitive:

Sī peccet, doleat; (Dīxit:) illum, sī peccāret, dolitūrum esse.

Type III (440). An Imperfect or Pluperfect Subjunctive in the Protasis remains unaltered, even if the verb of *saying* is Present. In the Apodosis an Imperfect or Pluperfect Subjunctive becomes an Infinitive in **-ūrum fuisse** (if such a form exists); but the periphrastic **futūrum fuisse** with the Imperfect Subjunctive is used if the verb is passive or lacks a future participle:

(*a*) sī peccāret, dolēret ⎫   (*a, b*) (Dīxit:) illum, sī peccāret (*or*
(*b*) sī peccāvisset, doluisset ⎭   peccāvisset), dolitūrum fuisse.
(*c*) sī peccāvisset, pūnītus esset: (*c*) (Dīxit:) sī peccāvisset, futūrum fuisse ut pūnīrētur.

VIRTUAL ŌRĀTIŌ OBLĪQUA

468 A Subordinate Clause is in Virtual Ōrātiō Oblīqua when a verb of *saying* is implied, and the writer does not vouch for the truth of statements or opinions which, in effect, he is quoting. The verb of such clauses is in the Subjunctive:

Paetus librōs quōs pater suus relīquisset mihi dōnāvit. CICERO.
Paetus gave me the books which (as he said) his father had left.

Laudat Āfricānum Panaetius quod fuerit abstinēns. CICERO.
Panaetius praises Africanus because (as he says) he was temperate.

Caesar Aeduōs frūmentum, quod pollicitī essent, flāgitābat. CAESAR.
Caesar demanded of the Aedui the corn which (he reminded them) they had promised.

Themistoclēs noctū ambulābat, quod somnum capere nōn posset. CICERO.
Themistocles used to walk at night because (as he said) he could not sleep.

SUBJUNCTIVE BY ATTRACTION

469 A Subjunctive is often found, where the Indicative would be expected, merely because the Clause is dependent on another Subjunctive or on an Infinitive:

> Utinam tunc essem nātus quandō Rōmānī dōna accipere coepissent. SALLUST.
>
> *Would that I had been born when Romans began to receive gifts.*

> Nescīre quid antequam nātus sīs acciderit, id est semper esse puerum. CICERO.
>
> *Not to know what happened before you were born, that is to be a child always.*

EXAMPLES OF NARRATIVE IN ŌRĀTIŌ OBLĪQUA

470

Direct Statement

(1) Ars eārum rērum est quae sciuntur; ōrātōris autem omnis āctiō opīniōnibus, nōn scientiā, continētur; nam et apud eōs dīcimus quī nesciunt, et ea dīcimus quae nescīmus ipsī. CICERO.

Art belongs to the things which are known; but the whole sphere of an orator is in opinion, not in knowledge; for we both speak in the presence of those who know not, and speak of that which we ourselves know not.

(2) Cum Germānīs Aeduī semel atque iterum armīs contendērunt; magnam calamitātem pulsī accēpērunt, omnem nōbilitātem, omnem equitātum āmīsērunt. Sed peius victōribus Sēquanīs quam Aeduīs victīs accidit; proptereā quod Ariovistus, rēx Germānōrum, in eōrum fīnibus cōnsēdit, tertiamque partem agrī Sēquanī, quī est optimus tōtīus

Indirect Statement

(Antōnius apud Cicerōnem docet:)
Artem eārum rērum esse quae sciantur; ōrātōris autem omnem āctiōnem opīniōnibus, non scientiā, continērī; quia et apud eōs dīcant quī nesciant, et ea dīcant quae ipsī nesciant.

(Antonius teaches in Cicero:)
That art belongs to the things which are known; but that the whole sphere of an orator is in opinion, not in knowledge; because they both speak before those who know not; and speak of that which they themselves know not.

Locūtus est prō Aeduīs Dīvitiacus:
Cum Germānīs Aeduōs semel atque iterum armīs contendisse; magnam calamitātem pulsōs accēpisse, omnem nōbilitātem, omnem equitātum āmīsisse. Sed peius victōribus Sēquanīs quam Aeduīs victīs accidisse; proptereā quod Ariovistus, rēx Germānōrum, in eōrum fīnibus cōnsēdisset, tertiamque partem agrī Sēquanī, quī esset optimus tōtīus Galliae, occu-

Galliae, occupāvit. Ariovistus barbarus, īrācundus, temerārius est; nōn possunt eius imperia diūtius sustinērī.

pāvisset. Ariovistum esse barbarum, īrācundum, temerārium; nōn posse eius imperia diūtius sustinērī.

The Aedui have repeatedly fought with the Germans; they have been defeated and have suffered great misfortune; they have lost all their nobles and all their cavalry. But worse has befallen the conquering Sequani than the conquered Aedui, for Ariovistus, king of the Germans, has settled in their dominions and occupied a third part of their territory, which is the best in all Gaul. Ariovistus is barbarous, passionate and violent; his commands can no longer be endured.

Divitiacus said on behalf of the Aedui: 'That the Aedui had fought repeatedly with the Germans; that, having been defeated, they had suffered great misfortune (and) had lost all their nobles, all their cavalry. But that worse had befallen the conquering Sequani than the conquered Aedui, for Ariovistus, king of the Germans, had settled in their dominions and had occupied a third part of their territory, which was the best in all Gaul. Ariovistus was barbarous, passionate, violent; his commands could no longer be endured.'

(3) Cōnsulēs scrīpta ad Caesarem mandāta remittunt, quōrum haec erat summa:

'In Galliam revertere, Arīminō excēde, exercitūs dīmitte; quae sī fēceris, Pompeius in Hispāniās ībit.'

In Galliam reverterētur, Arīminō excēderet, exercitūs dīmitteret; quae sī fēcisset, Pompeium in Hispāniās itūrum.

The Consuls sent back to Caesar written instructions, of which this was the sum total: 'Return into Gaul, quit Ariminum, and disband your armies; when you have done these things, Pompey will go into Spain.'

(4) Thrasybūlus, cum exercitus trīgintā tyrannōrum fugeret, magnā vōce exclāmat:

'Cūr mē victōrem fugitis? Cīvium hanc mementōte aciem, nōn hostium esse; trīgintā ego dominīs, nōn cīvitātī, bellum īnferō.'

Cūr sē victōrem fugiant? Cīvium illam meminerint aciem, nōn hostium esse; trīgintā sē dominīs, nōn cīvitātī, bellum īnferre.

Thrasybulus, when the army of the thirty tyrants was in flight, cried aloud: 'Why do you flee from me as your conqueror? Remember that this is an army of fellow-citizens, not of foreign enemies; I am waging war on the thirty tyrants, not on the community.'

(5) Ōrō vōs, Veientēs (inquit), nē mē extorrem egentem, ex tantō modo rēgnō cum līberīs adulēscentibus ante oculōs vestrōs perīre sinātis. Aliī peregrē in rēgnum Rōmam accītī sunt; ego rēx, augēns bellō Rōmānum imperium, ā proximīs scelerātā coniūrātiōne pulsus sum. Patriam rēgnumque meum repetere, et persequī ingrātōs cīvēs volō. Ferte opem, adiuvāte; vestrās quoque veterēs iniūriās ultum īte, totiēns caesās legiōnēs, agrum adēmptum.

Ōrat Tarquinius Veientēs nē sē extorrem egentem ex tantō modo rēgnō cum līberīs adulēscentibus ante oculōs suōs perīre sinerent: aliōs peregrē in rēgnum Rōmam accītōs; sē rēgem augentem bellō Rōmānum imperium, ā proximīs scelerātā coniūrātiōne pulsum. Patriam sē rēgnumque suum repetere et persequī ingrātōs cīvēs velle. Ferrent opem, adiuvārent; suās quoque veterēs iniūriās ultum īrent, totiēns caesās legiōnēs, agrum adēmptum. LIVY.

I entreat you, men of Veii (said Tarquin), not to let me with my young children die before your eyes, banished in destitution from a kingdom lately so great. Others were fetched to Rome from abroad to reign. I, their king, while enlarging by war the Roman empire, was expelled by a wicked conspiracy of my nearest kinsmen. I wish to reclaim my country and my kingdom, and to punish ungrateful citizens. Give me help, assist me; hasten to avenge also your own old wrongs, your legions so often slaughtered, your land taken from you.

PROSODY

Prosody treats of the Quantity of Syllables and the Laws of Metre.

I. GENERAL RULES OF QUANTITY

1. A syllable is long if it ends:
   (a) In a long vowel or diphthong: scrī-bae.
   (b) In two consonants or a compound consonant: dant, dux.
   (c) In a single consonant followed by a syllable beginning with a consonant: mul-tōs.

2. All other syllables are short.

Note 1. The rules for syllable division are given in **8a**. For prosody it is important to notice that poets often divide a combination of Plosive and Liquid between two syllables, so that the first syllable is long even if it contains a short vowel: pat-ris, teneb-rae, trip-lex. 'h' and 'u' in 'qu-' do not count as consonants.

Note 2. General principles governing the quantities of vowels and diphthongs are given in **4b**, n. 1, and **5b**. For prosody it is important to notice that a vowel or diphthong is short before another vowel or h (in the same word): proavus, trahō, praeesse. Important exceptions to this are certain parts of fīō (**141**) and some cases of Fifth Declension words in -iēs (**57**). Observe further: (a) that in Greek words a long vowel or diphthong keeps its length: ēar, Aenēās, Enȳō, Melibœus; (b) that compounds of iaciō, though written iniciō, adiciō, have their first syllable long as if pronounced inyiciō, adyiciō; (c) that consonant-i between vowels was pronounced as a doubled consonant, and the first syllable of words like eius, huius, is consequently long.

---

3. A syllable is called doubtful when it is found in poetry to be sometimes long, sometimes short: Dĭāna, fidĕī, rĕī, and genitives in -ius, as illĭus.

4. The quantity of a stem syllable is kept, as a rule, in compounds and derivatives: cadō occidō, ratus irritus, flūmen flŭmineus; but exceptions to this rule are numerous.

II. RULE FOR MONOSYLLABLES

Most monosyllables are long: dā, dēs, mē, vēr, sī, sīs, sōl, nōs, tū, vīs, mūs.

Exceptions:

Substantives: cor, fel, lac, mel, os (*bone*), vas (*surety*), vir.
Pronouns: is, id, qua (*any*), quis, quid, quod, quot, tot. (For hic, see p. 49.)
Verbs: dat, det, it, scit, sit, stat, stet, fit, fac, fer, es (from sum).
Particles: ab, ac, ad, an, at, bis, cis, et, in, nec, ob, per, pol, sat, sed, sub, ut, vel.
and the enclitics -ne, -que, -ve.

473   III. RULES FOR FINAL SYLLABLES

1. A final is short.

   Exceptions.—Ablatives of decl. 1. mēnsā, bonā; Vocative of Greek names in ās, Aeneā; and of some in ēs, Anchīsā; Indeclinable Numerals, trīgintā; Imperatives of conj. 1. amā (but puta); most Particles in a; frūstrā, intereā (but ita, quia, short).

2. E final is short: lege, timēte, carēre.

   Exceptions.—Ablatives of declension 5. rē, diē, with the derivatives quārē, hodiē. Cases of many Greek nouns; also famē. Adverbs formed from Adjectives: miserē; also ferē, fermē (but bene, male, facile, impūne, temere, short). Imperatives of conj. 2. monē (but cavĕ is doubtful). Also the Interjection ohē.

3. I final is long: dīcī, plēbī, dolī.

   Exceptions.—Vocatives and Datives of Greek nouns; Chlōri, Thyrsidi; but Datives are sometimes long: Paridī. Particles as: sīcubi, nēcubi, nisi, quasi. Mihĭ, tibĭ, sibĭ, ubĭ, and ibĭ are doubtful.

4. O final is long: virgō, multō, iuvō.

   Exceptions.—Duo, ego, modo, cito, and three verbs: puto, scio, nescio. In the Silver age final o was often shortened in Verbs and Nouns.

5. U final is long: cantū, dictū, diū.

6. A vowel before final c is long; illĭc; except dōnec.

7. A vowel before final l, d, t is short: Hannibal, illud, amāvit.

8. A vowel before final n is short: Ĭlion, agmen.

   Exceptions.—Many Greek words: Hymēn, Ammōn.

9. A vowel before final r is short: calcar, amābitur, Hector.

   Exceptions.—Many Greek words: āēr, crātēr; and compounds of pār: dispār, impār.

10. Final -as is long: terrās, Menalcās.

    Exceptions.—Greek nouns of decl. 3. Arcas (gen. -adis) and acc. pl. lampadas; anas, *a duck.*

11. Final -es is long: nūbēs, vidērēs.

    Exceptions.—Cases of Greek nouns: Arcades, Nāiades. Nominatives of a few substantives and adjectives with dental stems in -et, -it, or -id: seges, pedes, obses, dīves (but abiēs, ariēs, pariēs); also penes. Compounds of es: ades, potes.

12. Final -is is short: dīceris, ūtilis, ēnsis.

    Exceptions.—Datives and Ablatives in īs, including grātīs, forīs. Accusatives in īs: nāvīs; some Greek Nouns in īs: Salamīs. Sanguĭs, pulvĭs, are doubtful. 2nd Pers. Sing. Pres. Ind. conj. 4. audīs; compounds of vīs, sīs *e.g.* quīvīs, possīs; also velīs, mālīs, nōlīs. 2nd Pers. Sing. Perf. Subj., amāverīs (*cf.* 113).

13. Final **-os** is long: ventōs, custōs, sacerdōs.

> *Exceptions.*—Greek nom. and gen. in os (*os*): Dĕlos, Arcados; also compos, impos, exos.

14. Final **-us** is short: holus, intus, amāmus.

> *Exceptions.*—Nominatives from long stems of decl. 3. are long: virtūs, tellūs, incūs, iuventūs; gen. sing. and nom. and accus. pl. of decl. 4.: artūs, gradūs; and a few Greek words: Dīdūs, Sapphūs (genitive).

15. The Greek word chlamys, chelys, Tīphys, Erīnys have the final syllable short and the vocative ending y.

IV. ON THE LAWS OF METRE

A Verse (versus, *line*) is composed of a certain number of Feet.

A Foot consists of two or more syllables. The metrically predominant part of a foot (generally a long syllable) is called the Rise (or Arsis); the other part is called the Fall (or Thesis).

The principal feet in Latin poetry are the following:

Iambus, one short and one long syllable, carō (∪ Fall, — Rise)

Trochee, one long and one short syllable, mēnsa (— Rise, ∪ Fall).

Dactyl, one long and two short syllables, lītora (— Rise, ∪∪ Fall).

Anapaest, two short and one long syllable, patulae (∪∪ Fall, — Rise).

Spondee, two long syllables, fātō (— Fall, — Rise; or — Rise, — Fall).

Tribrach, three short syllables, temere (∪ Fall, ∪∪ Rise; or ∪∪ Rise, ∪ Fall).

The Spondee often takes the place of the Dactyl in Dactylic verse. It may also take the place of the Iambus or Trochee in certain parts of an Iambic or Trochaic verse.

The Tribrach can take the place of the Iambus or the Trochee, but is more rarely used than the Spondee (*cf.* 479).

A short syllable in versification constitutes one 'mora', or 'time'. A long syllable (= two shorts) constitutes two 'morae', or 'times'. The Iambus, Trochee, Tribrach are feet of three 'morae'; Dactyl, Anapaest, Spondee, are feet of four 'morae'.

74b A vowel at the end of a word was so lightly pronounced, if there was a vowel at the beginning of the next word, that it did not count as a syllable in Scansion: Phyllid(a) am(ō) ant(e) aliās; this is called Elision (Synaloepha).

A vowel and **m** were similarly treated at the end of a word: Ō cūrās homin(um) Ō quant(um) est in rēbus ināne. This is called Ecthlipsis.

A vowel unelided in such a position is said to be in Hiatus.

> Ter sunt | cōnā ǀ tī im ǀ pōnere | Pēlio | Ossam.

475   V. METRE

The word Metre (metrum, *measure*) is used in two different senses.

i. It means any system of versification: which may take its name either (1) from the Foot which prevails in it: Dactylic (Iambic, Trochaic, Anapaestic) metre; or (2) from the subjects of which it treats: Heroic (Elegiac) metre; or (3) from the musical instrument to which it was sung: Lyric metres; or (4) from the poet who is said to have invented or chiefly used it: Alcaic metre (from Alcaeus), Sapphic (from Sappho), &c.

ii. Some part of a Verse is called 'a metre'. In Dactylic and some other verses each foot constitutes 'a metre'. In Iambic, Trochaic, and Anapaestic verses, two feet constitute 'a metre'.

Note. A verse is often named from the number of 'metres' it contains; hence the terms: dimeter, trimeter, tetrameter, pentameter, hexameter. A verse which has its metres complete is said to be acatalectic (unclipt). If its last metre is incomplete, the verse is catalectic (clipt).

476   The dividing of a verse according to feet is called scanning or scansion. The method of scansion may be shown by two Dactylic Hexameters of Virgil:

        1   2   3   4   5   6
(a) Tītyre | tū ‖ patu | lae ‖ recu | bāns ‖ sub | tegmine | fāgī
(b) Fōrmō | sam ‖ reso | nāre ‖ do | cēs ‖ Ama | ryllida | silvās.

The numerals and single strokes show the six feet or metres of the Hexameter; The double strokes are explained below.

A verse like:

sparsīs | hastīs | longīs | campus | splendet et | horret,

in which the end of every foot coincides with the end of a word, sounded uncouth to Roman ears and was rigorously avoided by poets of the classical ages. The ending of a word and foot together is called **Diaeresis**, as in (a) Tītyre, tegmine. The place within a foot where a word ends is called a **Caesura** (*cutting*). There are three caesuras in each of the verses (a), (b), marked by a short double stroke. A Caesura after a long syllable is called strong, and is most frequent. A Caesura after a short syllable is called weak, as that in the third foot of (b) after -nāre. (See 'Dactylic Hexameter'.)

VI. DACTYLIC, IAMBIC AND SOME LYRIC SYSTEMS OF VERSE

477 *A.* **Dactylic Hexameter**:

This Metre has six feet. The first four may be Dactyls or Spondees. The fifth must be a Dactyl (rarely a Spondee). The sixth is a Spondee or Trochee; for the last syllable in any verse may be either long or short.

Scheme

| 1 | 2 | 3 | 4 | 5 | 6 |

$$-\cup\cup \mid -\cup\cup \mid -\cup\cup \mid -\cup\cup \mid \cup\cup \mid -\cup$$
$$\overline{-\;\;-}\; \mid \overline{-\;\;-} \mid \overline{-\;\;-} \mid \overline{-\;\;-} \mid \quad\quad \mid \overline{-\;\;-}$$

(See the Examples, *a*, *b*, **476**.)

Note 1. A verse called Hypermeter (a syllable over-measure) is occasionally found, the syllable in excess being elided before the initial vowel of the next line:

Aerea | cui gradi | bus sur | gēbant | līmina | nexae | qu(e)
Aere tra | bēs ...

The Caesura by far most common in Dactylic Hexameters is that in the third foot (called Penthemimeral). It is generally strong, as in (*a*) after patulae, but occasionally weak, as in (*b*) after resonāre.

Next in importance is that in the fourth foot, called Hephthemimeral, which is sometimes the chief caesura of the verse: as

   (*c*) clāmō | res simul | horren | dōs ‖ ad | sīdera | tollit.

The Trihemimeral Caesura in the second foot often contributes to the rhythm usefully, as after clāmōrēs (*c*).

Note 2. Hemimeris means 'a half'. Hence 'Trihemimeral' means 'after three half-feet': clā-mō-rēs; 'Penthemimeral' means 'after five half-feet': hīc il-lum vī-dī; 'Hephthemimeral' means 'after seven half-feet': quam Iūnō fertur terrīs. (Two short syllables constitute one half-foot: Tǐt*yre* tū *patǔ*-lae *recǔ*bāns.)

The Heroic Measure of Epic poets, Virgil, Lucan, &c., consists of Dactylic Hexameters only.

78 *B.* **Dactylic Pentameter:**

This Verse consists of two parts, called Penthemimers, which are kept distinct. The first Penthemimer contains two feet (Dactyls or Spondees) and a long syllable. The second contains two feet (both Dactyls) and one further syllable.

Scheme

| 1 | 2 | | 1 | 2 | |

$$-\cup\cup \mid -\cup\cup \mid - \;\| \; -\cup\cup \mid -\cup\cup \mid -$$
$$\overline{-\;\;-}\; \mid \overline{-\;\;-}$$

Example

tū domi | nus tū | vir ‖ tū mihi | frāter e | rās.

This Verse is not used alone, but follows an Hexameter to form the **Elegiac Distich** (or Couplet):

Dōnec eris fēlīx, multōs numerābis amīcōs,
   Tempora sī fuerint nūbila, sōlus eris.

The chief Elegiac poets are Ovid, Tibullus, and Propertius.

479 *C.* **Iambic Trimeter** (as written by Horace):

This verse has three 'metres', each of two feet. Each foot may be an Iambus:

Suīs | et ip|sa Rō|ma vīribus | ruit.

But a Spondee may stand in the first, third, and fifth foot; and (rarely) a Dactyl or Anapaest in the first. A Tribrach sometimes takes the place of an Iambus, except in the last two feet.

Scheme

Examples

(a) lābun|tur al|tīs ‖ in|terim | rīpīs | aquae.
(b) Cānidi|a brevi|bus ‖ im|plicā|ta vī|perīs.
(c) positōs|que ver|nās ‖ dī|tis ex|āmen | domūs.

The usual Caesura is after the first syllable of the third foot. Another, less usual, is after the first syllable of the fourth foot; as,

Ibē|ricīs | perus|te ‖ fū|nibus | latus.

Horace sometimes uses this metre alone throughout a poem.

Note. The Iambic line of six feet called the Sēnārius, which is used by earlier writers like Plautus and Terence, admits many more licences than the Trimeter of Horace.

480 *D.* **Iambic Dimeter:**

This Verse is constituted like the first and third 'metres' of a Trimeter. It follows a Trimeter to form an Iambic Distich:

pater|na rū|ra bō|bus ex|ercet | suis,
solū|tus om|nī fae|nore.

481 *E.* **Lyric Stanzas:**

The lyric poets Horace and Catullus used many kinds of lyric stanza. But we shall notice here only the Sapphic and Alcaic Stanzas, each of four lines.

Note.—An Anacrusis is a short or long syllable (not necessarily a monosyllabic word), which introduces the scansion of a verse. It is analogous to an initial up-beat in music. Compare the English:

Anacrusis   1   2   3
O | Mari|on's a | bonnie | lass

1. The Sapphic Stanza:
This Stanza takes its name from Sappho, the Greek poetess who used, and perhaps invented it. It consists of three verses of this form:

Trochee   Spondee   Dactyl   Trochee   Trochee or Spondee

−∪ | −− | − ∪∪ | −∪ | −◡

followed by a verse called Adonius,

Dactyl   Trochee or Spondee

−∪∪ | −◡

1. Terru|it gen|tēs grave | nē re|dīret
2. Saecu|lum Pyr|rhae nova | mōnstra | questae
3. Omne | cum Prō|teus pecus | ēgit | altōs
4. Vīṣere | montēs.

Sappho often used a Trochee as the second foot; but Horace always uses a Spondee.
The strong Caesura in the Dactyl, after the fifth syllable of the line, is most frequent; but the weak Caesura after the sixth syllable of the line is occasionally used for variety.

Nōn semel dīcēmus ‖ Iō triumphe.

The Adonian verse is so closely united with the third line that Hiatus between a vowel at the end of this line and a vowel at the beginning of the Adonius is unusual. Words are sometimes divided between the two lines:

Thrāciō bacchante magis sub inter-
lūnia ventō.

Note. A Hypermeter (**477**, n. 1) also occurs:
Dissidēns plēbī numerō beātō | r(um)
Eximit virtūs.

---

483   **2. The Alcaic Stanza** (so named from the Greek poet, Alcaeus):

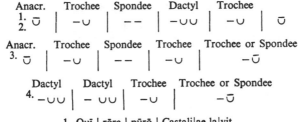

Anacr.   Trochee   Spondee   Dactyl   Trochee

1. 2. ◡ | −∪ | −− | −∪∪ | −∪ | ◡

Anacr.   Trochee   Spondee   Trochee   Trochee or Spondee

3. ◡ | −∪ | −− | −∪ | −◡

Dactyl   Dactyl   Trochee   Trochee or Spondee

4. −∪∪ | − ∪∪ | −∪ | −◡

1. Quī | rōre | pūrō | Castali|ae la|vit
2. Crī|nēs so|lūtōs | quī Lyci|ae te|net
3.   Dū|mēta | nātā|lemque | silvam
4.   Dēlius | et Pata|reus A|pollō

Rules for the Alcaic Stanza

(a) *First and Second Lines*

(1) The Anacrusis is rarely short.

(2) There is a Diaeresis between the Spondee and Dactyl: that is to say, the fifth syllable generally ends a word. An Elision often occurs before the sixth syllable: as

Quō Styx et invīs|(ī) horrida Taenarī.

(3) The fifth and the last syllables are rarely monosyllables.

(b) *Third Line*

(1) The Anacrusis is rarely short.

(2) The line rarely begins with a word of four syllables, and only when Elision follows: as

Fūnāli(a) et vectēs et arcūs.

It never begins with two dissyllables.

(3) The line does not end with a word of four syllables and rarely with two dissyllables.

(4) Monosyllables at the end of the line are rare. *Et* and *in*, with an Elision, occasionally are used at this place:

(*a*) Cum flōre Maecēnās rosār(um), et
(*b*) Incūde diffingās retūs(um) in

(c) *Fourth Line*

(1) A Diaeresis after *both* Dactyls is avoided.

(2) A weak Caesura in the second Dactyl is not common:

(*a*) Juppiter ipse ruēns tumultū.
(*b*) Stēsichorīque gravēs Camēnae.

Note. Hypermeters occur only twice in Horace:

(*a*) Sor exitūra, et nōs in aeter|n(um)
Exsili(um) impositūra cymbae.

(*b*) Cum pāce dēlābentis Etrus|c(um)
In mare.

But in the third and fourth books of Odes Horace avoids ending a verse with a vowel or m if the next verse in the same stanza begins with a vowel.

DERIVED AND COMPOUNDED WORDS

I. DERIVED SUBSTANTIVES

From the Verbal Roots:

-a, denoting the agent: scrība, *notary* (scrībō); advena, *new comer* (adveniō); convīva, *guest* (con-vīvō).

-or, abstract words denoting action or feeling: amor, *love* (amō); timor, *fear* (timeō); clāmor, *outcry* (clāmō); terror, *terror* (terreō).

-ium, denoting action or effect: gaudium, *joy* (gaudeō); ingenium, *mind* (ingignō); iūdicium, *judgment* (iūdicō).

-iēs, denoting a thing formed: faciēs, *face, form* (faciō); effigiēs, *likeness* (effingō); speciēs, *appearance* (-speciō); seriēs, *order* (serō).

-iō, denoting the result of an action: regiō, *region* (regō); legiō, *legion* (legō); opīniō, *opinion* (opīnor).

-men, denoting the instrument or the thing done: agmen, *column* (agō); tegmen, *covering* (tegō).

-mentum: documentum, *document* (doceō); īnstrūmentum, *instrument* (īnstruō).

-bulum, -brum, denoting the instrument or object: vocābulum, *name* (vocō); vēnābulum, *hunting-spear* (vēnor); flābrum, *blast* (flō, Stem flā-).

-culum, -crum: curriculum, *course* (currō); spectāculum, *spectacle* (spectō); sepulcrum, *tomb* (sepeliō).

85 From the Supine Stem:

-tor, -sor, denoting the agent: arātor, *ploughman* (arō); auctor, *author* (augeō); victor, *victor* (vincō); audītor, *hearer* (audiō); dictātor, *dictator* (dictō); spōnsor, *surety* (spondeō); cursor, *runner* (currō). A few Nouns in -tor form a feminine in -trīx, as victrīx.

-tus, -sus, denoting action: ēventus, *event* (ē-veniō); mōtus, *motion*, (moveō); sonitus, *sound* (sonō); cursus, *running* (currō); plausus, *clapping* (plaudō); lūsus, *game* (lūdō).

-tūra, -sūra, denoting function or result of action: dictātūra, *dictatorship* (dictō); cultūra, *culture* (colō); pictūra, *picture* (pingō); tōnsūra, *tonsure* (tondeō); caesūra, *dividing* (caedō).

-tiō, -siō, abstract: āctiō, *action* (agō); cōgitātiō, *thought* (cōgitō); relātiō, *relation* (referō); vīsiō, *sight* (videō); pēnsiō, *payment* (pendō).

486 Substantives derived from Adjectives:

-ia: memoria, *memory* (memor); concordia, *peace* (concors); sapientia, *wisdom* (sapiēns); dīvitiae, pl., *riches* (dīves).

-itia: laetitia, *joyfulness* (laetus); amīcitia, *friendship* (amīcus); mollitia, also mollitiēs, *softness* (mollis).

-tās: lībertās, *freedom* (līber); vēritās, *truth* (vērus); fēlīcitās, *happiness* (fēlīx).

-tūdō: fortitūdō, *valour* (fortis); multitūdō, *multitude* (multus).

-mōnia: ācrimōnia, *sharpness* (ācer); sānctimōnia, *sanctity* (sānctus); parcimōnia, *parsimony* (parcus).

487 Substantives derived from Substantives:

-tor: viātor, *traveller* (via); iānitor, *doorkeeper* (iānua); balneātor, *bathkeeper* (balneum). The feminine iānitrīx is used.

-ātus: senātus, *senate* (senex); magistrātus, *magistracy* (magister); cōnsulātus, *consulship* (cōnsul).

-iō, -ō: lūdiō, *player* (lūdus); pelliō, *furrier* (pellis); centuriō, *captain of a hundred* (centum, centuria); praedō, *robber* (praeda).

-ārius: aquārius, *water-carrier* (aqua); tabulārius, *registrary* (tabula). A secondary derivative is tabellārius, *letter-carrier* (tabella).

-ārium: grānārium, *granary* (grānum); tabulārium, *archives* (tabula).

-ētum, -tum: olīvētum, *olive-grove* (olīva); rosētum, *rose-garden* (rosa); arbustum, *shrubbery*; also the later form arborētum (stem arbos-, arbor-); salictum, *willow-ground* (salix).

-īna, -īnum: textrīna, *weaver's shop* (textor); pistrīnum, *bakehouse* (pistor).

-ulus, -olus, (-a, -um): ānulus, *little ring* (annus); gladiolus, *little sword* (gladius); fōrmula, *little form* (fōrma); līneola, *little line* (līnea); scūtulum, *little shield* (scūtum); palliolum, *little cloak* (pallium).

-ellus (-a, -um): agellus, *small field* (ager); fābella, *short story* (fābula); flagellum, *little whip* (flagrum); corōlla, *chaplet* (corōna).

-culus, (-a, -um): versiculus, *little verse* (versus); mātercula, *little mother* (māter); rēticulum, *little net* (rēte).

II. DERIVED ADJECTIVES

Adjectives derived from Verbal Roots:

-**āx**: audāx, *daring* (audeō); rapāx, *grasping* (rapiō); tenāx, *tenacious* (teneō); ferāx, *fruitful* (ferō).

-**bundus, -cundus**: furibundus, *raging* (furō); moribundus, *dying* (morior).

-**uus**: continuus, *continuous* (con-tineō); vacuus, *empty* (vacō); adsiduus, *persevering* (adsideō).

-**ulus**: tremulus, *trembling* (tremō); querulus, *complaining* (queror); crēdulus, *trustful* (crēdō).

-**idus, -idis**: calidus, *hot* (caleō); pavidus, *timid* (paveō); viridis, *green* (vireō).

-**ilis**: ūtilis, *useful* (ūtor); facilis, *easy* (faciō); docilis, *teachable* (doceō).

-**bilis**: penetrābilis, *penetrable* (penetrō), but sometimes active: penetrābile frīgus, *penetrating cold*; flēbilis, *lamentable* (fleō).

-**ivus**, joined to the Supine Stem: captīvus, *captive* (capiō): nātīvus, *native* (nāscor); fugitīvus, *fugitive* (fugiō).

9 Adjectives derived from Nouns, Adjectives, or Adverbs:

-**ius**: rēgius, *royal* (rēx); plēbēius, *plebeian* (plēbs); ēgregius, *out of the common* (grex).

-**icus**: bellicus, *warlike* (bellum); barbaricus, *barbarous* (barbarus); Gallicus, *Gaulish*; cīvicus, *civic* (cīvis).

-**ticus**: rūsticus, *belonging to the country* (rūs); domesticus, *domestic* (domus).

-**ānus, -iānus**: hūmānus, *human* (homō); urbānus, *urban* (urbs); Rōmānus, *Roman* (Rōma); Āfricānus, *African* (Āfer); praetōriānus, *praetorian* (praetor).

-**nus**: frāternus, *fraternal* (frāter); aeternus, *eternal* (aetās); alternus, *alternate* (alter).

-**inus**: marīnus, *marine* (mare); palātīnus, *belonging to the palace* (palātium).

-**estis**: caelestis, *heavenly* (caelum); agrestis, *rural* (ager).

-**ēnsis**: forēnsis, *belonging to the forum*; castrēnsis, *belonging to the camp* (castra).

-**ālis, -āris** (see 20b): nātūrālis, *natural* (nātūra); generālis, *general* (genus); rēgālis, *kingly* (rēx); vulgāris, *common* (vulgus); salūtāris, *healthful* (salūs).

-**ōsus**: fōrmōsus, *beautiful* (fōrma); glōriōsus, *glorious* (glōria).

-**lentus**: fraudulentus, *deceitful* (fraus); turbulentus, *noisy* (turba).

-**bris, -cris**: fūnebris, *funereal* (fūnus): mediocris, *middling* (medius).

-**eus**: aureus, *golden* (aurum): ferreus, *iron* (ferrum).

-**ulus**: parvulus, *very small* (parvus).

-**ellus**: misellus, *poor* (miser).

-tus: modestus, *moderate* (modus); rōbustus, *strong* (rōbur); vetustus, *aged* (vetus).

III. DERIVED VERBS

490 Verbs derived from Nouns or Adjectives

Ā-Stems cūrō, *take care* (cūra); onerō, *burden* (onus); pācō, *pacify* (pāx). **Deponents:** moror, *delay* (mora); dignor, *deem worthy* (dignus); miseror, *pity* (miser).

Ē-Stems flōreō, *bloom* (flōs); flāveō, *am yellow* (flāvus).

U-Stems metuō, *fear* (metus); minuō, *diminish* (minus).

I-Stems fīniō, *limit* (fīnis); serviō, *am a slave* (servus); largior, *bestow* (largus).

IV. VERBS COMPOUNDED WITH PREPOSITIONS

491 ā, ab, abs-
ā-vertō, *turn away*; ab-sum, *am absent*; abs-terreō, *frighten away*.

ad
ad-eō, *go to*; ad-spiciō, *look at*; accipiō, *accept*; adferō, *carry to*; adsentior, *agree*; adloquor, *address*; appōnō, *place near*; arripiō, *seize*; attrahō, *attract*.

ambi-
amb-iō, *go around*.

con
con-trahō, *contract*; compōnō, *compose*; committō, *commit*; colligō, *collect*; corripiō, *seize violently*; cōnfīdō, *rely on*.

dē
dē-cēdō, *depart*; dēcipiō, *deceive*; dēscendō, *come down*.

ē, ex
ē-dūcō, *lead forth*; ē-loquor, *utter*; ē-vocō, *evoke*; effundō, *pour out*; ex-eō, *go forth*; ex-pellō, *expel*.

in
in-ferō, *bring into*; imperō, *command* (*cf.* parō); immineō, *overhang*; inligō, *bind on*; irrigō, *water*; indūrō, *make hard*.

inter
inter-sum, *am among*; interrogō, *question*; intellegō, *understand*.

ob
ob-tineō, *maintain*; offerō, *offer*; oppōnō, *oppose*; occurrō, *meet, occur*.

per
per-mittō, *let go, permit*; pereō, *perish*; pellūceō, *shine through, am transparent*; perterreō, *frighten greatly*.

post
post-pōnō, *put after*.

prae
prae-cēdō, *go before*; praeferō, *prefer*; praestō, *excel*.

praeter:
praeter-eō, *pass by*.

prō:
prō-cēdō, *proceed*; prō-pōnō, *propose*; prōmō, *produce*.

red-, re-:
red-eō, *return*; re-cordor, *remember*; re-ferō, *refer*; restituō, *restore*.

sē-:
sē-cernō, sē-parō, *separate*; sē-clūdō, *shut up, seclude*.

sub:
sub-dō, *subdue*; sub-mergō, *submerge*; suc-currō, *succour*; suf-ferō, *suffer*; sug-gerō, *suggest*; sup-plicō, *supplicate*; sur-ripiō, *steal*; suspiciō, *look up at, suspect*.

trāns, trā-:
trāns-mittō, *transmit*; trāns-portō, *transport*; trādūcō, *lead across*; trāiciō, *throw across*.

A few Verbs are compounded with Adverbs, as:

benedīcō, *commend* (bene dīcō); benefaciō, *benefit* (bene faciō).
maledīcō, *speak ill (of)* (male dīcō); malefaciō, *do evil (to)* (male faciō).
satisfaciō, *satisfy* (satis faciō); satisdō, *give bail* (satis dō).

The following are a few specimens of compound words:

Noun and Verb

auceps, *birdcatcher* (avis avi-, capiō).
agricola, *husbandman* (ager agro-, colō).
fidicen, *lute-player* ⎰ fidēs ⎱
tībīcen, *flute-player* ⎨ tībia ⎬canō
tubicen, *trumpeter* ⎱ tuba ⎰
artifex, *artisan* (ars, arti-, faciō).
Lūcifer, *morning star* (lūx lūc-, ferō); frūgifer, -a, -um, *fruit-bearing* (frūg-ferō).
Graiugena, *Greek* (Graius Graio-, gignō).
armiger, *armour-bearer* (arma, gerō).
iūsiūrandum, *oath* (iūs-, iūrō).

Two Substantives, or Substantive and Adjective

paterfamiliās, *father of a family* (pater, familiās, an old genitive).
rēspūblica, *state, republic* (rēs, pūblicus).
bipēs, *two-footed* (bis, pēs).
tridēns, *three-pronged, trident* (trēs, dēns).

ROMAN MONEY, WEIGHTS, MEASURES AND TIME

493   MONEY

(a) The Ās, *unit*, of money was the Lībra, or pound of 12 ounces (ūnciae).

Ūncia	= 1 oz. or $\frac{1}{12}$ of the Ās.			Septūnx	=	7 oz. or $\frac{7}{12}$ of tne Ās.	
Sextāns	= 2	,,	$\frac{1}{6}$,,	Bēs	= 8	,,	$\frac{2}{3}$,,
Quadrāns	= 3	,,	$\frac{1}{4}$,,	Dōdrāns	= 9	,,	$\frac{3}{4}$,,
Triēns	= 4	,,	$\frac{1}{3}$,,	Dēxtāns	= 10	,,	$\frac{5}{6}$,,
Quīncūnx	= 5	,,	$\frac{5}{12}$,,	Deūnx	= 11	,,	$\frac{11}{12}$,,
Sēmissis	= 6	,,	$\frac{1}{2}$,,				

(b) Ūnciae ūsūrae = $\frac{1}{12}$ per cent per month = 1 per cent per annum.
Sextantēs ūsūr. = $\frac{1}{6}$,,   ,,   = 2   ,,   ,,
&c.   &c.   &c.

Assēs ūsūrae   = 1 per cent per month = 12 per cent per annum.
Assēs ūsūrae were also called centēnsimae: bīnae centēnsimae = 2 per cent
per month = 24 per cent per ann.   Ūnciārium faenus was 1 ūncia yearly per ās.

(c) Hērēs ex asse .   .   . means heir to the whole estate.
Hērēs ex sēmisse, or   .⎫ ,,   heir to $\frac{1}{2}$ of the estate.
Hērēs ex dīmidiā parte   .⎭
&c.   &c.

(d) The Sēstertius, *Sesterce* (= sēmis tertius, *the third half*, i.e. 2$\frac{1}{2}$), was a
silver coin equal to 2$\frac{1}{2}$ assēs, being $\frac{1}{4}$ of the Dēnārius (coin of 10 assēs). Its symbol
is HS. (for IIS., duo et sēmis, 2$\frac{1}{2}$ assēs).

The Sēstertium (originally a gen. pl. of sēstertius depending on mīlle) was not a
coin, but a sum of 1,000 sēstertiī (= £8 approx.).

Sēstertia, the Plural (also represented by HS.), joined with the Distributive
Numbers denotes so many 1,000 sēstertiī.

Sēstertium joined with Numeral Adverbs (and omitting centēna mīlia) denotes
so many 100,000 sēstertiī.

Thus HS.X = Sēstertiī decem, 10 sesterces.
       HS.$\overline{\text{X}}$ = Sēstertia dēna, 10,000 sesterces.
       $\overline{\text{HS.X}}$ = Sēstertium deciēns, 1,000,000 sesterces.

(e) Apart from the use of ūncia, sextāns, &c., fractions might also be expressed by the Ordinals as Denominators with the Cardinals for Numerators (above 1). Thus, $\frac{1}{2}$ is *dīmidia pars*; $\frac{1}{3}$ *tertia pars*, &c.; $\frac{1}{6}$ *sexta* or *dīmidia tertia* ($\frac{1}{2} \times \frac{1}{3}$); $\frac{1}{8}$ *octāva pars* or *dīmidia quārta* ($\frac{1}{2} \times \frac{1}{4}$), &c. So $\frac{1}{21}$ was *tertia septima* ($\frac{1}{3} \times \frac{1}{7}$). Again, $\frac{2}{3}$ is either *duae tertiae*, or *duae partēs*, or *dīmidia et sexta* ($\frac{1}{2} + \frac{1}{6} = \frac{2}{3}$). And $\frac{3}{4}$ is *trēs quārtae*, or *trēs partēs*, or *dīmidia et quārta* ($\frac{1}{2} + \frac{1}{4} = \frac{3}{4}$).

WEIGHT

The unit of 'ās' of weight also was the 'lībra', or Roman pound (perhaps the weight which a man could support on his hand horizontally extended). It was divided duodecimally, the 'ūncia' (*ounce*) being its 12th part; the 'scrīpulum' (*scruple*) the 24th part of an ūncia. The lībra was a little less than 12 oz. Avoirdupois.

LENGTH

The unit or 'ās' of length was the 'pēs' (*foot*), also divided duodecimally, the 'ūncia' (*inch*) being its 12th part.

'Cubitum' (*cubit*) was 1$\frac{1}{2}$ pedēs. 'Ulna' (*ell*) was variously measured, sometimes = cubit. Land was measured out by the 'decempeda' (rod of 10 pedēs). In roads the unit was 'passus', a pace or double step (5 pedēs). Mīlle passūs (1,000 paces) were the Roman mile, $\frac{1}{8}$ of which was called 'stadium' (*furlong*). The pēs was a little less than the English foot.

SURFACE

The 'ās' of surface was 'iūgerum' (the Roman acre), about $\frac{5}{8}$ of an English acre. 'Scrīpulum', or 'decempeda quadrāta' (ten square feet) was its most important subdivision.

CAPACITY

1. Liquid measure:
The 'ās' was 'sextārius' (less than a pint), divided into 12 'cyathī'. 24 sextāriī were 1 'urna', and 2 urnae were an 'amphora', a vessel of 10 cubic Roman feet.
2. Dry measure:
Here too the 'ās' was 'sextārius' and the 'cyathus' its 'ūncia'; 16 sextāriī made the 'modius', which approached 2 gallons English ($\frac{1}{4}$ bushel).

TIME—THE ROMAN CALENDAR

Every Roman month had three chief days: Kalendae (Calends), Nōnae (Nones), Īdūs (Ides). The Calends were always the 1st day of the month; the Nones were usually on the 5th; the Ides on the 13th; but in four months the Nones were on the 7th, the Ides on the 15th.

March, May, July, October; these are they
Make Nones the 7th, Ides the 15th day.

These three days, the Calends, Nones, and Ides, were taken as points from which the other days were counted backwards. That is, the Romans did not say, such and such a day *after*, &c., but such and such a day *before* the Calends, or Nones, or Ides. They reckoned inclusively, counting in the days at both ends; therefore the rules are: (1) For days before the Calends subtract the day of the month from the number of days in the month increased by two. (2) For days before the Nones or Ides subtract from the day on which they fall, increased by one.

Examples.—May 31, Prīdiē Kalendās Iūniās.

",, 30, Ante diem tertium (a.d. III) Kal. Iūn.
",, 11, ", ", quīntum (a.d. V) Īd. Mai.
",, 2, ", ", sextum (a.d. VI) Nōn. Mai.

English Month	MĀRTIUS, MĀIUS, IŪLIUS, OCTŌBER, 31 Days	IANUĀRIUS, AUGUSTUS, DECEMBER, 31 Days	APRĪLIS, IŪNIUS, SEPTEMBER, NOVEMBER, 30 Days	FEBRUĀRIUS, 28 Days—in every fourth Year 29
1	Kalendīs	Kalendīs	Kalendīs	Kalendīs
2	a.d. VI	a.d. IV	a.d. IV	a.d. IV
3	a.d. V	a.d. III	a.d. III	a.d. III
4	a.d. IV	Prīdiē	Prīdiē	Prīdiē
5	a.d. III	Nōnīs	Nōnis	Nōnis
6	Prīdiē	a.d. VIII	a.d. VIII	a.d. VIII
7	Nōnīs	a.d. VII	a.d. VII	a.d. VII
8	a.d. VIII	a.d. VI	a.d. VI	a.d. VI
9	a.d. VII	a.d. V	a.d. V	a.d. V
10	a.d. VI	a.d. IV	a.d. IV	a.d. IV
11	a.d. V	a.d. III	a.d. III	a.d. III
12	a.d. IV	Prīdiē	Prīdiē	Prīdiē
13	a.d. III	Īdibus	Īdibus	Īdibus
14	Prīdiē	a.d. XIX	a.d. XVIII	a.d. XVI
15	Īdibus	a.d. XVIII	a.d. XVII	a.d. XV
16	a.d. XVII	a.d. XVII	a.d. XVI	a.d. XIV
17	a.d. XVI	a.d. XVI	a.d. XV	a.d. XIII
18	a.d. XV	a.d. XV	a.d. XIV	a.d. XII
19	a.d. XIV	a.d. XIV	a.d. XIII	a.d. XI
20	a.d. XIII	a.d. XIII	a.d. XII	a.d. X
21	a.d. XII	a.d. XII	a.d. XI	a.d. IX
22	a.d. XI	a.d. XI	a.d. X	a.d. VIII
23	a.d. X	a.d. X	a.d. IX	a.d. VII
24	a.d. IX	a.d. IX	a.d. VIII	a.d. VI
25	a.d. VIII	a.d. VIII	a.d. VII	a.d. V
26	a.d. VII	a.d. VII	a.d. VI	a.d. IV
27	a.d. VI	a.d. VI	a.d. V	a.d. III
28	a.d. V	a.d. V	a.d. IV	Prīdiē
29	a.d. IV	a.d. IV	a.d. III	
30	a.d. III	a.d. III	Prīdiē	
31	Prīdiē	Prīdiē		

(In Leap-year Feb. 24th (a.d. VI Kal. Mārt.) was twice reckoned—hence this day was called DIES BISSEXTUS, and Leap-year itself ANNUS BISSEXTUS.)

Note 1. Ante diem tertium (a.d. III) Kal. Iūn., means 'on the third day before the Kalends of June', *i.e.* 'before the Kalends of June by three days'. Diem tertium, being placed between ante and Kalendās, instead of being an Abl. of Measure (**244, 280**), is attracted to the Accusative Case. This mode of expression became so purely idiomatic that it was used with Prepositions: *ex* ante diem tertium.

Note 2. The names of the months are adjectives (used in agreement with mēnsis etc.; see **73**, *Note* 2): Iānuārius, Aprīlis, September, &c. The old names of July and August were Quintīlis, Sextīlis, but later they were called Iūlius and Augustus after the two Caesars.

Note 3. In dates prīdiē, *the day before*, is joined with the accusative.

ABBREVIATIONS

(1) PRAENOMINA

A. Aulus	M. Mārcus	S. (Sex.) Sextus
C. Gaius	M'. Mānius	Ser. Servius
Cn. Gnaeus	Mam. Māmercus	Sp. Spurius
D. Decimus	P. Pūblius	T. Titus
K. Kaesō	Q. Quīntus	Ti. (Tib.) Tiberius
L. Lūcius		

Note. A Roman of distinction had at least three names: the Praenōmen, individual name; the Nōmen, name showing the Gēns or clan; and the Cognōmen, surname showing the Familia or family. Thus, Lūcius Iūnius Brūtus expressed Lūcius of the Gēns Iūnia and Familia Brūtōrum. To these were sometimes added one or more Agnōmina, titles either of honour (as Āfricānus, Macedonicus, Magnus, &c.), or expressing that a person had been adopted from another Gēns: as Aemiliānus, applied to the younger Scīpiō Āfricānus, who was the son of L. Aemilius Paulus, but adopted by a Scīpiō. The full name of the emperor Augustus (originally an Octāvius) after he had been adopted by his uncle's will and adorned by the Senate with a title of honour, was Gaius Iūlius Caesar Octāviānus Augustus.

(2) VARIA

A. D. Ante diem	HS. Sēstertius, Sēstertium	P. M. Pontifex Maximus
A. U. C. Annō urbis conditae	Id. Īdūs	P. R. Populus Rōmānus
Aed. Aedīlis	Imp. Imperātor	Pl. Plēbis
Cos. Cōnsul	Kal. Kalendae	Proc. Prōcōnsul
Coss. Cōnsulēs	L. Lībra	S. Senātus
D. Dīvus	LL. Dupondius	S. P. Q. R. Senātus Populusque Rōmānus
Des. Dēsignātus	Non. Nōnae	S. C. Senātūscōnscultum
Eq. Rom. Eques Rōmānus	O. M. Optimus Maximus	S. D. P. Salūtem dīcit plūrimam
F. Fīlius	P. C. Patrēs Cōnscrīptī	Tr. Tribūnus

8

FIGURES OF SPEECH

OR PECULIAR FORMS FOUND IN SYNTAX AND IN RHETORIC

501   FIGURES OF SYNTAX

Ellipsis (*omission*)—Words are omitted which can be supplied from the context. Thus are used:

    (1) An Adjective without its Substantive: Gelida, calida (aqua): dextra, sinistra (manus).

    (2) A Genitive without the word on which it depends: Caecilia Metellī (fīlia), Faustus Sullae (fīlius).

    (3) A Verb without its Object: obīre (mortem); movēre (castra).

    (4) A Sentence without its Verb: Suus cuique mōs. Quid multa (dīcam)?

Pleonasmus (*redundance*)—Use of needless words: Sīc ōre locūta est.

Zeugma, Syllepsis—Connexion of a Verb or Adjective with two words or clauses to both of which it does not equally belong; therefore Zeugma is a sort of Ellipsis: Ex spoliīs et torquem et cognōmen induit; *put on the necklace and* (*assumed*) *the surname*. Agreement with one only of two or more Subjects is also called Zeugma.

Synesis—Agreement with meaning not with form:

    1. Gender: Capita coniūrātiōnis virgīs caesī sunt. LIVY. Capita (= *chief men*) though Neuter in form, is Masculine in meaning; hence caesī.

    2. Number: A Collective Noun or a Phrase implying more than one, though Singular in form, may take a Plural Verb: Cētera classis . . . fūgērunt. LIVY. Optimus quisque iussīs pāruēre. TACITUS.

Attraction—Words are drawn by the influence of others to take irregular constructions: (1) attraction of Copulative Verb (**196a**); (2) attraction of Antecedent and of Adjective to Relative Clause (**331–2**). Attraction of Case happens after Copulative Verbs, especially the Dative (**224,** n.), and especially with licet esse: Vōbīs licet esse beātīs. HORACE. Licuit esse ōtiōsō Themistoclī. CICERO.

Asyndeton—Omission of Conjunctions: Abiit, excessit, ēvāsit, ērūpit. CICERO.

Polysyndeton—Redundance of Conjunctions: Ūnā Eurusque Notusque ruunt crēberque procellīs Āfricus. VIRGIL.

Hendiadys—Use of two Substantives coupled by a Conjunction for a Substantive and Adjective: Paterīs lībāmus et aurō (for paterīs aureīs). VIRGIL.

Hyperbaton—Alternation of natural order of words: Per tē deōs ōrō (for per deōs tē ōrō). The four following figures belong to Hyperbaton:

(1) **Anacoluthon**—Passing from one construction to another before the former is completed: Sī, ut Graecī dīcunt, omnēs aut Graiōs esse aut barbarōs, vereor nē Rōmulus barbarōrum rēx fuerit. CICERO (for Graī sunt aut barbarī).

(2) **Hysteron-proteron**—When, of two things, that which naturally comes first is placed last: Moriāmur et in media arma ruāmus. VIRGIL.

(3) **Anastrophe**—Placing a Preposition after its Case: quōs inter for inter quōs. HORACE.

(4) **Parenthesis**—Interpolation of one sentence within another: At tū (nam dīvum servat tūtēla poētās), praemoneō, vātī parce, puella, sacrō. TIBULLUS.

Tmesis—Separation of the parts of a compound word: Quae mē cumque vocant terrae. VIRGIL (for quaecumque).

Enallage—Use of one word for another:

(1) One Part of Speech for another: aliud crās (alius diēs crāstinus).

(2) One Case for another: Mātūtīne pater, seu Iāne libentius audīs. HORACE (for Iānus).

(3) One Number for another: nōs for ego; mīles for mīlitēs.

Hypallage—Interchange of Cases: Dare classibus Austrōs. VIRGIL (for dare classēs Austrīs). Also attraction of Adjectives to Substantives to which they do not properly belong: Fontium gelidae perennitātēs. CICERO (for fontium gelidōrum perennitātēs).

02

FIGURES OF RHETORIC

Metaphora—One expression put for another which has some resemblance to it, generally a concrete for an abstract; portus for refugium; sentīna (*dregs*) reīpūblicae for turpissimī cīvēs; exsultō for gaudeō. A strong metaphor is often qualified by quasi, tamquam, quīdam, or ut ita dīcam: In ūnā philosophiā quasi tabernāculum vītae suae allocārunt. CICERO. Scōpās, ut ita dīcam, mihi videntur dissolvere. CICERO (untie a broom = create disorder).

Metonymia—A related word conveying the same idea is put for another. Mārs for bellum; cēdant arma togae (CIC.) for cēdat bellum pācī; iuventūs for iuvenēs; Graecia for Graecī; aurum for vāsa aurea.

Synecdoche—The part stands for the whole: Caput for homō; tēctum for domus; carīna for nāvis.

Allegoria—A chain of metaphors:
Claudite iam rīvōs, puerī, sat prāta bibērunt. VIRGIL.
Cease to sing, shepherds, recreation enough has been taken.

Hyperbole—Exaggeration.

Litotes—Less is said than is meant: Nōn laudō for culpō.

Ironia—One thing is said but will be understood to mean the contrary: Ēgregiam vērō laudem et spolia ampla refertis tūque puerque tuus. VIRGIL (*ignoble praise* and *paltry spoils*).

Climax—A high point of effect led up to gradually: Quod libet iīs, licet; quod licet, possunt; quod possunt, audent. CICERO.

Polyptoton—Cases of the same Noun are brought together: Iam clipeus clipeīs, umbōne repellitur umbō; ēnse mināx ēnsis, pede pēs et cuspide cuspis. STATIUS.

Paronomasia—A play upon the sound of words: Tibi parāta sunt verba, huic verbera. TERENCE.

Antithesis—Contrast of opposites: Urbis amātōrem Fuscum salvēre iubēmus rūris amātōrēs. HORACE.

Oxymoron—Union of seeming contraries: Temporis angustī mānsit concordia discors. LUCAN. Splendidē mendāx. HORACE.

Periphrasis—Description of a simple fact by various attending circumstances. Instead of 'Now night is approaching', Virgil says 'Et iam summa procul vīllārum culmina fūmant, maiōrēsque cadunt altīs dē montibus umbrae'. See the beautiful periphrases of old age and death in Ecclesiastes, ch. xii.

Simile—Illustration of a statement by an apt comparison, as: Per urbēs Hannibal Italās ceu flamma per taedās vel Eurus per Siculās equitāvit undās. HORACE.

Apostrophe—An appeal to some person or thing: Quid nōn mortālia pectora cōgis, aurī sacra famēs? VIRGIL.

Aposiopesis—The conclusion of a thought is suppressed: Quōs ego ... sed mōtōs praestat compōnere flūctūs. VIRGIL.

Prosopopoeia—Personification. An abstract idea, as faith, hope, youth, memory, fortune, is addressed or spoken of as a person: Tā Spēs et albō rāra Fidēs colit vēlāta pannō. HORACE.

MEMORIAL LINES ON THE GENDER OF LATIN SUBSTANTIVES

3 I. General Rules.
The Gender of a Latin Noun
by meaning, form, or use is shown.

1. A Man, a name of People and a Wind,
River and Mountain, Masculine we find:
Rōmulus, Hispānī, Zephyrus, Cōcȳtus, Olympus.

2. A Woman, Island, Country, Tree,
and City, Feminine we see:
Pēnelopē, Cyprus, Germānia, laurus, Athēnae.

3. To Nouns that cannot be declined
The Neuter Gender is assigned:
Examples fās and nefās give
And the Verb-Noun Infinitive:
Est summum nefās fallere:
Deceit is gross impiety.

Common are: sacerdōs, dux,	*priest (priestess), leader*
vātēs, parēns et coniūnx,	*seer, parent, wife (husband)*
cīvis, comes, custōs, vindex,	*citizen, companion, guard, avenger*
adulēscēns, īnfāns. index,	*youth (maid), infant, informer*
iūdex, testis, artifex,	*judge, witness, artist*
praesul, exsul, opifex,	*director, exile, worker*
hērēs, mīles, incola,	*heir (heiress), soldier, inhabitant*
auctor, augur, advena,	*author, augur, new-comer*
hostis, obses, praeses, āles,	*enemy, hostage, president, bird*
patruēlis et satelles,	*cousin, attendant*
mūniceps et interpres,	*burgess, interpreter*
iuvenis et antistes,	*young person, overseer*
aurīga, prīnceps: add to these	*charioteer, chief*
bōs, damma, talpa, serpēns, sūs,	*ox (cow), deer, mole, serpent, swine*
camēlus. canis, tigris, perdix, grūs.	*camel, dog, tiger, partridge, crane*

(For exceptions see p. 15.)

504 II. Special Rules for the Declensions.
Decl. 1 (Ā-Stems).

Rule.—Feminine in First *a*, *ē*,
Masculine *ās*, *ēs* will be.

Exc.   Nous denoting Males in *a*
are by meaning *Māscula*:
and Masculine is found to be
Hadria, *the Adriatic Sea.*

505   Dec. 2 (O-Stems).

Rule.—O-nouns in us and er become
Masculine, but Neuter um.

Exc.   Feminine are found in *us*,
alvus, Arctus, carbasus,   *paunch, Great Bear, linen*
colus, humus, pampinus,   *distaff, ground, vine-leaf*
vannus: also trees, as pirus;   *winnowing-fan, pear-tree*
with some jewels, as sapphīrus;   *sapphire*
Neuter pelagus and vīrus.   *sea, poison*
Vulgus Neuter commonly,   *common people*
rarely Masculine we see.

506   Decl. 3 (Consonant and I-Stems).

Rule 1.—Third-Nouns Masculine prefer
endings *ō*, *or*, *ŏs*, and *er*;
add to which the ending *ēs*,
if its Cases have increase.

Exc. (*a*) Feminine exceptions show
Substantives in *dō* and *gō*.
But ligō, ōrdō, praedō, cardō,   *spade, order, pirate, hinge*
Masculine, and Common margō.   *margin*

   (*b*) Abstract Nouns in *iō* call
Fēminina, one and all:
Masculine will only be
things that you may touch or see,
(as curculiō, vespertīliō,   *weevil, bat*
pugiō, scīpiō, and pāpiliō)   *dagger, staff, butterfly*
with the Nouns that number show,
such as terniō, sēniō.   3, 6

   (*c*) Ēchō Feminine we name: *echo*
carō (carnis) is the same.   *flesh*

(*d*) Aequor, marmor, cor decline   *sea, marble, heart*
    Neuter; arbor Feminine.   *tree*

(*e*) Of the Substantives in ŏs,
    Feminine are cōs and dōs;   *whetstone, dowry*
    while, of Latin Nouns, alone
    Neuter are os (ossis), *bone*
    and ōs (ōris), *mouth*: a few
    Greek in os are Neuter too.*

(*f*) Many Neuters end in *er*,
    siler, acer, verber, vēr,   *withy, maple, stripe, spring*
    tūber, über, and cadāver,   *hump, udder, carcase*
    piper, iter, and papāver.   *pepper, journey, poppy*

(*g*) Feminine are compēs, teges,   *fetter, mat*
    mercēs, merges, quiēs, seges,   *fee, sheaf, rest, corn*
    though their Cases have increase:
    with the Neuters reckon aes.   *copper*

507 Rule 2.—Third Nouns Feminine we class
    ending *is*, *x*, *aus*, and *ās*,
    s to consonant appended,
    ēs in flexion unextended.

Exc. (*a*) Many Nouns in *is* we find
    to the Masculine assigned:
    amnis, axis, caulis, collis,   *river, axle, stalk, hill*
    clūnis, crīnis, fascis, follis,   *hind-leg, hair, bundle, bellows*
    fūstis, ignis, orbis, ēnsis,   *bludgeon, fire, orb, sword*
    pānis, piscis, postis, mēnsis,   *bread, fish, post, month*
    torris, unguis, and canālis,   *stake, nail, canal*
    vectis, vermis, and nātālis,   *lever, worm, birthday*
    sanguis, pulvis, cucumis,   *blood, dust, cucumber*
    lapis, cassēs, Mānēs, glīs.   *stone, nets, ghosts, dormouse*

(*b*) Chiefly Masculine we find,
    sometimes Feminine declined,
    callis, sentis, fūnis, fīnis,   *path, thorn, rope, end*
    and in poets torquis, cinis.   *necklace, cinder*

(*c*) Masculine are most in *ex*:
    Feminine are forfex, lēx,   *shears, law*
    nex, supellex: Common, pūmex,   *death, furniture, pumice*
    imbrex, ŏbex, silex, rumex.   *tile, bolt, flint, sorrel*

* As melos, *melody*, epos, *epic poem*.

(d) Add to Masculines in *ix*,
fornix, phoenix, and calix.   *arch, —, cup*

(e) Masculine are adamās,   *adamant*
elephās, mās, gigās, ās: *elephant, male, giant, as*
vas (vadis) Masculine is known,   *surety*
vās (vāsis) is a Neuter Noun.   *vessel*

(f) Masculine are fōns and mōns,   *fountain, mountain*
chalybs, hydrōps, gryps, and pōns,   *iron, dropsy, griffin, bridge*
rudēns, torrēns, dēns, and cliēns,   *cable, torrent, tooth, client*
fractions of the ās, as triēns.   *four ounces*
Add to Masculines tridēns,   *trident*
oriēns, and occidēns,   *east, west*
bidēns (*fork*): but bidēns (*sheep*)
with the Feminines we keep.

(g) Masculine are found in *es*
verrēs and acīnacēs.   *boar, scimitar*

508 Rule 3.—Third-Nouns Neuter end *a, e,*
ar, ur, us, c, l, n, and *t.*

Exc. (a) Masculine are found in *ur*
furfur, turtur, vultur, fūr.   *bran, turtle-dove, vulture, thief*

(b) Feminine in *ūs* a few
keep, as virtūs, the long *ū*:   *virtue*
servitūs, iuventūs, salūs,   *slavery, youth, safety*
senectūs, tellūs, incūs, palūs.   *old age, earth, anvil, marsh*

(e) Also pecus (pecudis)   *beast*
Feminine in Gender is.

(d) Masculine appear in *us*
lepus (leporis) and mūs.   *hare, mouse*

(e) Masculines in *l* are mūgil,   *mullet*
cōnsul, sāl, and sōl, with pugil.   *consul, salt, sun, boxer*

(f) Masculine are rēn and splēn,   *kidney, spleen*
pecten, delphīn, attagēn.   *comb, dolphin, grouse*

(g) Feminine are found in *ōn*
Gorgōn, sindōn, halcyōn.   *Gorgon, muslin, king-fisher*

509   Decl. 4 (U-Stems).

Rule.—Masculines end in *us*: a few
are Neuter nouns, that end in *ū.*

Exc. Women and trees are Feminine,
with acus, domus, and manus,   *needle, house, hand,*
tribus, Īdūs, porticus.   *tribe, the Ides, porch*

Decl. 5 (Ē-Stems).

Rule.—Feminine are Fifth in *ēs*,
Except merīdiēs and diēs   *noon, day*

Exc. Diēs in the Singular
Common we define:
But its Plural cases are
always Masculine (*cf.* **57**).

List of Prepositions

With Accusative:

Ante, apud, ad, adversus,
Clam, circum, circā, citrā, cis,
Contrā, inter, ergā, extrā,
Īnfrā, intrā, iuxtā, ob,
Penes, pōne, post, and praeter.

Prope, propter, per, secundum,
Suprā, versus, ultrā, trāns;
Add super, subter, sub and in,
When '*motion*' 'tis, not '*state*', they
mean.

With Ablative:

Ā, ab, absque, cōram, dē,
Palam, cum, and ex, and ē,
Sine, tenus, prō, and prae:

Add super, subter, sub and in,
When '*state*', not '*motion*', 'tis they
mean.

Note. Clam, *secretly*, and palam, *openly*, are used by classical prose writers mainly as adverbs, very rarely indeed as prepositions.

8*

INDEX I

SUBJECTS

(The reference is to Sections)

INDEX II

LATIN WORDS

(The reference is to Sections)

AM

amplius, 314
an-, 175
an, 405, 405 (n. 2), 472
anas, 37, 473
Anchīsēs, 473
animal, 47
animī (loc.), 246 (n. 1)
anne, 405, 406
an nōn, 405, 406
annus, 12 (2), 12 (3), 35a
ānser, 37
ante, 168, 172, 285
antequam, 178, 431
antīquus, 82 (n.)
apage, 142b
aperiō, 155
apis, 49
appāret, 146
appāreō, 187
appellor, 187
Aprīlis, 73 (n. 2)
aptus, 217 (n. 2)
apud, 172, 285
aquila, 31e
Arbēla, 31c
arbiter, 31d
arbitra, 31d
arbor, 51
arbōs, 41 (n. 2)
arceō, 153 (n. 1)
arcessō, 154c
arctus, 35a
arcus, 55 (n. 3)
ārdeō, 153, 153 (n. 3)
arguō, 154f, 208 (n. 3)
ariēs, 473
-āris, 20b
arma, 60
armiger, 35a (n. 2)
ars, 46, 48
artūs (plur.), 55 (n. 3), 60
arx, 46
ās, 41 (n. 1), 52, 493
asper, 71
ast, 177
at, 177, 442 (n. 4), 472
at enim, 177
Athēnae, 34 (n. 2), 60
atque, cf. ac
atquī, 177
Atrīdēs, 67
attamen, 177
attinet, 146, 293
-au-, 12 (2)

AUC

auceps, 12 (1), 12 (2), 37, 40
audācter, 85a, 85b
audāx, 76, 85a, 85b
audeō, 127, 158, 369
audiō, 113, 119, 123, 147, 150, 151, 187
augeō, 153
Augustus (mēnsis), 73 (n. 2)
aurum, 59
aut, 177, 179, 400 (n. 1)
autem, 177, 400 (n. 2, 3)
auxilior, 216
auxilium, 61
avē, 142b
avis, 44
axis, 54

baccar, 47 (n.)
Bacchanālia, 60
baculus, 63
bellum, 35a, 246, 356 (n. 3)
bene, 17, 86, 473
bene-, 220
beneficus, 81
benevolus, 81
bēs, 493
bibō, 154e
bidēns, 54
bīnī, 313 (n. 2)
bis, 472
bonitās, 12 (1)
bonus, 71, 80a
Boreās, 31c
bōs, 50
Būcolica, 68

-c, 96 (n. 3)
cadāver, 51
cadō, 150, 154d, 471
caedō, 154d
caelebs, 75
caelum, 59
calcar, 47
caleō, 149
calēscō, 149
calix, 52
callis, 54
campester, 73
canālis, 54

CIR

Canēphoroe, 68
canis, 31e, 37, 44 (n. 3), 49
canō, 24 (n.), 150, 154d
capessō, 154c
capiō, 133, 149, 151, 154g
caput, 37, 39, 53
carbasus, 35a
carcer, 42
cardō, 52
careō, 229
carmen, 43
carō, 37, 51
carpō, 150, 154a
Carthāgō, 50 (n.), 246
cassēs, 54
castra, 61
Catōnēs, 59 (n.)
caulis, 54
causa, 21b, 254 (n. 1)
cautēs, 45
cavē, 417 (n. 2), 473
cavē nē, 350 (n. 3)
caveō, 153, 417
cēdō, 149, 154b
cedo, 142b
celeber, 73
celer, 73 (n. 1), 78
celeriter, 164
cēlō, 208
-cendō, 150, 154e
cēnō, 129
cēnseō, 153, 417
centēnsima, 493
cēra, 61
Cerēs, 37
cernō, 149, 154c
certē, 170, 442 (n. 4)
cētera (adverbial), 213 (n. 2)
cēterī, 307 (n.)
cēterum, 177
cette, 142b
ceu, 178
chelys, 473
chlamys, 473
cieō, 153, 153 (n. 2)
cingō, 154a
cingor, 210 (n. 6)
cinis, 11, 37
circā, 172, 285
circiter, 172, 285
circum, 172, 205 (n. 1), 285
circumdō, 135a